Portrait of Nathaniel Hawthorne, 1804–1864, by Charles Osgood.

Photograph of Hawthorne, taken about 1862 when he was in his fifties.

Nathaniel Hawthorne

and the Truth of Dreams

Rita K. Gollin

Louisiana State University Press
Baton Rouge and London

Design: Patricia Douglas Crowder
Typeface: VIP Caledonia
Composition: G&S Typesetteres, Inc., Austin, Texas
Printing: Thomson-Shore, Inc.
Binding: John Dekker and Sons, Inc.

Parts of letters from Nathaniel Hawthorne to Sophia Hawthorne are quoted
with permission of the Huntington Library, San Marino, California. Quota-
tions from Sophia Hawthorne's letters to her family are from the Henry W.
and Albert A. Berg Collection, the New York Public Library, Astor, Lenox
and Tilden Foundations. Other Hawthorne letters are quoted by permission of the Houghton Library, Harvard University, and the Duyckinck
Collection, Manuscripts and Archives Division, the New York Public Library, Astor, Lenox and Tilden Foundations.

LIBRARY OF CONGRESS CATALOGING IN PUBLICATION DATA

Gollin, Rita K   1928–
    Nathaniel Hawthorne and the truth of dreams.

    Bibliography: p.
    Includes index.
    1. Hawthorne, Nathaniel, 1804–1864—Criticism and interpretation.
2. Dreams in literature.   I. Title.
PS1892.D74G65   813'.3   78–14952
ISBN 0-8071-0467-1

For Dick, Kathy, Michael, and Jim

"If a man, sitting all alone, cannot dream strange things, and make them look like truth, he need never try to write romances."

Contents

Bibliographical Note

I quote from *The Centenary Edition of the Works of Nathaniel Hawthorne*, ed. William Charvat *et al.* (Columbus: Ohio State University Press), citing the volumes parenthetically, with the following abbreviations:

The Scarlet Letter (1962), *SL*
The House of the Seven Gables (1965), *HSG*
The Blithedale Romance (1964), *BR*
The Marble Faun (1968), *MF*
Our Old Home (1970), *OOH*
True Stories (1972), *TS*
The American Notebooks (1972), *AN*
Twice-told Tales (1974), *T-t T*
Mosses from an Old Manse (1974), *Mosses*
The Snow-Image, and Uncollected Tales (1974), *S-I*
The American Claimant Manuscripts (1977), *ACM*
The Elixir of Life Manuscripts (1977), *ELM*

For the *English Notebooks* I use Randall Stewart's edition (New York: Modern Language Association of America, 1941), cited as *EN*. The Riverside edition of *The Complete Works of Nathaniel Hawthorne*, ed. George P. Lathrop (12 vols.; Boston: Houghton Mifflin, 1887–88), is cited by volume and page. Unless otherwise indicated, Hawthorne's correspondence is cited from typescripts prepared for the forthcoming Centenary edition.

Acknowledgments

I wish to thank the Research Foundation of the State of New York and the College of Arts and Science of the University of Rochester for summer fellowships which enabled me to complete this book. My research was facilitated by the librarians of SUNY Geneseo, the University of Rochester, and the Essex Institute, the Houghton Library of Harvard University, the Boston Public Library, the Morgan Library, and the New York Public Library. I am indebted to L. Neal Smith, who provided typescripts of letters being prepared for the Centenary edition of Hawthorne's correspondence. I gratefully acknowledge the counsel and criticism of Walter Harding, Leo Marx, the late Norman Holmes Pearson, William Rueckert, Otto Thaler, and other friends and colleagues; but my main debt is to my husband, Richard M. Gollin, my best counselor as well as my severest critic.

Sections of Chapter II have already been published, in slightly different form—"Hawthorne on Perception, Lubrication, and Reverie" in *The Nathaniel Hawthorne Journal 1976*, and "Hawthorne: The Writer as Dreamer" in the first issue of *Studies in the American Renaissance: 1977* (1978). Part of the *Blithedale* section of Chapter IV appears in "'Dream-Work' in *The Blithedale Romance*," *ESQ*, XIX (1973).

Nathaniel Hawthorne
and the Truth of Dreams

Introduction

To write a dream, which shall resemble the real course of a dream, with all its inconsistency, its strange transformations, which are all taken as a matter of course, its eccentricities and aimlessness— with nevertheless a leading idea running through the whole. Up to this old age of the world, no such thing ever has been written. (*AN*, 240)

"To write a dream" was Hawthorne's recurring ambition long before this notebook entry of the 1840s, and long after. Never did he intend to write the kind of dream that filled contemporary magazines—the romantic idyl, or the bizarre nightmare. His purpose was to capture the intractable and unpredictable experience of real dreams, experience at once intimate and universal, yet never fully understood. Through dreams and their threshold, reverie, he would enter the interior life and encounter its demons in fictions asserting that the adventure is crucial to human understanding. From the start of his writing career, he used dreams as encounters that simultaneously horrify the dreamer and inform him about his own motives and desires. By the time he came to write his last romances, he had become increasingly reluctant to undertake such encounters; he was not only afraid of what he might himself learn in the course of writing, but he was dispirited by what he suspected and what he already knew.

1

Hawthorne frequently called himself a dream-haunted man; and because that identity somehow seems to account for his fiction, many critics have always described him as a dreamer. Yet rarely do they distinguish legend and metaphor from fact, or Hawthorne's self-portrait from his fiction. Further, they use "dreams" in several different senses to define and evaluate the writer and his literary achievement.

In an 1868 essay, Eugene Benson accepted Hawthorne's account of himself as an isolated dreamer, concluding that "he is our American type of the 'Dreamer',—a being who could have no place in our thoughts of American life but for Hawthorne." His fiction was the product of his dreams: "Hawthorne was dreaming. He brooded over his thoughts; he spent season after season in reverie—reverie which is foreign to our idea of the American man. Out of his loneliness, out of his reveries, out of his dreams, he wove the matchless web of a style." Benson unequivocally praised Hawthorne as a literary magician, a writer who "lures the mind from the visible and concrete to the invisible and spiritual."[1]

A decade later, Anthony Trollope also used the word *dreams* to account for the suggestive power of Hawthorne's fiction, but, by contrast with Benson, he concluded that Hawthorne's "weird imagination" was an extreme form of an essentially American trait. "On our side of the water we deal more with beef and ale, and less with dreams," he said. Like Benson, however, Trollope praised Hawthorne for reaching beyond "the common needs of our common life" and concluded that following him into his dream world "will have enabled you to feel yourself an inch taller."[2]

1. Eugene Benson, "Poe and Hawthorne," *Galaxy*, VI (1868), 742–48. Benson concluded that Hawthorne was completely separated from the life of his contemporaries and that his fiction was wholly the product of his imagination.

2. Anthony Trollope, "The Genius of Hawthorne," *North American Review*, CXXIX (1879), 203–22. "The creations of American literature generally are no doubt given more to the speculative,—less given to the realistic,—than are those of English literature," Trollope said. Yet he insisted that if Hawthorne was speculative and reticent, he was also sociable and cheerful, and that his fiction shows the same

Hawthorne's son-in-law, George Parsons Lathrop, offered a more sustained judgment of Hawthorne as a "man of reverie" who was also a "business-like official." In 1888, in his "Biographical Sketch of Nathaniel Hawthorne," Lathrop argued that for Hawthorne, synthesis of the real and the imaginary was a condition of literary creation. Thus, he could not write fiction in Italy because there "the ideal force within him" was dominant. "His dreams in such case, would be apt to overcome him, to exist simply for their own sake instead of being subordinated to his will: and, in fine, to expend their witchery on the air, instead of being imprisoned in a book" (XII, 535). Lathrop understood Hawthorne's problem, though he oversimplified it.

Early twentieth-century critics continued to characterize Hawthorne as a dreamer of dreamlike fiction, usually as a mode of praise. In a sympathetic commentary on what he called "Hawthorne's Supernaturalism," Prosser Frye said that the "dusky chiaroscuro" of Hawthorne's imagination enabled him to capture in fiction a dream's intermingling of real and imaginary, its characteristic ambiguity, and its sense of paralyzed effort: "He is able to deepen this elementary impression of dreaming into the very intensity of nightmare" in which characters are spellbound "because the horror they would escape is within them and is ineluctable." Frye suggested that Hawthorne's dreamlike imagination could serve as a critical tool, though he did not use that tool.[3] W. C. Brownell took an opposite tack. He condemned Hawthorne for indulging his daydreaming state of mind, saying, "There can hardly be a more barren [one] for the production of anything more than conceits or fancies." Brownell asserted without qualification, "Reality repelled him. What attracted him was mirage."[4]

---

balance in its "mixture of romance and austerity, quite as far removed from the realities of Puritanism as it is from the sentimentalism of poetry."

3. Prosser Frye, "Hawthorne's Supernaturalism," in *Literary Reviews and Criticisms* (New York: Putnam, 1908), 114–29.

4. W. C. Brownell, "Hawthorne," in *American Prose Masters* (New York: Scribner, 1909), 63–132, esp. 70.

The idea that Hawthorne was a dreamer isolated in his own imagination has persisted in more recent biography and criticism. Yvor Winters, for example, perpetuated Hawthorne's self-image as a "sombre youth who lived in solitude and contemplation of Salem, for a dozen years or more" before his love for Sophia initiated "spasmodic and only moderately successful attempts to accustom himself to daylight."[5] But Malcolm Cowley is more representative and also closer to Lathrop in his sympathetic recognition of Hawthorne's "obsession both with the inner dream world and with activity in the real world."[6] Many recent critics have acknowledged this dual concern, freely drawing on Freud, Jung, or current studies of the dreaming mind, as they try to assess Hawthorne's purpose and accomplishment. Hyatt Waggoner, noting Hawthorne's self-characterization as a dreamer "dissatisfied with dreaming," concludes that Hawthorne wanted "to test his dreams against a reality he could not control, to determine their truth."[7] Lionel Trilling believed Hawthorne's imagination was usually dominated by "the literal actuality of the world," but he recognized the importance of dreams in Hawthorne's fiction, especially "in those of his works which touch us most deeply," such as "Roger Malvin's Burial," where morality has "the power of the dream, for it is indeed spontaneous, peremptory, and obligatory."[8] And Terence Martin correctly observes that often in Hawthorne's fiction, as in "The Haunted Mind," "dream and reality meet and merge."[9] What should now be stressed is that for Haw-

5. Yvor Winters, *Maule's Curse* (New Haven: Yale University Press, 1938), 15.
6. Malcolm Cowley, "Hawthorne in the Looking-Glass," *Sewanee Review*, LVI (1948), 551.
7. Hyatt Waggoner, *Hawthorne: A Critical Study* (Cambridge: Harvard University Press, 1963), 31.
8. Lionel Trilling, "Our Hawthorne," in Roy Harvey Pearce (ed.), *Hawthorne Centenary Essays* (Columbus: Ohio State University Press, 1964), 451–57.
9. Terence Martin, "The Method of Hawthorne's Tales," in Roy Harvey Pearce (ed.), *Hawthorne Centenary Essays* (Columbus: Ohio State University Press, 1964), 13. Also see Martin's discussion of "The Haunted Mind" in *The Instructed Vision* (Bloomington: Indiana University Press, 1961), 145–48.

thorne, such meeting and merging was essential for literary creation and a necessary concern of the fiction. Joseph C. Pattison does not exaggerate when he argues that "the point of view essential for reading Hawthorne is one of dream," that his fictions have the shape of dreams, and that in the fiction "life is to be regarded as a dream."[10]

The problem is even more far-reaching. Jorge Luis Borges suggests its scope when, referring to Hawthorne as "the dreamer" ("el soñador"), he asserts that Hawthorne recorded trivial details in his notebooks "to show himself that he was real" and concludes that "Hawthorne's world is the world of dreams."[11] Hawthorne frequently tried to dismiss his dreams as "only" dreams, though at the same time he was anxious about them. And unlike Poe, who courted the dream state, Hawthorne frequently chided himself for daydreaming, yet he knew his creative sensibility required it. Neither the philosophers he studied in school nor his Salem neighbors believed dreams or reverie have anything to do with truth or with man's proper work in the world. Yet his favorite books and such famous contemporaries as Poe and Emerson affirmed his own underlying conviction that dreaming and daydreaming are important. No one writer or philosophic scheme is adequate to account for the questions Hawthorne raised, nor the alternative answers he speculatively proposed in his fiction. His conception of the mind and his ideas about how it copes with inner and outer reality are complex and sometimes self-contradictory; but they must be understood. They underlie his ambivalence about his role as a writer, they provided an important subject and method for his fiction, and they account for its recurrent ambiguity.

In "The Custom-House," Hawthorne said that "if a man, sitting all alone, cannot dream strange things, and make them

10. Joseph C. Pattison, "Point of View in Hawthorne," *PMLA*, LXXXII (1967), 363–69.

11. Jorge Luis Borges, "Nathaniel Hawthorne," in *Other Inquisitions, 1937–52*, trans. Ruth L. C. Simms (Austin: University of Texas Press, 1964), 47–65.

look like truth, he need never try to write romances." He could readily "dream strange things"; and if he sometimes had difficulty inventing scenes where they would "look like truth," he could readily convey a different kind of truth—about the mind's leaps and involutions when the will is relaxed and memory, perception, and imagination all freely intermingle. And he was aware that the "strange things" within the dreamer's mind have their own logic and their own truth.

It is evident that when Hawthorne spoke of sitting alone to "dream strange things," the word *dream* carries the sense of *daydream*, as it commonly does in his writings and in ordinary speech. The mind is then semipassive: the dreamer is conscious of reality, and the will is partly suspended, but able to deflect the dreamer's attention from thoughts, memories, and fantasies that trouble him. For Hawthorne, this state of mind necessarily preceded literary creation, and he often placed his characters in a similar dream state. Many of the early tales concentrate on individuals who "dream strange things"; those "things" define them, establishing their relative emotional balance or imbalance, their streams of associated ideas, and their most obsessive concerns. But when Hawthorne spoke of his ambition "to write a dream, which shall resemble the real course of a dream," he meant not a daydream, but the experience of a mind abandoned to its own interior world, with the will in abeyance—a world of abysmal depths and cavernous recesses where illusive shapes—"disagreeable phantasms," or "phantoms of iniquity"—urge truths that the waking mind could repress. Repeatedly Hawthorne follows a character into that dream state, to the point where he encounters intolerable phantasms and suddenly returns to waking consciousness.

Yet throughout his life, Hawthorne was profoundly ambivalent about the value of any kind of dreaming. Whenever he referred to dreams as "mere dreams," or "unsubstantial dreams," he expressed his fear that dreaming (and thus writing) was wasteful: the dream world was a shadowy limbo, and the dreamer an incomplete human being. More frequently, he presented dreaming as an important mode of experience and knowledge, a supplement to waking life, the only way the past can persist and the future be anticipated, the only way a man can begin to come to terms with his inmost fears and desires. But inherent in this view is another kind of ambivalence: Hawthorne believed the inner world has its own infernal depths as well as spiritual heights, and it might be dangerous for the dreamer (or the writer) to pay attention to iniquitous desires.

Neither in terms of epistemological complexity nor aesthetic control do the dreams in Hawthorne's fiction follow a single or simple line of development. Some of his earliest stories that dramatize dreaming as a mode of knowledge are as profound and as consummately successful as the novels he would write over twenty years later. Yet there are discernible patterns of change. In the young bachelor's stories, dreams are retributive and informative, taking shape as spectral enchantment and demonic torment; for the writer on the verge of death, they figure as shattered fragments and indeterminate glimpses beyond the curtain of time. But Hawthorne always used dreams to raise questions about how the mind moves toward understanding and about the moral significance of individual acts, which ultimately concern the limits of mortal existence.

Hawthorne always questioned himself about dreams, and more broadly about the imagination and the role of the writer, though he never reached clear or final answers. Was the imagination a capricious faculty, unregulated by the real world and so unfitting man for it; or was it a creative power, a mode of apprehending the world we inhabit, and a way of envisioning ideal truth? As a dreamer and a writer of stories that capture the atmosphere, the characters, and the events of dreams, was he self-centered and irresponsible, or was he fulfilling man's unique capacities to understand himself and his role in the universe? The questions recur in his notebooks and his letters and give shape and substance to his fiction.

7

I

Available Traditions

1. Literary Conventions

Whenever dreams occur in the books Hawthorne read from childhood on,[1] they puzzle the dreamer, but their meanings are eventually made clear. Dreams in the Bible, Spenser, Shakespeare, Milton, Bunyan, the Augustans, and Gothic novels exhibit a wide range of narrative conventions and concepts of mind as they relate the visible to the invisible and articulate assumptions about the limits of reason and human knowledge. Yet they retain a peculiar impersonal quality. Hawthorne often based his fictional accounts of dreaming on these precedents, even when his own convictions and uncertainties extended and deepened their range.

The dominant assumption in all this literature is that dreams speak true. In the Bible as in classical literature, dreams are interpreted as coded divine messages, and each separate dream

1. See Randall Stewart, *Nathaniel Hawthorne* (New Haven: Yale University Press, 1948), 4–8; Randall Stewart (ed.), "Recollections of Hawthorne by His Sister Elizabeth," *American Literature*, XVI (1945), 316–31; Austin Warren, "Hawthorne's Reading," *New England Quarterly*, VIII (1935), 480–97; Arlin Turner, "Hawthorne's Literary Borrowings," *PMLA*, LI (1936), 543–62; Neal Frank Doubleday, *Hawthorne's Early Tales, A Critical Study* (Durham: Duke University Press, 1972), 32–42; and Julian Hawthorne, *Hawthorne Reading* (1902; Folcroft, Pa.: Folcroft Press, 1969).

image has specific prophetic significance.[2] But the dream is completely separate from waking reality. The dreamer's mind in no way affects his dream: it is only a stage on which the dream is played. As in the story of Joseph, only the abstracted manifest content of the dream matters. Pharaoh's dream of seven fat and seven lean kine is God's arcane warning to a responsible governor, not a phantasm of Pharaoh's imagination. Like the symbolic dreams of the butler, the baker, and Joseph himself, it foretells future events in an explicable code. Obviously these conventions recur in Hawthorne's fiction, though altered to conform with what he knew about real dreams.

He also was well aware of the equally ancient assumption that dreams cannot always be trusted, that malevolent powers can lie to men through dreams. The young Nathaniel Hawthorne encountered a vivid example of such deception when he read the first canto of *The Faerie Queene*. Archimago makes Redcrosse dream that Una is lustful, and when the knight wakes up he believes the "false shewes" and berates the innocent girl. The episode is brief, but all its elements appear later in Hawthorne's fiction: disguise, metamorphosis, a devil who evokes a dream of sexual shame, and a confused dreamer.[3]

2. See W. S. Messer, *The Dream in Homer and Greek Tragedy* (New York: Columbia University Press, 1918). Biblical dreams are either interpreted as a whole, each element treated as part of a coherent pattern, as with the dreams of Joseph and the Pharaoh, or each element is assigned a separate meaning, as in Daniel's interpretation of Nebuchadnezzar's dream of an idol with feet of clay. Sigmund Freud discusses these as the symbolic or decoding methods in *The Interpretation of Dreams*, Vols. IV and V of *The Complete Psychological Works of Sigmund Freud*, trans. James Strachey (23 vols; London: Hogarth Press, 1962), IV, 96–100. Hawthorne usually used the symbolic method in his fiction, but sometimes tried to apply the decoding method to his own dreams.

3. *The Faerie Queene* was the first book Hawthorne bought with his own money. That his first child was named Una suggests how deeply Spenser affected Hawthorne's imagination. John Schroeder in "Alice Doane's Story: An Essay on Hawthorne and Spenser," *Nathaniel Hawthorne Journal 1974* (Washington, D.C.: NCR/Microcard, 1975), 129–34, says "Hawthorne learned to write psychological romance from copying the model of Spenser." He argues that "My Kinsman, Major Molineux" and "Young Goodman Brown" as well as "Alice Doane's Appeal" dramatize similar

Shakespeare's plays incorporate still other conventions.[4] In *Julius Caesar*, for example, Calpurnia's dream prophesies her husband's death, but Caesar is deceived by Decius' willful misinterpretation. In some plays, a prophetic dream draws on the dreamer's private state of mind, as when Clarence worries about his imprisonment in *Richard III* and then dreams of drowning. In *Romeo and Juliet*, Mercutio articulates the idea of the dream as wish-fulfillment—lovers dream of love and lawyers of fees—though he later denigrates dreams as "the children of an idle brain/ Begot of nothing but vain fantasy." Yet in the same play, Romeo dreams with prophetic accuracy that Juliet will discover him dead. In several plays, Shakespeare suggests what Hawthorne would later assert: that the dream state may not be separable from waking experience. Thus, Imogen in *Cymbeline* and the four lovers of *A Midsummer Night's Dream* question whether they are awake, since reality closely resembles their dreams. Perhaps even more seminal for Hawthorne was Prospero's famous statement after the masque of *The Tempest*: "We are such stuff/ As dreams are made on, and our little life/ Is rounded with a sleep." Hawthorne also suggested that our outer lives may be no more substantial than our dreams, implying that as we understand our dreams, so we understand our waking lives.

In *Paradise Lost*, Hawthorne found a clear statement of the Renaissance psychology of dreams inherited from the Middle Ages and still current in his own day. After Satan tempts Eve in a dream in Book V of *Paradise Lost*, Adam belittles her fears:

> But know that in the Soul
> Are many lesser Faculties that serve
> Reason as chief; among these Fancy next

"perilous unconscious states," and draw on Spenser's structured patterns and narrative devices. It must be recognized, however, that Spenser unequivocally blames Archimago for the "false shewes."

4. See Marjorie B. Garber, *Dream in Shakespeare* (New Haven: Yale University Press, 1974).

Her office holds; of all external things,
Which the five watchful Senses represent,
She forms Imaginations, Aery shapes,
Which Reason joining or disjoining, frames
All what we affirm or what deny, and call
Our knowledge or opinion; then retires
Into her private Cell when Nature rests.
Often in her absence mimic Fancy wakes
To imitate her; but misjoining shapes,
Wild work produces oft, and most in dreams,
Ill matching words and deeds long past or late.

But Adam's theory is belied by the poem. He tells Eve he hopes that "what in sleep thou didst abhor to dream/ Waking thou never wilt consent to do," but she consents to do what she abhorred to dream. Further, dreams in *Paradise Lost* always tell the truth. Nevertheless, Hawthorne sometimes echoed Adam's mistrust of the role of the Fancy in dreams, and his dream fictions attempt to accommodate it.

The tradition of the allegorical dream vision offered even wider narrative latitude. In *Pilgrim's Progress*, one of Hawthorne's favorite books, the dream emerges from the consciousness of an ordinary individual.[5] It begins when Christian falls asleep and ends when he wakens. But within that frame, a marvelous world extends in time and space, and the dreamer unquestioningly accepts even improbable events. Further, each event—such as sinking into the Slough of Despond—is morally significant, calculated to edify the dreamer and, through him, the reader. The eighteenth century provided other models for journeys through a dream terrain, such as Addison's "Dream of Mirzah," but the morally urgent dream journeys in Hawthorne's fiction owe more to Bunyan than to the Augustans.

They are also indebted to dreams in Gothic fiction, which are always brief episodes of nightmare.[6] Gothic dreams speak true,

5. See David E. Smith, *John Bunyan in America* (Bloomington: Indiana University Press, 1968), 47–89.
6. See Jane Lundblad, *Nathaniel Hawthorne and the European Literary Tradi-*

11

and each detail can be interpreted allegorically, but interpretation is always tributary to emotional effect. The dreams present frightening and threatening events, usually as premonitions. They are each connected to the dreamer's waking predicament and ostensibly emanate from his tormented mind, though they are never calculated to reveal his unique experience or sensibility. In M. G. Lewis' *The Monk*, for example, the melancholy hero, worried about his beloved Antonia, dreams she is snatched from him by a monster readily identifiable as the monk Ambrosio; later Ambrosio does indeed try to rape her. Her anxious mother dreams Antonia is trembling on a precipice and shouting for help. Both dreams tell the truth about Antonia's danger in terms appropriate to each dreamer; but they are essentially adjuncts to Gothic horror. This horror and the nightmare ambiance of the Gothic novel as a whole exerted a far more pervasive influence on Hawthorne's fiction than the particular episodes of dramatized dreams.

By the time Hawthorne began writing his early poems and sketches, the English Romantic poets had already won a wide audience for poems that celebrated dreams as a mode of heightened and penetrating vision, such as Keats's "Endymion" and Coleridge's "Kubla Khan." American magazines were studded with poems cloaked as dreams and prose sketches based on dreams, and clearly these pieces fed their readers' appetite for fantasy while gratifying the prevailing American insistence on credibility. But except for Poe's and Hawthorne's, these American poems and sketches are devoid of literary interest. Most of them treat dreams simplistically. Some imitate Gothic dreams, some derive from didactic dream allegories, and others feebly follow the example of the Romantic poets. The *American Monthly Magazine* for 1837 included Poe's "Von Jung, the Mystific" and Hawthorne's "Fragments from the Journal of a

---

tion (Cambridge: Harvard University Press, 1947); Oral S. Coad, "The Gothic Element in American Literature Before 1835," *Journal of English and Germanic Philology*, XXIV (1925), 72–93; and Doubleday, *Hawthorne's Early Tales*, 52–62.

Solitary Man," and also three undistinguished poems based on dreams. In "The Nightmare," two spirits describe the horrible night ride of a fair lady and a fiend that ends when she is "saved" by waking; "A Dream" offers a lover's "bright visions" of reunion with the beloved; and a brief poem, "Imagination," ends by praising the "sweet symphonious spell" of the imagination in dreams.[7]

Most of the prose sketches of the same period treat dreams as wholly separate from waking life. The *New England Magazine* for 1835 printed four Hawthorne tales involving dreams— "The Old Maid in the Winding-Sheet," "The Vision of the Fountain," "Sketches from Memory," and "The Devil in Manuscript"—as well as three sketches that deserve notice only for their subject. One describes the poet as a dreamer who "must be isolated from external life, to enjoy in its fullness that inward life, which developes in him a new existence; and it is only when the physical world has utterly vanished from before his eyes, that the ideal world is fully revealed to him"; another describes the poets' "world of fanciful imagery, of daydreams and visions, which have visited them." The third sketch adopts the ancient mode of the divinely inspired dream, though like "The Dream of the Rood" it is retrospective rather than prophetic: a good Puritan who yearns for a divine revelation is rewarded by a dream about the disciples.[8] None of these three sketches conveys the perplexities or discoveries of real dreams, but they are indices of popular taste.

Popular novels provide similar evidence. Most of the dreams in Catharine Sedgwick's *Redwood* (1824) offer symbolic portents of danger in the well-established Gothic tradition, but some are idyllic interludes, sentimental restatements of what was already known. By mid-century the idyllic reverie had become popular as a separate genre: one of the best sellers was Ik

---

7. *American Monthly Magazine*, IX (1837), 322–24; X (1837), 440.
8. *New-England Magazine*, IX (1835), 209, 322, 5–7. After this last volume, the magazine merged with the *American Monthly Magazine*.

NATHANIEL HAWTHORNE

Marvel's *Reveries of a Bachelor* (1850), a series of wistful meditations and sentimental fantasies primarily concerning the narrator's disappointed or gratified love.[9] Like Sedgwick's, Marvel's dreams are essentially set pieces calculated to evoke a shiver or a sigh, not to probe the dreamer's mind.

Yet this does not suggest that Hawthorne was the only American writer who used dreams to explore man's inner world. At the turn of the century, Charles Brockden Brown, the only American novelist Hawthorne praised in his own fiction,[10] had used fictional dreams as symptoms of emotional disturbance and as a way to explore that disturbance. In *Edgar Huntly* (1799), both major characters are self-conscious young men whose waking torments erupt in dreams. Their nightmares are sensational in the Gothic mode, but they are also forms of self-knowledge. At a time when Edgar is near starvation and considers eating panther meat, his disgust emerges in dreams of "plenteous banquets, which, though placed within my view, some power forbade me to approach." At several points, Edgar comments on man's limited consciousness, explaining how repressed ideas operate in the unconscious. He understands that nightmares are expressions of guilt or examinations of dilemmas. Criminals sometimes betray themselves during sleep, he says, because "thoughts, which considerations of safety enable them to suppress or disguise during wakefulness, operate without impediment, and exhibit their genuine effects when the notices of sense are partly excluded, and they are shut out from a knowledge of their entire condition." He examines his own troubled dreams with similar insight: ideas

9. Ik Marvel was the pseudonym of Donald Grant Mitchell (1822–1908), the popular essayist whose best known work was *Reveries of a Bachelor*. *Reveries* sold fourteen thousand copies in 1850, the year six thousand copies of *The Scarlet Letter* were printed, and went through scores of editions. A sequel entitled *Dream Life* (1851) was almost as successful. See James D. Hart, *The Popular Book* (Berkeley: University of California Press, 1961).

10. In "The Hall of Fantasy" he puts Brown among the rulers of "the realms of imagination," though in "an obscure and shadowy niche" (*Mosses*, 173–74), and he calls Brown "venerable and revered" in "P's Correspondence" (*Mosses*, 380).

"nearly banished from my waking thoughts, recurred in an incongruous and half seen form to my dreams" and offered "something like a solution to the problem" then troubling him.[11] Brown understood how dreams interact with waking consciousness, and he was fascinated by man's limited awareness of the workings of his anguished mind; in his novels, however, dreams usually rehearse or anatomize abnormal or criminal acts.

When Hawthorne began writing a few decades later, Edgar Allan Poe was using dreams for a more far-reaching purpose. Repeatedly in his poetry and prose, dreams celebrate man's vast capacity for mental adventure. Poe paid less attention than Brown to normal consciousness, or even to abnormal minds coping with ordinary reality. His hero is a sensitive and even diseased young man whose inner visions seem more vital than phenomenal experience. He suffers in the confines of the real world, luxuriating only in escape from it. Roderick Usher, William Wilson, and the narrator of "Eleonora" all assert they belong to "a race of visionaries."[12] The hero of "The Assignation" speaks for many of Poe's protagonists when he says "to dream has been the business of my life": his apartment is contrived as "a bower of dreams," and he dies looking forward to "that land of real dreams whither I am now departing."

Yet Poe knew, as Hawthorne did, that a dream feeds on waking experience and that it can be fathomed—though never fully—at the moment it crosses the borders of consciousness. Repeatedly he invented literary situations that exploit the sensations of partial consciousness, such as the drift in and out of a

11. Charles Brockden Brown, *Edgar Huntly* (1799; Philadelphia: McKay, 1887), 160, 13, 124, 266. Richard Slotkin in *Regeneration Through Violence* (Middletown: Wesleyan University Press, 1973), discusses Huntly's "nightmare discovery" of his own inner complexity—his hidden fears and his guilty desires (382–90).

12. Poe's protagonists usually attribute their dreams to hereditary imaginativeness and nervous sensitivity, sometimes to physical disease. The narrator of "The Premature Burial" is epileptic; the narrator of "Eleonora" begins by stating "I am come of a race noted for vigor of fancy and ardor of passion," and though he may be mad, "those who dream by day," he says, "are cognizant of many things which escape those who dream only by night."

swoon in "The Pit and the Pendulum." His heroes move across subliminal landscapes where mind and matter seem to intermingle, absorbed by the mysteries of mind, convinced that consciousness is never lost, but—unlike Hawthorne's heroes—delighting in its near loss. They brood over the threshold of wakefulness and sleep, sanity and insanity, life and death, eager to cross into the regions of mystery—into sleep, insanity, and death.

A single important variation is the young man who tells his sea adventures in *The Narrative of A. Gordon Pym*; his two dreams are exceptions to Poe's usual concentration on the ecstasy or horror of the dreamer rather than on the dream itself. Both of Pym's dreams are essentially elaborations of his predicament when he is shut into a small space on shipboard, anguished by hunger and thirst and menaced by some unseen beast. They are psychologically credible, though they reveal nothing new to Pym or the reader.

For Poe, dreams were a device to dramatize the agonies and delights of an acutely sensitive individual in a bizarre situation. By contrast, Hawthorne's solitary dreamer is usually a relatively ordinary man whose dreams are part of an ongoing process of self-discovery.

Hawthorne's achievement seems all the more remarkable when we realize that Herman Melville, who also probed men's hidden natures, rarely used dreams for that purpose. Most of Melville's references to dreams are casual if not contemptuous, as when he praised *The Blithedale Romance* "as an antidote to the mooniness of some dreamers—who are merely dreamers," but ended by asking, "Yet who the devil ain't a dreamer?" He did sometimes pursue the convolutions of waking thought as it drifted into reverie, as in Ishmael's meditations on the masthead in *Moby-Dick*. But his fictional dreams are few, and they rely on well established literary conventions. In *Mardi*, Babbalanja has a conventional didactic dream vision of man's ultimate purpose and destiny. And, in *Moby-Dick*, Stubb's dream is an *allegoria* of his relations to Ahab and the still undefined quest: he dreams he kicks Ahab, who turns into a pryamid; then a humpbacked merman tries to dissuade Stubb from continuing to kick. The dream is consistent with Stubb's mixed emotions and even amplifies them, but the episode is a product of Melville's consciousness rather than the dreamer's. *Redburn* and *Pierre* offer two apparent exceptions. When Redburn is horrified by the London gaming house, he drifts into a reverie in which "the mirrors and marbles around me seemed crawling over with lizards," and then into a nightmare. But the episode is only a Gothic interlude dramatizing Redburn's immediate anxieties. The Enceladus dream in *Pierre* is more complex. The ambitious but hopeless Pierre dreams of boulders on the Mount of Titans which spring to life and, led by Enceladus, attack the invulnerable mountain; at the climax, Pierre sees on Enceladus' "armless trunk, his own duplicate face and features." But despite the psychological force of this recognition, the dream simply restates Pierre's predicament. Melville did not penetrate the labyrinths of the dreamer's mind, as Hawthorne did.[13]

Even the briefest consideration of Hawthorne's use of dream traditions reveals his distinctive originality. The biblical convention of precisely detailed prophetic dreams is evident in "The Birth-mark," for example: Aylmer dreams he is cutting away his wife's birthmark, and later he does so. But even

---

13. The *Blithedale* reference occurs in a letter from Melville to Hawthorne dated July 17, 1852, in Jay Leyda (ed.), *The Melville Log* (2 vols.; New York: Harcourt Brace, 1951), I, 454. Babbalanja's dream is in Chapter 188 of *Mardi*, Stubb's in Chapter 31 of *Moby-Dick* (entitled "Queen Mab"), Redburn's in Chapter 46 of *Redburn*, and Pierre's in Book 25, Section 4 of *Pierre*. In Chapter 44 of *Moby-Dick*, Melville says Ahab was sometimes "forced from his hammock by exhausting and intolerably vivid dreams," but attributes the dreamer's horror to "the eternal, living principle or soul in him," which was in sleep "dissociated from the characterizing mind" and sought to escape it. Despite the paucity of fictional dreams, Nathalia Wright in *Melville's Use of the Bible* (Durham, N.C.: Duke University Press, 1949) notes that "Biblical dreams or revelations which Melville used most often form almost as long a list as his favorite stories of violence"; and she says "the visions of Babbalanja and Pierre have Hebrew, Miltonic, and Greek echoes" (28, 183).

though his dream offers a symbolic prophecy, it is not divine in origin, and prophecy is not its most important function. It reveals Aylmer's anguish and accounts for it, presenting truths so painful that Aylmer tries to hide them even from himself. The tradition of demonic intervention in dreams is evident in "Young Goodman Brown" and in the demons and mocking old men from the early sketches through the last romances; but again, Hawthorne's changes are crucial. Demonic thoughts emerge from the mind's inner hell; they may be unclear but they are never simply untrue. Hawthorne was more a questioner than a teacher like Milton's Adam, as he tried to understand how dreams emerge from the dreamer's mind. And even when he says like Mercutio that dreams are mere fantasies, his stories demonstrate that dreams tell truths. Hawthorne's dream visions come at the end of the long line that goes from the Bible through medieval dream allegories, *Pilgrim's Progress*, and beyond, but they succeed most where their debt is least, where the dreamer confronts apparitions of his own repressed guilt.

Hawthorne drew heavily on Gothic conventions—persecuting villains and helpless victims, ominous interiors and threatening landscapes—but usually to objectify inner states. Whenever he used themes recurrent in Gothic fiction, such as retribution and the persistence of the past, the main scene of suffering is within the mind, equivalent to the Gothic castle with its hidden passages, secret chambers, and locked dungeons.

The best gloss on Hawthorne's adaptation of Gothic conventions is his comment on Cotton Mather's belief in witches. According to Grandfather in *Grandfather's Chair*, Mather was so tormented by monstrous ideas that he believed they had independent existence. Thus he acted conscientiously, however wrongly, as "chief agent" of the Salem witchcraft delusion: "He believed that there were evil spirits all about the world. Doubtless he imagined that they were hidden in the corners and crevices of his library, and that they peeped out from the leaves of many of his books, as he turned them over, at midnight. He supposed that these unlovely demons were everywhere, in the sunshine as well as in the darkness, and that they were hidden in men's hearts, and stole into their inmost thoughts" (*TS*, 94). Hawthorne was also familiar with such "unlovely demons," and occasionally his fictions objectify them as supernatural agents. Usually, however, they are analogues for the guilt and shame whose hidden operations he uncovered "in men's hearts and . . . their inmost thoughts," as manifest in dreams.

To the extent that earlier dreams served Hawthorne as literary models, they were modes of dramatizing knowledge and experience not readily accessible to the waking consciousness. He experimented with conventional formulas and traditional beliefs, trying out the questions and answers of earlier writers; and clearly, some proved more useful than others. Sometimes his borrowings were delimiting, as in "The Threefold Destiny," where the ancient tradition of prophetic and allegorical dreams serves merely as a curious contrivance. But when Hawthorne drew on the conventions of antecedent dreams that had entered deep into his imagination and fused with his own discoveries and speculations about the mind's strange operations—such as those of the Redcrosse Knight, or Bunyan's Christian—he could produce his finest fictions—such as "My Kinsman, Major Molineux" and "Young Goodman Brown." These are at once tributes to the borrowed fictions, sustained critical reinterpretations of them, and stories of brilliant originality.

2. *Theories of Mind*

Although Hawthorne never adopted or formulated a single systematic approach to the irrational mind, his ideas coincide more with the Scottish school of philosophy than with any other. The Scots offered a credible scheme of the mind's powers, and they considered problems that worried him, such as the roles of the imagination and the will in perception and during the surrendered consciousness of sleep. They scrutinized the phenomena of mind, aware of the limits of such knowledge, without relinquishing their moral emphasis or their religious faith.

Scottish philosophy dominated the major American colleges from the time it was first introduced, when Hawthorne was a student at Bowdoin. One reason is suggested by the alternate term for it—the Common Sense School of Philosophy. Its beliefs were clear, logical, and essentially optimistic. It asserted that the mind can know reality, that the senses offer valid knowledge, that study of the mind is justified because self-development requires self-knowledge, and that ideas emerge according to clear patterns of association. As I. Woodbridge Riley says, Scottish philosophy was not only "convenient, compact, and teachable, appealing to a common sense of which every youngster had some spark, but it was also an eminently safe philosophy . . . safe from the dark speculations of materialism or the beguiling allurements of idealism"; [14] Herbert Schneider attributes its wide appeal "to its systematic exposition of both reason and moral sentiment as supplementary factors in human life, and as substitutes for supernatural grace and revelation." [15]

14. I. Woodbridge Riley, *American Philosophy: The Early School* (New York: Dodd, Mead, 1907), 476.

15. Herbert W. Schneider, *A History of American Philosophy* (New York: Columbia University Press, 1946), 246. Schneider says attacks on Jonathan Edwards at the end of the eighteenth century provoked interest in faculty psychology, which "dominated at least two generations of philosophers, created a new 'science,' and profoundly affected the course of academic studies in philosophy" (237). Scottish philosophy invaded America around 1820 "and rapidly crowded out the older eighteenth century texts" (238). Stewart and Reid were published in a flood of American editions. See also William Charvat, *The Origins of American Critical Thought, 1810–1835* (Philadelphia: University of Pennsylvania Press, 1936); S. A. Grave, *The Scottish Philosophy of Common Sense* (Oxford: Clarendon Press, 1960); Daniel Sommer Robinson (ed.), *The Story of Scottish Philosophy* (New York: Exposition Press, 1961); and Terence Martin, *The Instructed Vision* (Bloomington: Indiana University Press, 1961). Martin argues that Scottish philosophy supported American mistrust of the imagination. Using "The Haunted Mind" to illustrate the American writer's "creative problem," he concludes that "the imagination in Hawthorne's sketch supplies a different kind of reality that must be dealt with on its own terms"; it is not "subservient

One of the major texts of the Scottish school, Dugald Stewart's *Elements of the Philosophy of the Human Mind*, was part of Hawthorne's senior curriculum at Bowdoin.[16] Many of Stewart's ideas and even some of his illustrative examples seem to anticipate passages in Hawthorne's fiction. It seems evident that Stewart encouraged and shaped Hawthorne's introspective meditations about the mind and also his dramatizations of the mind's experience.

Stewart insisted that the mind is unitary, that all its powers should interact, and that man should try to live through the whole range of his faculties. He explicitly divided the powers of mind into consciousness, external perception, attention, conception, abstraction, memory, judgment and reason, association of ideas, and imagination, defining each power and the interactions among them. Two of Stewart's chapters are especially helpful to a study of Hawthorne: the chapter on the association of ideas, particularly the subsection on dreaming, and the chapter on imagination.

Stewart defines the association of ideas as a law of our constitution by which one thought succeeds another according to specific principles, many more than Hume had postulated. In addition to Hume's resemblance, contiguity, and cause and effect, Stewart postulates such principles as contrast, habit, and the relation of premise to conclusion. Stewart distinguishes the fancy from the imagination and considers the fancy to be simply a "habit of association": it can "collect materials for the Imagina-

---

to literal fact" (148). But Martin is not concerned about the kinds of reality the imagination "supplies." David Pancost, "Hawthorne's Epistemology and Ontology," *ESQ*, XIX (1973), 8–13, argues that "Scottish influence permeates Hawthorne's ontology," and that "about the only difference between Hawthorne and the Scottish philosophers is that he delights in and treats seriously the products of the unconscious."

16. For information about Hawthorne's instruction at Bowdoin, see Norman Holmes Pearson's unpublished monograph, "The College Years of Nathaniel Hawthorne" (1932), 55–60. Randall Stewart reprints the 1822 Bowdoin curriculum in *Nathaniel Hawthorne*, 16–17. See also Nehemiah Cleaveland, *History of Bowdoin College* (New York: Putnam, 1908), and Louis Hatch, *The History of Bowdoin College* (Portland: Loring, Short, and Harmon, 1927).

tion" and offer metaphors and analogies that are more or less "luxuriant." The poet's imagination can use these, in conjunction with his taste and judgment, to create scenes and characters which will be more or less "beautiful or sublime."[17] Fancy, like all association of ideas, is essentially passive, but the imagination is active. Hawthorne maintains a similar distinction when he differentiates fancy from imagination, and Stewart's theory about the sequence of associated ideas seems the basis for Hawthorne's allegorical processions of ideas in such tales as "The Haunted Mind" and "Fancy's Show Box."

The longest subsection of the chapter on association, a discussion of how the mind behaves during dreams, seems virtually a gloss on Hawthorne's fiction. Stewart says that dream thoughts succeed one another according to laws of association, as these laws are modified by the dreamer's bodily associations and his thoughts and mood before falling asleep. Consistent with this theory, Aylmer's distress at his wife's birthmark in "The Birth-mark" begets a dream in which he cuts it out, and Giovanni's confusion about Beatrice's ministrations to the exotic purple flower in "Rappaccini's Daughter" leads to a dream in which she is identified with the flower. According to Stewart, old men dream of childhood because their youthful minds had greater "facility of association" and were consequently more impressionable, a statement that explains Clifford's recurrent dreams of childhood in *The House of the Seven Gables*. Further, Stewart observes that dreams seem as lively and steady as our perceptions do when we are awake, an observation that explains why the dreamer of "The Celestial Rail-road" unquestioningly accepts the wonders of his journey.

In the course of explaining how a dreamer accepts anomalies of time, Stewart draws an analogy to visual illusion: "When I look into a show-box where the deception is imperfect, I see

17. Dugald Stewart, *Elements of the Philosophy of the Human Mind, I*, in William H. Hamilton (ed.), *The Collected Works of Dugald Stewart* (11 Vols.; Edinburgh: Thomas Constable, 1854), II, 59–61.

only a set of paltry daubings of a few inches' diameter; but if the representation be executed with so much skill as to convey to me the idea of a distant prospect, every object before me swells in its dimensions in proportion to the extent of space which I conceive it to occupy; and what seemed before to be shut up within the limits of a small wooden frame, is magnified, in my apprehension, to an immense landscape of woods, rivers, and mountains."[18] This analogy, with its qualifications and even its sequence, seems a direct anticipation of "Fancy's Show Box," the "shifting panorama" in "Main Street," and the show-box scenes in "The Seven Vagabonds" and "Ethan Brand."

Stewart's comments on the will are of special interest. Because the will cannot regulate thoughts in dreams, Stewart compares dreaming to madness. In both conditions the mind may be obsessed by a single idea, or thoughts may succeed one another with excessive rapidity. The dreams in "Rappaccini's Daughter" and "The Birth-mark" are clear examples of such obsession; and Clifford's thoughts emerge with the rapidity of madness on his abortive train ride. Hawthorne supports and expands Stewart's theory in his characterizations of habitual dreamers, such as the hero of "Peter Goldthwaite's Treasure," who hover on the verge of madness.

In the course of discussing the dreamer's powerless subjection to his dreams, Stewart mentions Andrew Baxter's "whimsical theory" ascribing dreams to "the influence of separate spirits on the mind."[19] Whether or not this led Hawthorne to check out Baxter's *An Enquiry into the Nature of the Human Soul* from the Salem Athenaeum,[20] he did subsequently write

18. *Ibid.*, 303.
19. *Ibid.*, 301.
20. Marion Kesselring, in "Hawthorne's Reading, 1828–1850," in *Bulletin of the New York Public Library*, LIII (1949), 55–71, 121–38, 173–94, argues that most of the books charged to his Aunt Mary Manning's card for the Salem Athenaeum during those years were read by Hawthorne. The two volumes of Baxter were charged on April 12, 1827.

the whimsical tale "Graves and Goblins," in which a ghost explains his intervention in a writer's dreams.

Stewart begins his chapter on imagination by stating that the role of imagination is "to make a selection of qualities and of circumstances from a variety of different objects, and by combining and disposing these, to form a new creation of its own." He believed the imagination is not unitary but a combination of the faculties of conception, abstraction, taste, and fancy; and, he believed, "it is not an original endowment of the mind, but an accomplishment formed by experience and situation."[21] Stewart's firm and explicit beliefs that the imagination is a "complex power" requiring deliberate cultivation differ from Hawthorne's tentative assertions. Hawthorne also believed that the imagination is a complex power that all men should use and develop, but not that it is an aggregate of other faculties or an acquired accomplishment.

Yet they were both in substantial agreement about the dangers of excessive indulgence in imagination. Stewart said that an individual who devotes too much time to imagination could easily reverse the normal state in which sense perceptions impress the mind more strongly than its own operations; he would "lose all interest in external occurrences" and his mind would lose command over itself until "at length the most extravagant dreams of imagination acquire as powerful an influence in exciting all its passions as if they were realities."[22] This describes the dreamer's plight in many Hawthorne tales, such as "Fragments from the Journal of a Solitary Man" and "The Devil in Manuscript." Both Stewart and Hawthorne suggest only one possible remedy: resolute return to the ordinary world.

A man absorbed by his own imagination might eventually forfeit the possibility of a normal life, Stewart said; and Hawthorne agreed. Stewart believed imagination can increase sensibility, but "sensibility which terminates in imagination, is but

21. Dugald Stewart, *Philosophy of the Human Mind*, I, 431–37.
22. *Ibid.*, 457–60.

a refined and selfish luxury." Thus he cautioned that novel reading can reduce morality: accommodation to fictional distress can diminish uneasiness at real distress and so preclude action to relieve it. In similar terms, Hawthorne criticized his fictional dreamers for excessivly refined and self-reflexive efforts of imagination; and he frequently worried about whether novels serve any useful purpose. Stewart suggested another danger of imagination: an individual might conceive an impossible idea of perfection; love might then take root only in his imagination.[23] The heroine of "Sylph Etherege" forms such an impossible ideal of love, and in "Rappaccini's Daughter," Hawthorne warns as explicitly as Stewart against "that cunning resemblance of love which flourishes in the imagination, but strikes no depth of root into the heart."

Yet Stewart concludes that exercise of imagination can have great value "when corrected by habits of real business." Fiction can not only soothe the reader and distract him from worries, but it can cultivate his taste, refine his moral perceptions, and lead to deeper understanding of human nature, particularly "weaknesses of the heart." Exercising the imagination can ease an individual burdened by real distress, Stewart said—essentially the same point Hawthorne later made in "The Hall of Fantasy." But Stewart ends his chapter with even stronger praise: "The faculty of imagination is the great spring of human activity, and the principal source of human improvement." Because the imagination can envisage scenes and characters more perfect than we encounter in life, it can refine and exalt men, encouraging them to pursue such perfection.[24] This is the view of imagination that engendered the utopian vision of *The Blithedale Romance*.

Hawthorne's interest in Stewart did not end with his senior year at Bowdoin. Two years later he checked out Stewart's *Philosophical Essays* from the Salem Athenaeum, as well as

23. *Ibid.*, 461–66.
24. *Ibid.*, 466–70.

Lectures on the Philosophy of the Human Mind by Stewart's eminent colleague, the Scottish philosopher Thomas Brown, whose ideas essentially corroborate Stewart's. In Brown's discussion of subjective vision, even his language and style seem to anticipate Hawthorne's. In twilight, Brown says, superstitious people "incorporate their fears with the objects they dimly perceive, till the whole, thus compounded, assumes the appearance of external reality." Here is an explanation of the unsteady perceptions of young Goodman Brown as he begins his forest adventure. Continuing his explanation of how the imagination interacts with real perceptions, Brown says "spectral forms and visions seem truly to exist, because there are forms which are truly seen, and sounds which are truly heard." This is what occurs in "The Hollow of the Three Hills" and "The White Old Maid."[25]

Hawthorne's instructor in the course of "Moral and Mental Philosophy" which used Stewart as text was Thomas C. Upham, a young clergyman, poet, and philosopher who had just come to Bowdoin. Hawthorne's classmates Horatio Bridge and Longfellow both praised him, Bridge commenting that he was "scholarly, gentle, and kind to the students, by all of whom he was much beloved."[26] Clearly Upham was a sympathetic teacher of Stewart's ideas. If Hawthorne read any of Upham's popular textbooks, which began to appear two years after his graduation, he would have found explicit agreement with Stewart. Upham's *Elements of Mental Philosophy* even uses Stewart's illustrative examples.

Upham's comments on dreaming in this book closely follow Stewart's. Dreams can become wild and incoherent because they are not corrected by perceptions of reality or disciplined

25. Thomas Brown, *Lectures on the Philosophy of the Human Mind* (Edinburgh: William Tait, 1833), 247. *Lectures* was charged from the Athenaeum on June 13, 1827. Brown's moral emphases are consistent with Hawthorne's, as when he says "conscience is our moral memory. It is the memory of the heart" (70).

26. Horatio Bridge, *Personal Recollections of Nathaniel Hawthorne* (New York: Harper, 1893), 53.

by the will, he says; dreams seem real because the dreaming mind is undistracted; and time in dreams is assumed to be whatever the dream actions require. At this point Upham quotes Stewart's analogy of the show box. He continues to follow Stewart in explaining the relation of dreams to waking life: "Dreams are fashioned from the materials of the thoughts and feelings we have while awake," he says, governed by "the repetition of our customary and prevailing sensations, by recent thoughts, and by concurrent sensations." But here some of his examples implicitly go beyond Stewart, suggesting that creativity and problem solving can occur during dreams: Upham cites Coleridge's account of composing "Kubla Khan" in a dream, and Benjamin Franklin's claim that he solved political problems while dreaming.[27] Hawthorne is thus closer to Upham than to Stewart when he represents dreams as a special mode of knowledge and when he cultivates reverie as a condition of creation.

Upham's definition of imagination and his praise of it similarly accord with Stewart's. "Imagination is a complex exercise of the mind, by means of which various conceptions are combined together, so as to form new wholes," Upham says; and he even offers Stewart's example—Milton's description of Eden. Both agree that imagination can charm the mind by presenting new views of human experience; it can ease a heavy heart;

27. Thomas C. Upham, *Elements of Mental Philosophy* (New York: Harper, 1841), 204–12. Upham's first textbook, *Elements of Intellectual Philosophy*, was published in 1827, and the version entitled *Elements of Mental Philosophy* was first published in 1831. In 1834, Upham published *A Philosophical and Practical Treatise on the Will*, considered his most original contribution to psychology. The *Elements* was expanded into two volumes in 1837 and from 1840 on included the *Treatise on the Will* as a third volume. *Outlines of Imperfect and Disordered Mental Action*, first published in 1840, was republished in Harper's Family Library in 1841. Schneider, in *History of American Philosophy*, 240–41, calls Upham "the first great American textbook writer in mental philosophy," observing that "between 1837 and 1857, American textbooks on mental philosophy appeared at the rate of about one a year." According to A. A. Roback, *History of American Psychology* (New York: Library Publishers, 1952), Upham's *Elements of Mental Philosophy* was the dominant text in American psychology before William James.

and it can inspire the soul. But Upham, a pious minister, offers an additional justification. "There are those who recommend the careful culture of the memory, the judgment, and the reasoning power, but look coldly and suspiciously on the imagination," he observes; however, "the Creator had some design or purpose in furnishing men with it," and therefore man should exercise his imagination.[28] Although Hawthorne never offered that argument, he did consciously reckon with suspicion about the imagination, including his own, ultimately concluding that the imagination is an important component of full human experience.

Upham's eventual three-part division of *Elements of Mental Philosophy* into sections on the intellect, the sensibilities, and the will—which began with the 1841 edition—seems so consistent with Hawthorne's analytical approach to characterization that it is easy to agree with Marvin Laser that Upham was a "solid underpinning" for Hawthorne and that his "system was useful to Hawthorne in contriving his characters and in analyzing their states of mind."[29] But Upham is not necessarily Hawthorne's source for this three-part formulation. The head-heart division is centuries old; and Stewart as well as other early faculty psychologists had discussed the role of the will.[30] Further, although Upham discusses the essential nature of the will, aware that its strength can vary, he was never concerned about the eroded, suspended, or overpowered will, as Hawthorne was. Finally, simply assessing the roles of head, heart, and will does not lead far enough into Hawthorne's characters; it avoids the problem of how the mind moves deeper into itself during

28. Upham, *Elements of Mental Philosophy*, 220–23.
29. Marvin Laser, "'Head,' 'Heart,' and 'Will' in Hawthorne's Psychology," *Nineteenth Century Fiction*, X (1955), 130–40. Laser does not look into Upham's beliefs about the imagination and dreaming, and he overstates his case when he says "it appears that Hawthorne was striving for an almost scientific accuracy of expression when he undertook the analysis of his fictional creatures" (135).
30. Schneider, in *History of American Philosophy*, 243, says a three-faculty psychology dates back to Samuel West in 1793, that it was seriously formulated by Asa Burton in 1824, and that Upham was familiar with Burton's three-part division.

dreams and reveries, and it does not recognize that sometimes Hawthorne used the terminology of head and heart interchangeably in his attempts to convey the sense of a unitary inner life.

The processes Upham precisely delineated remained ultimately mysterious for Hawthorne. Not only Upham's schematizations as such but even his particular analytic divisions seem inconsistent with Hawthorne's understanding of how the mind functions. For example, Upham divided the intellect into the external or receptive powers, including sense perception and dreaming, and the internal or suggestive powers of memory, reason, and imagination. Hawthorne would not abstract the intellectual powers that precisely; but if he did, he would certainly not separate dreaming from imagination, nor would he consider dreaming merely a "receptive" activity.

Nevertheless, he was interested in all the "intellectual" powers Upham discussed, in the inner experiences Upham grouped as natural and moral sensibilities, and in the will. Thus it makes little sense to insist that Upham had no influence on Hawthorne, as Frederick Crews does. It is true that "Hawthorne never mentions his teachings and is not known to have read his books"; but Hawthorne mentions few of the teachers or books whose ideas merged with his own. When Crews suggests that "the mixed motives, hidden scruples, and maniacal projects of Hawthorne's heroes would have appalled Upham," he is really arguing that Hawthorne's insights are more profound and complex than the philosopher's. That is one reason why we read Hawthorne, but not Upham. Crews correctly observes tht "Hawthorne's terrible insights" cannot be confined to "Upham's tediously subdivided and inert categories"; but they cannot be confined to any categories. Crews overstates his case when he ironically dismisses the hypothesis of influence by saying, "Hawthorne, it seems, loyally followed Upham's schematization of the mind into intellect, sensibilities, and will, and used his fictional characters as personifications of one or another of these functions."[31] The question of loyalty is irrelevant. Hawthorne does often establish inner conflicts or contrasts between characters in terms of the dominance of head, heart, or will. This does not prove that Hawthorne read Upham's works in one of their numerous printings; yet that remains a possibility. Further, despite his rigid categories, Upham did achieve some "terrible insights" into mental disorders: his discussions of mental aberrations in the *Elements* and later in a separate volume include astute comments about emotionally disturbed individuals who cannot distinguish fantasies from reality, a condition recurrent in Hawthorne's fiction.

Upham, Stewart, and the other Scottish philosophers may well have stimulated Hawthorne to pursue in his own way problems of how the mind operates within its own confines. Certainly many of his ideas and attitudes are consistent with the Scottish system. And yet the differences are crucial. Hawthorne never believed as Stewart and Upham did that dreams are simply passive experiences, or that both dreams and imagination are wholly dependent on the world of objective experience; nor did he adopt the linear schematizations of the Common Sense school. He goes far beyond such schemes in his fiction whenever he dramatizes how repressed ideas erupt in sleep and how the mind with some reluctance then presses deeper into itself, and whenever he suggests we can never wholly understand what then happens. He also differs from the Scots to the extent that he agrees with Emerson, believing the imagination to be a creative power that can attain glimpses of ideal truth.[32]

31. Frederick C. Crews, *The Sins of the Fathers: Hawthorne's Psychological Themes* (New York: Oxford University Press, 1966), 259–60.

32. For discussions of Emerson's familiarity with Scottish philosophy in college, see Sheldon W. Liebman, "The Origins of Emerson's Early Poetics: His Reading in the Scottish Common Sense Critics," *American Literature*, XLV (1973), 23–33; and Merrill R. Davis, "Emerson's 'Reason' and the Scotch Philosophers," *New England Quarterly*, XVII (1944), 209–28.

Critics who compare Hawthorne with Emerson are right to focus on the two men's beliefs about the imagination.[33] Unlike most of their contemporaries, they both thought it was important to examine inner experience and to write about it, though they reached those conclusions separately. Hawthorne had already chosen his career before Emerson's first essays were published. Hawthorne became familiar with their common ground through Emerson's essays and poems, through Sophia and his many other admirers at Brook Farm and in Concord, and through Emerson himself. And undoubtedly, Transcendental theories provoked him to formulate his own conceptions of ideal truth. But Hawthorne knew where he differed from the

33. Marjorie Elder in *Nathaniel Hawthorne: Transcendental Symbolist* (Athens: Ohio University Press, 1969) overstates her case: she says Hawthorne's ideas in general are consistent with transcendentalism, and "his aesthetic theories can only be called Transcendental" (50). Hyatt Waggoner says unequivocally that both Emerson and Hawthorne were "idealists in metaphysics and based their metaphysics on their idealism" (*Hawthorne: A Critical Study* [Cambridge: Harvard University Press, 1963], 15). Millicent Bell says Hawthorne "absorbed the elements of transcendentalism in common with his contemporaries," and comparing the "Romantic aesthetics" of Emerson and Hawthorne, she concludes that they both believed artists attain insight into eternal truths by submitting to "the current of the invisible"; but Bell realizes that this "transcendental view of the artist represents only part of Hawthorne's thinking on the subject" (*Hawthorne's View of the Artist* [Albany: State University of New York Press, 1962], 12, 49, 67). For studies of romantic idealism as it reached America from Germany, France, and England at the beginning of the nineteenth century, see O. B. Frothingham, *Transcendentalism in New England* (New York: Putnam, 1886); I. Woodbridge Riley, *American Thought from Puritanism to Pragmatism and Beyond* (New York: Holt, 1915); and Perry Miller's anthology, *The Transcendentalists* (New York: Doubleday, 1957). Hawthorne's and Emerson's contemporaries continued the Puritans' mistrust of the imagination and their emphasis on practical and socially productive labor. See Perry Miller, *The Puritans* (New York: Harper and Row, 1963), and Charles Feidelson, Jr., *Symbolism and American Literature* (Chicago: University of Chicago Press, 1953), esp. Chapter Three, which locates Puritan thought in the American tradition of "symbolic vision." Robert Shulman in "Hawthorne's Quiet Conflict," *Philological Quarterly*, XLVII (1968), 216–36, discusses Hawthorne's conflict between his "vocation as a Romantic artist and the imperatives of a Protestant ethic he shared with his contemporaries," which contended that man should do God's work in the world and make financial profit from it. But Hawthorne was always concerned about his impact on society, and he always had money problems. Terence Martin, in *The Instructed Vision*, comments that the Puritans distrusted the imagination because they assumed it led men away from truth and reality.

"great original Thinker" who was nevertheless an "everlasting rejecter of all that is, and seeker for he knows not what" (*Mosses*, 30; *AN*, 357).

Emerson's comments about the relation of dreams to waking experience might almost be mistaken for Hawthorne's. "Our dreams are the sequel of our waking knowledge," he wrote in "Spiritual Laws." "The visions of the night always bear some proportion to the visions of the day." He explained nightmares the same way: "Hideous dreams are exaggerations of the sins of the day. We see our own evil affections embodied in bad physiognomies."[34] This could be read as a gloss on the hideous illusive visages of "Young Goodman Brown" or the apparitions of the dreamer's "evil affections" in "The Celestial Rail-road"; but Hawthorne never attributed dream visions merely to the sins of a single day.

Dreams were most important for Emerson not as a commentary on waking experience but as a liberation from it. Thus he urged every author to respect "that dream-power which every night shows thee is thine own;—a power transcending all limit and privacy." Through his dream-power, the writer "unlocks our chains and admits us to a new scene."[35] This Hawthorne believed and attempted, even when he identified the dream world with the private consciousness. Like Emerson, he believed that only the imagination can free man from the fetters of material fact.

Both men believed that the imagination moves beyond the world of fact both to immanent truths and to the transcendent ideal, and both valued the writer who shares such experiences with his readers. Yet they reached different conclusions about the dominion of the imagination. Emerson believed that the imagination is a sovereign power to which nature is tributary, the source of "real and final facts" beyond mere material facts,

34. Edward Waldo Emerson (ed.), *The Complete Works of Ralph Waldo Emerson* (12 vols.; Boston: Houghton Mifflin, 1903–1904), II, 148.
35. Emerson, "The Poet," in *Complete Works*, III, 32–33.

a spontaneous and liberating power that exalts the individual, yet does not overpower him or lead him to confuse inner vision with material fact. We live in two worlds, Emerson said, the imaginary realm and the world of fact; and we "must not mix them."[36] Hawthorne believed we must mix them; this was his literary program and frequently his subject. He treated the imagination not as a sovereign but a subsidiary power, almost wholly dependent on actual experience. And unlike Emerson, he believed the imagination could go out of control all too easily, whether through excess or deficiency: he knew from experience that it could overpower an individual, who might then confuse fantasy and reality; and he also knew the imagination could become torpid or impotent.

Emerson sometimes seemed ridiculous to Hawthorne, the victim of his own imagination, a "mystic, stretching his hand out of cloud-land, in vain search for something real," but not at home among carrots and turnips. "Mr. Emerson is a great searcher for facts," Hawthorne said, "but they seem to melt away and become insubstantial in his grasp" (AN, 336). Thus Hawthorne implicitly identifies Emerson with his fictional dreamers who have lost hold of reality, in contrast with Thoreau, whose writing he praises as "true, minute, and literal in observation, yet giving the spirit as well as letter of what he sees" (AN, 355). Hawthorne agreed with Sophia in admiring Emerson as "a poet of deep beauty and austere tenderness"; but he "sought nothing from him as a philosopher" (Mosses, 30–31).

Nor did he seek anything from the pseudoscientists of his day, despite their claims to knowledge about the inner life. Hawthorne's opinions about them ranged from skepticism to horrified disbelief. Physiognomy and phrenology might have some validity: he thought a high brow might indicate intelligence. But the mesmerist's control of his subject appalled

36. Emerson, "Poetry and Imagination," in *Complete Works*, VIII, 19–29.

Hawthorne, and he condemned both mesmerism and spiritualism for debasing the idea of the soul.[37]

Mesmerism horrified him as a violation of the sanctity of the inner life. With eloquent anguish, he urged Sophia not to try a mesmeric cure for her chronic headaches, or at least not to let the mesmerist put her to sleep. Allowing a mesmerist to substitute his will for hers would be a degradation, a kind of psychological rape: "It seems to me that the sacredness of an individual is violated by it; there would be an intrusion into thy holy of holies—and the intruder would not be thy husband." He concluded that mesmeric phenomena "seem rather calculated to bewilder us, than to teach us any truths about the present or future state of being"; and even worse, the mesmerist's "earthly effluence" might contaminate the soul's "true, though hidden, knowledge."[38] Hawthorne worried about the

37. Contemporary texts are the best sources for information about these pseudosciences. See, for example, George Combe's books about phrenology and the Fowlers' phrenological charts; Lavater's texts on physiognomy; studies of mesmerism by doctors such as James Braid, J. C. Colquhon, Edwin Lee, and W. Newnham; and books about spiritualism by such practitioners as Douglas Home and Andrew Jackson Davis. See also two unpublished doctoral dissertations, Elizabeth Ruth Hosmer, "Science and Pseudo-Science in the Writings of Nathaniel Hawthorne" (University of Illinois, 1948), and John Thomas McKiernan, "The Psychology of Nathaniel Hawthorne" (Pennsylvania State University, 1957). Hawthorne was familiar with the theories of phrenology long before the fad was reflected in Salem newspapers of the 1830s: *Fanshawe* (1828) uses phrenological terminology for incidental characterization, and in 1828, Hawthorne withdrew from the Salem Athenaeum the four volumes of Johann Lavater's *Essays on Physiognomy* as well as Jacques Pernetti's *Philosophical Lectures Upon Physiognomy* (Kesselring, "Hawthorne's Reading," 55, 58). The first issue of *The American Magazine of Useful and Entertaining Knowledge* Hawthorne edited, in 1836, includes an excerpt from the famous French phrenologist Combe, as well as Hawthorne's proposal of a "science of noses"; and in the following issue Hawthorne describes phrenology as a "doubtful science" which "future generations may reject as utterly as the physiognomy of Lavater" (302–304, 268, 337). Yet he did not reject it utterly: he said Ilbrahim in "The Gentle Boy" was skilled in physiognomy but ignored physiognomical warnings against the boy who betrayed him. Sophia accepted the tenets of both phrenology and physiognomy. See Herbert Ross Brown's discussion of "Popular Isms and Ologies" in *The Sentimental Novel in America* (Durham: Duke University Press, 1940), 181–200.

38. Letter to Sophia, October 18, 1841, written from Brook Farm, in Huntington Library, San Marino, Calif. Hawthorne continues, "Now, ownest wife, I have no faith whatever that people are raised to the seventh heaven, or to any heaven at all, or that they gain any insight into the mysteries of life beyond death, by means of this

suspension of the will during dream and reverie, but he was far more horrified by the apparent annihilation of will during the mesmeric trance. The theological implications were intolerable. As Coverdale said in *The Blithedale Romance*, "The idea of man's eternal responsibility was made ridiculous, and immortality rendered at once impossible, and not worth acceptance" (*BR*, 198).

Hawthorne rejected the claims of spiritualists more dispassionately, on the grounds that their alleged proofs were addressed only to the senses. He tried to dissuade Sophia from joining in séances both before and after their marriage; and with passing years his remarks about spiritualism become increasingly plaintive. He always maintained that spiritualists "mistake the physical and material for the spiritual," even though his friend Pike believed in spiritualism, and even after Sophia engaged in spirit-rapping experiments with such distinguished friends as Hiram Powers and Elizabeth Barrett Browning.[39] As he wrote in his journal, "I would not believe my own

---

strange science. Without distrusting that the phenomena which thou tellest me of, and others as remarkable, have really occurred, I think that they are to be accounted for as the result of a physical and material, not of a spiritual, influence. . . . And what delusion can be more lamentable and mischievous, than to mistake the physical and material for the spiritual?" C. E. Schorer in "Hawthorne and Hypnosis" suggests that Sophia's experiments with mesmerism annoyed Hawthorne and made him feel belittled, perhaps even jealous. *Nathaniel Hawthorne Journal 1972* (Washington, D.C.: NCR/Microcard, 1973), 239–44. Taylor Stoehr in "Hawthorne and Mesmerism" discusses Hawthorne's knowledge of mesmerism and its role in his fiction "as a metaphor for the writer's art." *Huntington Library Quarterly*, XXXIII (1969), 33–60.

39. Sophia received letters from her mother on December 28, 1850, and March 23, 1851, discussing current spirit-rappings and suggesting that Una might be a good medium. She declared she believed in mesmerism, but suspended full belief in spiritualism, though she participated in séances. Letters in Henry W. and Albert A. Berg Collection, New York Public Library. On July 24, 1851, Hawthorne wrote a long letter about spiritualism to his friend William B. Pike, who was apparently a believer, saying, "I am very glad of your testimony in favor of spiritual intercourse. I have heard and read much on the subject, and it appears to me to be the strangest and most bewildering affair I ever heard of. I should be very glad to believe that these rappers are, in any one instance, the spirits of the persons whom they profess themselves to be; but though I have talked with those who have had the freest communication, there has always been something that makes me doubt. So you must

sight, nor touch of the spiritual hands. . . . I think I *might* yield to higher poetry or heavenlier wisdom than mortals in the flesh have ever sung or uttered"; but these no medium ever produced. The entry is distressed and even petulant, though not hostile; spiritualism moved him only to "a sluggish disgust, and repugnance to meddle with it" (*EN*, 616–17).

He explained his mistrust of séances through the analogue of dreams. What the medium produces is the product of her own mind, he said, and not of immortal spirits:

It resembles a dream, in that the whole material is, from the first, in the dreamer's mind, though concealed at various depths below the surface; the dead appear alive, as they always do in dreams; un-expected combinations occur, as continually in dreams; the mind speaks through the various persons of the drama, and sometimes astonishes itself with its own wit, wisdom, and eloquence, as often in dreams; but, in both cases, the intellectual manifestations are really of a very flimsy texture. . . . I should be glad to believe in the genuineness of these spirits, if I could; but the above is the con-clusion to which my soberest thoughts tend. (X, 395–96)

He was surprised by his own indifference to the marvels claimed by spiritualists; "they seem not to be facts to my in-tuitions and deeper perceptions," he said. "My inner soul does not in the least admit them; there is a mistake somewhere" (X, 394). Yet he remained a skeptic rather than an outright dis-believer. It was foolish to accept a medium's waking dreams as spiritual communications; but he thought metaphysicians and physiologists might well investigate the phenomena.

---

allow me to withhold my full and entire belief." Quoted by Rose Hawthorne Lathrop, in *Memories of Hawthorne* (Boston: Houghton Mifflin, 1897), 153. He always withheld entire belief. His notebooks record conversations in England and in Italy with such confirmed devotees of spiritualism as Elizabeth Barrett Browning, Frances Trollope, Hiram Powers, William Story, and Harriet Hosmer. The Hawthornes' governess, Ada Shepard, was the medium at séances in which Mrs. Hawthorne and Mrs. Browning participated during their stay in Italy; but both Robert Browning and Hawthorne remained nonbelievers. See Norman Holmes Pearson's introduction and notes to "The French and Italian Notebooks" (Ph.D. Dissertation, Yale University, 1941).

As he inquired into the limits and possibilities of the inner life, Hawthorne was not bound by the tenets of the Common Sense school, transcendentalism, the pseudosciences, or any other system of belief. There is no clearer index of his eclecticism and occasional inconsistency than his terminology. He freely used words like *heart*, *mind*, and *imagination* with the same imprecision that persists in common discourse. He might use antithetical terms as synonyms or distinguish between terms he otherwise used interchangeably. Yet each term has a central core of meaning, often expressed through clearly associated metaphors, and each conveys an implicit moral imperative essential to our understanding of the dreams in Hawthorne's fiction. These were the terms he himself used in discussing those dreams.

Hawthorne usually preserved the commonplace distinction between *mind* and *heart* and frequently used both terms together to define the complex range of ordinary inner experience. Whenever he used these paired terms or such alternative pairs as *thought* and *feeling*, or *intellect* and *sympathy*, he was usually asserting man's need for self-fulfillment, for inner wholeness and balance. At the same time he affirmed the wide range of individual differences and the individual's capacity to explore and to modify his inner being.[40]

Heart is the term that recurs most frequently, usually metaphorically defined as a chamber. It is an enclosed space containing passions and can vary in size and temperature: it can be large or small, hot or cold. Further, it is capable of growth and change, and one heart can warm another. Thus Chillingworth says that his heart was a large but cold room and that he hoped marriage to Hester might warm it.

40. John W. Schroeder exhaustively analyzes Hawthorne's heart imagery in "'That Inward Sphere': Notes on Hawthorne's Heart Imagery," *PMLA*, LXV (1950), 106–19; and Donald Ringe discusses Hawthorne's insistence on the need to balance the two in "Hawthorne's Psychology of the Head and Heart," *PMLA*, LXV (1950), 120–32. See also F. O. Matthiessen, *American Renaissance* (New York: Oxford University Press, 1941), 345–51.

For Hawthorne, the heart was at once the vessel of passion and of morality. Consistent with popular idiom and the Scottish philosophers' location of conscience in the sensibility, he located spectres of guilt within the heart; and he frequently represented the heart as a cavern, a well, a prison, or a gloomy edifice containing a tomb or dungeon. Components of the image are evident in a famous notebook entry: "The Human Heart to be allegorized as a cavern; at the entrance there is sunshine, and flowers growing about it. You step within, but a short distance, and begin to find yourself surrounded with a terrible gloom, and monsters of divers kinds; it seems like Hell itself. You are bewildered, and wander long without hope" (AN, 237). Yet sometimes Hawthorne's heart images express optimism and underlying faith, as in the continuation of the cavern image, with its imperative for self-knowledge: "At last a light strikes upon you. You press towards it yon, and find yourself in a region that seems, in some sort, to reproduce the flowers and sunny beauty of the entrance, but all perfect. These are the depths of the heart, or of human nature, bright and peaceful; the gloom and terror may lie deep; but deeper still is this eternal beauty" (AN, 237). Some hearts "have their well-spring in the infinite, and contain inexhaustible sympathies," he said in a variant image in "The Intelligence Office" (Mosses, 325); and Beatrice Rappaccini has such a heart. Only innocent hearts, however, can remain uncontaminated. Clifford Pyncheon's sympathies with children kept his heart pure "like a reservoir into which rivulets were pouring, not far from the fountainhead" (HSG, 171); but Hilda's knowledge of guilt is like a "murdered corpse" polluting the well of her heart (MF, 330).

The mind is the intellectual counterpart of the heart, sometimes spatially defined in terms and images similar to those used for the heart. A Gothic landscape serves as an analogue for Hester's terrifying moral speculations: she wandered in "the dark labyrinth of mind," where steep precipices and deep chasms are part of the "wild and ghastly scenery" (SL, 166).

But Hawthorne usually thought of the mind not as a place but a power that can vary in strength. Its essential faculty is intellect, which acts as an intermediary between the visible world and the imagination. It receives sense impressions and transforms them into thoughts and ideas; a moonlit room is readily translated into objects of intellect which can then be transmitted to the imagination. Yet the intellect is cold: it functions best in conjunction with the enlivening warmth of the heart. Hawthorne paid close attention to the problem of the mind separated from the heart, though he never considered the reverse possibility. A man of excessive intellect may become so morally warped that he pries into other people's lives simply out of curiosity; if he is an artist, his work then remains cold and lifeless.

Even though the mind and heart are treated as antithetical powers, sometimes they are virtually synonymous, so that either one can serve to define a character's inner consciousness. The chapter in *The Scarlet Letter* devoted to Dimmesdale's introspective vigils is called "The Interior of a Heart," but it could just as well be called "The Interior of a Mind"; and "The Haunted Mind" is about the feelings as well as thoughts that occur during reverie and dreams. Further, both the mind and the heart are sometimes represented spatially, as inner chambers or theaters, though sometimes as vital forces.

Hawthorne believed the imagination functions properly only when it is nurtured by the mind and the heart. He was consistent with faculty psychology in asserting that the imagination receives thoughts and images from the intellect and memory. It can then simply copy old images or formulate new combinations, perhaps capriciously; but if the heart is cooperating, the imagination can reveal what the material world has concealed, or can create images of ideal beauty that can not only inform but inspire. Sometimes Hawthorne used the terms *fancy* and *imagination* interchangeably for the image-making power and the mirroring of remembered experience; but sometimes he

39

adopted Coleridge's distinction, using *imagination* to signify the mind's creative faculty. Thus the poets satirized in the early sketches and painters who are mere technicians can produce works of fancy; but it takes an inspired artist to create Owen Warland's animate butterfly, Drowne's wooden image, or the portrait of Beatrice Cenci.[41]

The range of Hawthorne's beliefs about the imagination is evident in his metaphors. He sometimes figured the imagination as a mirror, which can concentrate sight and insight: it may reveal physical truths, such as the identity of the scarecrow in "Feathertop" or the absurd decrepitude of the participants in "Dr. Heidegger's Experiment"; it may provoke confrontation with private truths, as when Dimmesdale stares into his looking glass and sees illusive images of guilt; or it may suggest spiritual truths, like the trees reflected in the Concord River, more "real" than "objects palpable to our grosser senses," because the "disembodied images stand in closer relation to the soul" (*Mosses*, 22). Sometimes Hawthorne figured the imagination as moonlight or other dim light which transforms visions of the real world. And sometimes imagination is identified with the dream state.

The imagination may also be established by a spatial meta-

41. Robert Kimbrough in " 'The Actual and the Imaginary': Hawthorne's Concept of Art in Theory and Practice" misreads Hawthorne's complex use of faculty psychology, as in his comment that the artist has Everyman's "innate moral characteristics of intellect, soul, and heart," which are in him "expanded to 'thought, imagination, and keenest sensibility.' " He assumes incorrectly that Hawthorne considered imagination to be the active power of the soul. In *Transactions of the Wisconsin Academy of Sciences, Arts, and Letters*, L (1961), 277–93. Richard J. Jacobson in *Hawthorne's Conception of the Creative Process* (Cambridge: Harvard University Press, 1965) places Hawthorne's ideas in the context of earlier classical and romantic theories. Meyer H. Abrams in *The Mirror and the Lamp* (New York: Oxford University Press, 1953), examines the symbolic mirror of imagination and also the impact of Dugald Stewart's theories in the context of romantic aesthetics. Malcolm Cowley discusses the imagination's role in perception and creation in "Hawthorne in the Looking-Glass," *Sewanee Review*, LVI (1948), 545–63. Hawthorne's recurrent worry that the imagination might become excessively active is implicit in his admonition to Sophia in a letter dated October 18, 1841 (in the Huntington Library), really a warning to himself: "Keep thy imagination sane—that is one of the truest conditions of communion with Heaven."

phor, with a particular place serving Hawthorne as the analogue for a particular imagination. Rowing with the poet Ellery Channing on the gentle Concord River and observing its reflected "dream-pictures," he "could have fancied that this river had strayed forth out of the rich scenery of my companion's inner world." And in *The Marble Faun* he describes Miriam's dark and crowded studio as representative of the artist's haunted imagination. But the building that is the central image of "The Hall of Fantasy" is a far more extensive analogue, embodying Hawthorne's carefully qualified beliefs about all men's capacity for imagination. The sketch begins with a description of the spacious main hall with its lofty dome, "fantastic architecture," and windows that "admit the light of heaven only through stained and pictured glass." At the center, the waters of an ornamental fountain perform a "magic dance." The whole edifice gives "the impression of a dream, which might be dissipated and shattered to fragments, by merely stamping the foot upon the pavement," yet it is likely to endure. It is separated from ordinary life, yet accessible to everyone. Most people enter it at times, "if not in their waking moments, then by the universal passport of a dream"; here all people meet "who have affairs above, below, or beyond the Actual." Yet there are chambers above this hall and below it: "In its upper stories are said to be apartments, where the inhabitants of earth may hold converse with those of the moon. And beneath our feet are gloomy cells, which communicate with the infernal regions, and where monsters and chimeras are kept in confinement, and fed with all unwholesomeness" (*Mosses*, 172–73). The dreamers assembled in the hall include successful writers, philosophers, and inventors, but also unfortunate men "who make their whole abode and business here, and contract habits which unfit them for all the real employments of life" (*Mosses*, 174–78). The narrator feels tempted to spend his life "in that visionary scene, where the actual world, with its hard angles, should never rub against me, and only be viewed through the medium

41

of pictured windows"; but he resolves to pay only occasional visits to spiritualize "the grossness of this actual life" and to prefigure a state of eternity (*Mosses*, 185).[42]

Three other terms are relatively straightforward in their usage. Hawthorne's references to *soul* are consistent with popular idiom as well as traditional religion, though his images represent the soul as a spiritualized variant of the heart. It has dark depths and can be stained by guilt, but it does not harbor passions. It has an inner sky; and it is directly connected with the infinite. The soul, like the heart, can grow cold; but unlike the heart, it can generate its own warmth.

Sometimes *spirit* and *soul* are used as synonyms; but when they are differentiated, the spirit is the agent of the soul. It voyages forth and stirs the imagination; it both initiates dreams and wanders through them. "Your spirit has departed, and strays like a free citizen, among the people of a shadowy world, beholding strange sights, yet without wonder or dismay," Hawthorne says at the end of "The Haunted Mind" (*T-t T*, 309). The spirit is the active element of consciousness that transcends the limits of waking life and the limits of mortality.

The last term is implicit in all Hawthorne's speculations about dreams, though he rarely made it explicit. The *will* is the faculty that makes choices, the agent of moral control. It is active in waking thought, partly suspended during reverie, but virtually powerless in sleep, madness, or the hypnotic state. The question of whether a dreamer can prevent himself from

42. Gaston Bachelard says the houses of daydreams transcend "our memories of all the houses in which we have found shelter, above and beyond all the houses we have dreamed we lived in," but "do not readily lend themselves to description"; "the oneirically definitive house, must retain its shadows." Particularly suggestive to the reader of Hawthorne are Bachelard's comments on the house's vertical space, from cellars through attics and towers, on places of concealment, and on the relationship of inside to outside space. *The Poetics of Space*, trans. Maria Jolas (Boston: Beacon Press, 1969), 3, 13. See Edgar R. Dryden, "Hawthorne's Castle in the Air: Form and Theme in *The House of the Seven Gables*," *ELH*, XXXVIII (1971), 294–317, a phenomenological analysis with perceptive comments on images of portals, thresholds, and towers. Hawthorne used houses as analogues of particular faculties—mind, heart, or imagination—or to represent the entire interior realm.

becoming engulfed in his dreams is a question about his strength of will. The narrator of "The Haunted Mind" can pull himself out of unpleasant dreams, but not the feeble protagonist of "Fragments from the Journal of a Solitary Man."

Hawthorne's terminology was always tributary to his experience, and his metaphors gave him latitude for his uncertainties, suspicions, and tentative insights. Many of his insights tally with the Scotch philosophers and some with the Transcendentalists; but they tally as well with the later insights of Freud, Gaston Bachelard, and Jerome Singer.[43] Hawthorne needed no one to tell him that dream images are subject to metamorphoses, or that the mind is best able to look into itself when on the threshold between sleep and waking, or that even in our most confusing dreams, we are attempting to unravel problems that baffle our waking minds.

Even when Hawthorne's terminology and metaphors are irresolute or self-contradictory, they offer the same imperatives: the necessary interaction of all men's separate faculties—mind with heart but also with imagination and will, and the necessary interaction of the inner life with the outer world which both sustains and validates it. Only then can imagination spiritualize "the grossness of this actual life" and attain glimpses of transcendent truth. As Bachelard puts it, "The exterior spectacle helps

43. What Freud called the dream-work is comparable to Hawthorne's mirror of imagination: it neither invents nor judges, but gives form to inner visions, which it can transpose, combine, and interpret. Hawthorne would have agreed with Freud's contention that almost every dream is at some point unfathomable: "as soon as we endeavor to penetrate more deeply into the mental process involved in dreaming, every path will end in darkness" (Freud, *Interpretation of Dreams*, V, 511). Jerome L. Singer considers daydreaming "an important human ability," as Hawthorne did, a cognitive skill which is also a source of pleasure and of creativity. More unequivocally than Hawthorne, Singer asserts that daydreams give "a fuller sense of being intensely alive" which "may be worth the frequent pain of a deeper self-awareness." *Daydreaming* (New York: Random House, 1966), xii, 138, 214. Barton Levi St. Armand, in "Hawthorne's 'Haunted Mind': A Subterranean Drama of the Self," *Criticism*, XIII (1971), 1–25, compares Hawthorne to Poe and draws on Jung in his analysis of the hypnagogic state as "a means of profound self-examination and restoration"; he argues that throughout his fiction, Hawthorne avoided final therapeutic confrontation with his inner demons.

inner grandeur unfold." Self-exploration taught Hawthorne how the world and thought can unite. The mind can then attain the feeling Bachelard calls "intimate immensity." "We open the world, as it were," he says, "by transcending the world seen as it is, or as it was, before we started dreaming. And even if we are aware of our own paltry selves—through the effects of harsh dialectics—we become aware of grandeur."[44] Hawthorne looked at the world and at its transcendence within the dreamer's imagination, aware of mortal limits yet also "aware of grandeur."

---

44. Bachelard, *Poetics of Space*, 183–210.

II
The Writer as Dreamer

1. Dreams

Hawthorne's contradictory assumptions about dreams derive in part from other writers, but they also define a recurrent tension in his own life. Especially during his bachelor years, he was tormented by the fear that dreaming might consume him. So frequently did he describe himself as a dreamer, in relatively formal letters and prefaces as well as in intimate letters to Sophia, that we cannot attribute the term to mere sentimental whimsy. It conveys the facts of his relatively isolated life, his ambivalence about it, and his implicit hope that his dreaming might end. But even when he was married, a father, and a famous writer, he worried about the significance of his dreams.

Calling himself a dreamer, he renewed anxieties about his role as writer. He accused himself of passivity and uselessness, of falling victim to his own imagination. The indictment is fully stated in his letter acknowledging Longfellow's praise of *Twice-told Tales*. He is an enchanted dreamer in a shadowed dungeon. "For the last ten years, I have not lived, but only dreamed about living," he wrote. He denies responsibility: "By some witchcraft or other . . . I have been carried apart from the main current of life, and find it impossible to get back again." Yet his passivity is itself at fault: "I have . . . put me into a dungeon; and now I cannot find the key to let myself out—and if the door were open, I should be almost afraid to come out." He can barely sustain his writing: "I have nothing but thin air to concoct my stories of, and it is not easy to give a lifelike semblance to such shadowy stuff." With public approbation, he might have been "stimulated to greater exertions," but his writings have made no "decided impression" on the public. He will continue to be a writer only because he has "nothing else to be ambitious of."[1]

For years he called himself an enervated dreamer, repeatedly referring to the Salem bedroom of his bachelor years as a dream-haunted chamber. The image persisted in his imagination after he left home, sometimes colored by nostalgia. On a visit to Salem in 1840, he wrote to Sophia, "This deserves to be called a haunted chamber; for thousands upon thousands of visions have appeared to me in it; and some few of them have become visible to the world. If ever I should have a biographer, he ought to make great mention of this chamber in my memoirs, because so much of my lonely youth was wasted here; and here my mind and character were formed. . . . By and bye, the world found me out in my lonely chamber, and called me forth . . . and forth I went."[2] Retrospectively, he could see an advantage

1. In the long letter to Longfellow dated June 4, 1837, Hawthorne says he seldom leaves his room "till after dusk," but is comforted to think his future must necessarily be "more varied, and therefore more tolerable than the past." He will continue to "scribble for a living," willing, he says, to "turn my pen to all sorts of drudgery." In his letter to Longfellow on May 16, 1839, when he was working at the Boston Custom House, he complains that "as a literary man, my new occupations entirely break me up," and in November, 1847, he made a similar complaint about work at the Salem Custom House. The manuscripts of Hawthorne's letters to Sophia are at the Huntington Library and those to Longfellow are at the Houghton Library, Harvard University. Hawthorne's courtship letters were published in *Love Letters of Nathaniel Hawthorne* (2 vols.; Chicago: Society of Dofobs, 1907; Washington, D.C.: NCR/Microcard, 1972).

2. Hawthorne to Sophia, October 4, 1840. Hyatt Waggoner in "A Hawthorne Discovery: The Lost Notebook, 1835–1841," *New England Quarterly*, XLIX (1976), 626, says that the lost notebook reveals Hawthorne's preoccupation during the "solitary" years after graduation "not only with suffering, decay, and death, but with cruelty, guilt, and punishment."

in his solitude: it kept him "fresh" for Sophia to endow with "real life."

After his marriage, he could sometimes mock his self-dramatization as a visionary youth in a lonely chamber. Thus he wrote Sophia, "Here is thy husband in his old chamber, where he produced those stupendous works of fiction, which have since impressed the Universe with wonderment and awe! To this chamber, doubtless, in all succeeding ages, pilgrims will come to pay their tribute of reverence."[3] But he was not always so good-humored about it. In a letter to his friend Duyckinck, he summarily condemned the room, his wasted youth, and his abortive fictions: it was "the old dingy and dusky chamber, where I wasted many good years of my youth, shaping day-dreams and night-dreams into idle stories—scarcely half of which ever saw the light; except it were their own blaze upon the hearth."[4]

Subsequently Hawthorne developed for his readers a more pastoral version of himself as an enchanted dreamer. At the end of his 1851 preface to *Twice-told Tales*, he sentimentally recalled "the Dream-Land of his youth" with its "shadowy foliage" (*T-t T*, 7). Later that same year in the preface to *The Snow-Image*, he described himself as a kind of male Sleeping Beauty until Horatio Bridge woke him by arranging the publication of *Twice-told Tales*: "I sat down by the wayside of life, like a man under enchantment, and a shrubbery sprung up around me, and the bushes grew to be saplings, and the saplings became trees, until no exit appeared possible, through the entangling depths of my obscurity. And there, perhaps, I should be sitting at this moment, with the moss on the imprisoning tree-trunks, and the yellow leaves of more than a score of autumns piled above me, if it had not been for you" (*S-I*, 5).

3. The letter, dated January 20, 1842, continues the burlesque tone, as he imagines the "pilgrims" paying tribute to his washstand and dressing-glass.
4. Hawthorne to Evert A. Duyckinck, October 10, 1845, in Duyckinck Collection, New York Public Library. This was written during the time Hawthorne and his family shared his mother's house in Salem.

Yet images of imprisonment persisted. In the *English Note-books*, he attributed a recurrent dream of failure to the "heavy seclusion in which I shut myself up, for twelve years, after leaving college, when everybody moved onward and left me behind" (*EN*, 98). And a year before his death, he complained that he had lived in Concord so long "that I find myself rusted into my hole, and could not get out even if I wished."[5] In each of these allusions, Hawthorne conveys the same implicit drama: he secludes himself, he finds himself enervated by his seclusion, and he is then too somnolent to escape.

His courtship letters to Sophia go beyond images of imprisonment and enchantment to define dreaming as a state of incomplete development. Life without her had been a dream, he said repeatedly, his sentimentality according with his psychological theories. Until they met, he told her, he had been absorbed by fantasies and unable to love. He had once jotted as a story idea, "A man tries to be happy in love; he cannot sincerely give his heart, and the affair seems all a dream" (*AN*, 153). But Sophia had dispelled such dream-states. "Indeed, we are but shadows," he wrote her in October, 1840, "—we are not endowed with real life, and all that seems most real about us is but the thinnest substance of a dream—till the heart is touched. That touch creates us—then we begin to be—thereby we are beings of reality, and inheritors of eternity."[6] Even sixteen years later he repeated, "Nothing else is real, except the bond

5. Hawthorne to William D. Ticknor, January 6, 1863, in Berg Collection; also in *Letters of Hawthorne to William D. Ticknor, 1851–1864* (2 vols., Newark, N.J.: Carteret Book Club, 1910; Washington, D.C.: NCR/Microcard, 1972).

6. This letter of October 4, 1840, seems to draw on Plato's cave image: "For without thy aid, my best knowledge of myself would have been merely to know my own shadow—to watch it flickering on the wall, and mistake its fantasies for my own real actions." Sophia has "taught" him about his heart, illuminated his soul, and "revealed me to myself." Sophia, describing the completion Hawthorne's love brought her, said he gave her intellectual awareness. Refuting her sister Mary's "unfounded aspersions" of her husband's "glorious, great, expanded nature," she said that "his love first awoke in me *consciousness*. I am conscious of the bliss of being now. *Before* I ignorantly lived." Sophia to Mary Peabody Mann, dated February 3, 1850, in the Berg Collection, New York Public Library.

between thee and me. The people around me are but shadows. I am myself but a shadow, till thou takest me in thy arms, and convertest me into substance. Till thou comest back, I do but walk in a dream."[7]

His letters return to the word *dream* not only in describing his earlier life, but also the time spent away from Sophia. While working at the Boston Custom House he wrote to his fiancée, "It is a sore trial to your husband to be estranged from that which makes life a reality to him and to be compelled to spend so many GOD-given days and nights in a dream."[8] From Salem he wrote of Brook Farm, though still a member of the community, "It already looks like a dream behind me. The real Me was never an associate of the community. . . . This Spectre was not thy husband."[9] He echoed one of these phrases eight years later: "The life of the Custom-House lies like a dream behind me" (*SL*, 44).

Occasionally Hawthorne used the word *dream* in an even broader sense, to describe the whole of gross corporeal existence. He wrote Sophia, "All my life hitherto, I have been walking in a dream, among shadows which could not be pressed to my bosom; but now, even in this dream of time, there is something that takes me out of it, and causes me to be a dreamer no more." He concluded that "the grosser life is a dream, and the spiritual life a reality."[10] Such sentiments no doubt

7. The letter dated April 7, 1856, was written from Liverpool to Sophia who, with her daughters, had gone to Lisbon for its milder climate in the winter of 1855. They remained until June, 1856, as guests of Hawthorne's friend, J. L. O'Sullivan, American minister to Portugal.

8. He said in this December 18, 1839, letter to Sophia that the "outward show" of his life could not "satisfy the soul that has become acquainted with truth."

9. He again assured Sophia in this letter of September 3, 1841, that only she gave life "reality and significance"; without her "all was a dream and a mockery."

10. In this letter of January 1, 1840, he asks Sophia if she feels as he does that they live "above time" because their "affection diffuses eternity round about us." In a letter inviting Duyckinck to visit the Old Manse on November 26, 1843, sixteen months after their marriage, he said, "I feel as if, for the first time in my life, I was awake. I have found a reality, though it looks very much like some of my old dreams." He wistfully says he wishes only that "Providence would make it somewhat more plain to my apprehension how I am to earn my bread." In Duyckinck Collection.

appealed to Sophia's simple idealism, but Hawthorne meant them. He was certain that reciprocated love leads to spiritual awakening and thus to psychic wholeness, a recurrent theme in his fiction.

Even while he was declaring that dreams lack significance, however, he was an extraordinarily persistent observer of his own dreams. He noted them frequently in his letters and journals, sometimes as the mere fact that he had dreamed, but sometimes in more detail. In his journal for December 1, 1850, is the bare entry, "At night, dreamed of seeing Pike" (*AN*, 300). In a letter to Sophia eight months after their marriage when she was away visiting her family, he told her of a disturbing dream, then tried to dismiss it: "I dreamed the other night that our house was broken open, and all our silver stolen." Without acknowledging his own repressed fears for his domestic security, perhaps even his fear of losing Sophia, he playfully reassured her, "No matter though it be;—we have steel forks and German silver spoons in plenty."[11] A few weeks later, when Sophia was again on a family visit, he reported dispiritedly in his journal, "I dreamed a great deal, but to no good purpose; for all the characters and incidents have vanished" (*AN*, 376). Apparently he was by then accustomed to using his dreams as sources for his fiction. And a few months later, he complained that the short midsummer nights caused troubled dreams: "I get scarcely any sound repose, just now;—tossings and turnings, and the turmoil of dreams, consume the night" (*AN*, 390).

One dream recorded during this prolific period of his life is an unusually placid and unusually precise expression of his ambition for public acclaim and financial reward: "A dream, the other night, that the world had become dissatisfied with the inaccurate manner in which facts are reported, and had employed me, with a salary of a thousand dollars, to relate the things of public importance exactly as they happen" (*AN*, 244).

11. Hawthorne to Sophia, March 16, 1843.

The reference to "things of public importance" seems to reflect his perennial worry that fiction is socially useless; the reference to a thousand dollars evidently touches on his anxieties about making a living. He may have been aware that his dream expressed a wish-fulfillment, for about this time he commented fancifully on a bird singing at midnight. "Probably the note gushed out from the midst of a dream, in which he fancied himself in Paradise with his mate; and suddenly awaking, he found himself on a cold, leafless bough, with a New-England mist penetrating through his feathers" (AN, 386). The same bird awakening from a wishful dream appears in "Buds and Bird-Voices," and in "The Hall of Fantasy" he explained that wishful dreams can grant temporary ease. Even so, he was usually reluctant to pursue the meaning of his dreams.

Unlike these laconic notations, Hawthorne's courtship letters discussing the dreams and reveries Sophia had inspired are sentimental, lyrical, often rhapsodic. In one, he describes himself sitting in his room "musing and dreaming about a thousand things, with every one of which, I do believe, some nearer or remoter thought of you was intermingled."[12] A particularly happy night of dreaming followed a visit to her: "Did you not know, beloved, that I dreamed of you, as it seemed to me, all night long, after that last blissful meeting?" He remembered the mood of the dream but could describe none of its detail: "It is true, when I looked back upon the dream, it immediately became confused; but it had been vivid, and most happy, and left a sense of happiness in my heart." He then urged her to return to her recumbent fiancé: "Come again, sweet wife! Force your way through the mists and vapors that envelope my slumbers —illumine me with a radiance that shall not vanish when I awake. I throw my heart as wide open to you as I can."[13]

12. *Ibid.*, April 2, 1839.
13. *Ibid.*, August 8, 1839. This presentation of himself as the passive and Sophia as the aggressive partner is curiously consistent with his later image of himself as Sleeping Beauty.

As in this transparently erotic invitation, he often moved from generalized description of a happy dream to whimsical speculation about it, frequently playing with fantasies about meeting Sophia in dreams. He once suggested that she deliberately try to transmit her thoughts and feelings into his mind and heart, but worried that "perhaps it is not wise to intermix fantastic ideas with the reality of our affection."[14] Nevertheless, one evening as he was about to sleep, he urged, "Sleep thou too, my beloved—let us pass at one and the same moment into that misty region, and embrace each other there."[15] And in another letter he wondered if she ever hovered about him in her dreams, "calling to me, out of the midst of thy dream, to come and join thee there."[16] The speculation is fanciful, but the yearning is real.

Sometimes Hawthorne undercut his own sentimental yearning, as when he chided Sophia for being "naughty—she would not be dreamed about."[17] With more serious whimsy, he rejected the implications of her dream that he had addressed her as "sister" in a letter. Curiosity made him say, "I wish you had read that dream-letter through, and could remember its contents"; but he denied all responsibility: "you are to blame for dreaming such letters, or parts of letters, as coming from me. It was you that wrote it—not I."[18] He did not inquire why she should dream such a dream. Later, responding to a letter describing a nightmare so disturbing that it made her head ache, he again ignored the dream's content, whimsically reassuring her of his protective love: "Thou shouldst have dreamed of thy husband's breast, instead of that Arabian execution."[19]

Occasionally Hawthorne told Sophia about dreams that expressed his own acknowledged anxieties. Shortly before their

14. *Ibid.*, April 2, 1839. On December 11, 1839, he whimsically observed that if there were an intellectual daguerreotype, they might exchange reveries.

15. *Ibid.*, March 15, 1840.   16. *Ibid.*, March 26, 1840.

17. *Ibid.*, March 15, 1840.

18. *Ibid.*, April 30, 1839; this section of letter dated May 3.

19. *Ibid.*, January 13, 1841.

wedding, after she wrote of her plan to be mesmerized, he had terrible nightmares: "Belovedest, didst thou sleep well, last night?" he asked. "My pillow was haunted with ghastly dreams, the details whereof have flitted away like vapors, but a strong impression remains about thy being magnetized. God save me from any more such! I awoke in an absolute quake."[20] Clearly, Hawthorne hoped that his "ghastly dreams" constituted strong enough proof of his revulsion to change Sophia's decision.

If a dream seemed to challenge his assurance of Sophia's love, however, he rejected it as absurd. After writing a story about a faithless dove that flew away from its lover, he told her, he dreamed "the queerest dreams last night, about being deserted, and all such nonsense." Without acknowledging that both story and dream manifest the same anxiety—that he might lose his dove—he summarily dismissed the dream as punishment for writing a "naughty romance." His disclaimer seems excessive: "It seems to me that my dreams are generally about fantasies, and very seldom about what I really think and feel." As if to assure himself that the dream was simply fantastic, he reiterated his faith in her love: "You have warmed my heart, mine own wife; and never again can I know what it is to be cold and desolate, save in dreams."[21]

Yet nearly nine years later, when Sophia and their two children were visiting her mother in Newton, Hawthorne wrote of another dream that she had deserted him, a dream that left him in a state of "frozen agony." The dream expresses both distress and resentment:

The other night, I dreamt that I was at Newton, in a room with thee, and with several other people; and thou tookst occasion to announce, that thou hadst now ceased to be my wife, and hadst taken another husband. Thou madest this intelligence known with such perfect composure and *sang-froid*,—not particularly addressing me, but the company generally—that it benumbed my thoughts and feel-

20. *Ibid.*, June 30, 1842.
21. *Ibid.*, October 3, 1839; this section of letter dated October 4.

ings, so that I had nothing to say. . . . But, hereupon, thy sister Elizabeth, who was likewise present, informed the company, that, in this state of affairs, having ceased to be thy husband, I of course became hers; and turning to me, very coolly inquired whether she or I should write to inform my mother of the new arrangement! . . . I began to expostulate with thee in an infinite agony, in the midst of which I awoke. . . . Thou shouldst not behave so, when thou comest to me in dreams.[22]

Although he narrates the dream dispassionately, its detail suggests how deeply he was disturbed. The dream confesses that he has felt dependent on women (possibly including his Aunt Mary, his mother, his sister Elizabeth, and Sophia's sister Elizabeth, as well as Sophia herself), and it expresses his continuing conflict about that dependency. The women in the dream are cool and composed. Possibly Sophia's sister, who insists Hawthorne's mother must be told he is now her husband and offers to do the telling, is a version of Sophia herself, who years before had offered to tell his mother of their engagement when Hawthorne was reluctant to do so. The dream reveals that beneath the surface of marital security, Hawthorne was enough troubled by anxiety to revert to his old self-image as passive victim.

Two years before their marriage, Hawthorne had written to Sophia about a troublesome nightmare that seems to articulate the prospective bridegroom's uneasiness about leaving his mother and sisters: "Dearest, thou didst not come into my dreams, last night; but, on the contrary, I was engaged in assisting the escape of Louis XVI and Marie Antoinette from Paris, during the French Revolution. And sometimes, by an unaccountable metamorphosis, it seemed as if my mother and sisters were in the place of the King and Queen."[23] This dream seems to be an attempt to resolve his guilt at deserting his mother and sisters by transferring to them his own planned

22. *Ibid.*, June 27, 1848.
23. *Ibid.*, March 26, 1840; this section of letter dated March 27.

escape.[24] Hawthorne did not acknowledge the dream as an expression of his own feelings, and therefore, like Andrew Baxter theorizing that "spirits" cause dreams, he fancifully dismissed it: "I think that fairies rule over our dreams—beings who have no true reason or true feeling, but mere fantaisies [*sic*] instead of those endowments." This dismissal recalls his earlier dismissal of the fantasy of the faithless dove as completely separate from "what I really think and feel."

Yet on two occasions, one three years before his marriage and one long after, he did speculate about the details of anxiety dreams that puzzled him, dreams in which he was the single central figure. A letter to Sophia recounts a nightmare in explicit detail and asks her to decipher it, though at the same time he calls it "silly" and tells her not to see dark meaning in it:

I have been asleep; and I dreamed that I had been sleeping a whole year in the open air; and that while I slept, the grass grew around me. It seemed, in my dream, that the very bed-clothes which actually covered me were spread beneath me, and when I awoke (in my dream) I snatched them up, and the earth under them looked black, as if it had been burnt—one square place, exactly the size of the bed-clothes. Yet there was grass and herbage scattered over this burnt space, looking as fresh, and bright, and dewy, as if the summer rain and the summer sun had been cherishing them all the time. Interpret this for me, my Dove—but do not draw any sombre omens from it. What is signified [by] my nap of a whole year? (it made me grieve to think that I had lost so much of eternity)—and what was the fire that blasted the spot of earth which I occupied, while the grass flourished all around?—and what comfort am I to draw from the fresh herbage amid the burnt space? But it is a silly dream, and you cannot expound any sense out of it. Generally, I

24. Sigmund Freud, in *The Interpretation of Dreams*, Vols. IV and V of *The Complete Psychological Works of Sigmund Freud*, trans. James Strachey (23 vols.; London: Hogarth Press, 1962), V, 353, says kings and queens in dreams often represent the parents. For Hawthorne, whose father died when he was four, mother and sisters might well substitute for the king and queen. The dream may even indicate a more deeply repressed wish—that the fate that befell Louis and Marie Antoinette might befall his mother and sisters, thus freeing him for marriage with Sophia.

cannot remember what my dreams have been—only there is a confused sense of having passed through adventures, pleasurable or otherwise. I suspect that you mingle with my dreams, but take care to flit away just before I awake, leaving me but dimly and doubtfully conscious of your visits. [Three lines are excised here.]

Do you never start so suddenly from a dream that you are afraid to look round the room, lest your dream-personages (so strong and distinct seemed their existence, a moment before) should have thrust themselves out of dream-land into the midst of realities? I do, sometimes. [25]

He must have recognized how close the dream was to his view of himself as an enchanted dreamer, and how clearly it expressed his fear of ineffectuality as a man and a writer. The dream, dominated by his grief at wasting time while the rest of the world was flourishing, represents him as a peculiar fusion of Sleeping Beauty and Rip Van Winkle. It seems an intense expression of his feeling of helpless isolation, and the image of burnt space beneath the bedclothes suggests concern about his repressed sexual impulses. But Hawthorne's expectation that Sophia would discover "comfort" in the image of "fresh herbage amid the burnt space" indicates that at some level of awareness, he felt hopeful about the future—possibly anticipating both his role as Sophia's husband and a successful writing career.

Even though he does not himself venture interpretation, his approach to this dream is consistent with the way he contrived dreams in his fiction. He assumed that each separate detail—the nap, the fire, and the grass flourishing around a burnt spot—had a precise allegorical signification. The same kind of exact equivalence had just characterized Peter Goldthwaite's dream of buried treasure, and it would soon be manifested in Aylmer's dream of cutting out his wife's birthmark and Giovanni's dream identifying Beatrice and the purple flower. Further, the dream, like most of his fictional dreams, is

25. Hawthorne to Sophia, May 26, 1839.

dominated by a single idea or emotion (here, grief at wasted time). Moreover, like Giovanni, he claims that his recollection of his dreams is often confused and partial. Finally, his fear that "strong and distinct" dream phantoms might escape the confines of sleep accounts for the fictional dreamers from the first sketches to the last romances who are frightened and confused by "dream-personages" even when they are awake.

Years later, when Hawthorne was American consul in Liverpool, he again pondered a dream that expressed anxiety about his career. Once again, the dream implicitly condemns the dreamer's ineffectuality, but this time Hawthorne is concerned about his feelings within the dream. Before summarily recording it in his notebook, he remarks, "I think I have been happier, this Christmas, than ever before,—by our own fireside, and with my wife and children about me." Within this security, he could confront a recurrent nightmare:

For a long, long while, I have occasionally been visited with a singular dream; and I have an impression that I have dreamed it, even since I have been in England. It is, that I am still at college—or, sometimes, even at School—and there is a sense that I have been there unconscionably long, and have quite failed to make such progress in life as my contemporaries have; and I seem to meet some of them with a feeling of shame and depression that broods over me, when I think of it, even at this moment. This dream, recurring all through these twenty or thirty years, must be one of the effects of that heavy seclusion in which I shut myself up, for twelve years, after leaving college, when everybody moved onward and left me behind. How strange that it should come now, when I may call myself famous, and prosperous!—when I am happy, too!—still that same dream of life hopelessly a failure! (*EN*, 98)

As always, Hawthorne tried to trace his dream to waking experience—here to his twelve years of "seclusion" while college friends like Longfellow, Franklin Pierce, and Bridge advanced in their careers. He knew that recurring worries affect dreams, but cannot be confined there: the shame he felt in his dream recurred when he remembered it. Yet he was puzzled about why the dream persisted after the waking predicament had passed, why he reexperienced the shame and depression of youth "when I may call myself famous, and prosperous!—when I am happy, too!"

Like the dream of falling asleep for a year, this "singular dream" expresses concern about time passing while the dreamer makes no "progress in life." Yet it also suggests Freud's "examination dream" since it is a dream of anxiety but also of self-consolation. The dream recalls a problem that has been overcome, and so implicitly asserts that the future should hold no threats.[26] Another Freudian conjecture also seems applicable, that a dream of past unhappiness may conceal a wish for lost youth; it simultaneously expresses the wish and punishes it.[27] But most clearly, this dream expresses Hawthorne's continuing concern that his life might somehow be construed as a failure.

Given his persistent fascination with his own dreams, it is not surprising that the *American Notebooks* contains suggestions for stories about dreaming. "In a dream to wander to some place where may be heard the complaints of all the miserable on earth," reads one suggestion, and another outlines the story of an old man who wishes he could relive his misspent life but happily discovers "he had only been dreaming of old age" (*AN*, 15, 182). One entry implies that Hawthorne as artist understood what he could not acknowledge about his own dreams, that they conveyed truths repressed by the waking mind: a man dreams that a trusted friend acts "the part of a most deadly enemy" and eventually discovers "that the dream-character is the true one" (*AN*, 181). Hawthorne attributes this anomaly to "the soul's instinctive perception"; in his fiction, dreams repeatedly embody such perception.

The most provocative of the notebook entries articulates a

---

26. Freud, *Interpretation of Dreams*, IV, 273.
27. *Ibid.*, V, 473–76.

most serious literary ambition: "To write a dream, which shall resemble the real course of a dream, with all its inconsistency, its strange transformations, which are all taken as a matter of course, its eccentricities and aimlessness—with nevertheless a leading idea running through the whole. Up to this old age of the world, no such thing ever has been written" (AN, 240). This he accomplished repeatedly. That some details of dreams in Hawthorne's fictions resist final interpretation may be explained by Hawthorne's own experience: he knew that some dreams pierce to mysteries too painful or too profound to comprehend.

Partial, elusive, or indeterminate as Hawthorne's dreams were as reported in his letters and notebooks, they were nevertheless more detailed, more openly ambiguous, more "modern" than Sophia's. Her dreams as she reported them undoubtedly reveal more about contemporary assumptions than Hawthorne's and allow valuable comparison. Like Hawthorne, she was curious about dreams and wondered about their relation to real events. But she never tried to trace them to her own intimate thoughts or emotions. For Sophia, dreams were enclosed experiences, explicable and without mystery.

It is hardly surprising that as a sick young girl confined to her room, Sophia suffered from harrowing dreams. She casually reported several to her family, trying to tie them to precise waking experiences. "I dreamed that George Villiers, Duke of Buckingham, stabbed me in the bosom; and I awoke with a tremendous start, and trembled for an hour," she wrote and then speculated ingenuously, "It was because I had been reading Shakespeare I suppose."[28] On another occasion she merely noted, "Last night, midnight, I was wakened by a tremendous crash of thunder; and I went to sleep again to dream of all kinds of horrors."[29] She did not record speculation about the

28. In Julian Hawthorne, *Nathaniel Hawthorne and His Wife* (2 vols.; Boston: Houghton Mifflin, 1884), I, 76.
29. *Ibid.*, 77.

implications of a dream she had after waking early and drifting asleep again: she "dreamed of watching a sunrise," but "the sky was covered with clouds shaped like coffins."[30]

When she was sent to Cuba for her health a few years later, she continued to tell her family about her dreams. They all express her affection for the family but also her loneliness. "You cannot think how often I dream of you, delightful dreams too," she wrote to her mother. "You always appear to me with a most happy countenance, full of hope and satisfaction. . . . I dreamed once that you and Father came to Cuba to carry me home, and last night I dreamed that Betty came."[31] The following month she wrote to her father about a dream that she had returned to Massachusetts. She wanted to relive it by writing about it: "I have been at home all night, dreaming about you and I must continue the delusion as much as possible by writing you a letter. I was again in the Church Street nest. Mother had gone to Boston, and you and I were keeping house together. All unexpectedly to me, one evening the stage drove up, and Lydia Haven and Caroline Fernandez descended from it. It was a plan of yours, to give me an agreeable surprise in our loneliness." Her pleasure in "keeping house" with her father betrays her loneliness, but Sophia seems to notice only what she finds "agreeable."[32]

Sophia's interpretations of her own dreams were usually simplemindedly literal, as when she wrote of dreaming that a friend who had been sorrowful was now happily married and visiting her, "and I told him a great many things about my foreign experiences—perfectly inspired by the recovered happiness of his countenance. . . . I hope my dreaming was prophetic of his present state of mind."[33] Her uneasiness about whether dreams

30. *Ibid.*, 78.

31. Sophia to her mother, April 7, 1834, in Berg Collection. "Betty" is her sister, Elizabeth Peabody.

32. Sophia to her father, May 25, 1834, *ibid.*

33. Sophia to Mary Peabody Mann, November 16, 1834; this section of letter dated November 24, *ibid.*

can prophesy continued even after her marriage. "My beloved mother," she wrote in 1844, "I dreamed last night that you were very unhappy, and would not tell me why, and my heart was nearly broken. You must assure me that it was nothing but a dream when you write again; if you are happy as usual."[34]

Sophia cherished dreams she could interpret as divine messages, such as a childhood dream she was fond of recounting to her children. A dark cloud appeared and obscured the sun, but it was transformed eventually into beautiful singing birds. "This dream was doubtless interpreted symbolically by the dreamer," Julian Hawthorne said, "and the truth which it symbolized was always among the firmest articles of her faith."[35] It is easy to guess how the gentle Sophia interpreted this dream, especially after reading her four-page manuscript recording another rapturous dream.

After meditating one evening, she wrote, Morpheus embraced her, and imagination led her "to a place of exceeding loveliness, where nature was dressed in her richest drapery." It was a beautiful sunset, and spring was putting "forth her first tender leaves and blossoms." Suddenly she saw "a vision, which seemed to be the spirit of loveliness herself." After the wind seemed to "breathe upon her as upon the aeolian harp," the spirit "began to sing a sweetly plaintive lay. . . . It was the music of the spheres." Sophia was about to "address the angelic songstress, and request a repetition," but "my temerity met its just reward, for the moment I attempted to speak, I awoke and found the whole a *dream!*"[36]

Clearly this is not a careful account of a mental adventure, but a generalized description. Even the images—the Aeolian harp, the music of the spheres—are public and derivative. The rhapsodic tone recalls the dream poems recurrent in magazines of the 1830s and 1840s, but not the dreams in Hawthorne's

34. Sophia to her mother, February 4, 1844, *ibid.*
35. Julian Hawthorne, *Hawthorne and His Wife*, I, 49.
36. Holograph manuscript recording a dream, n.d., in Berg Collection.

61

tales. This does not suggest that Sophia was dishonest, but rather that her eagerness to see ideal beauty sometimes produced dreams of "loveliness," or the belief that she had such dreams. As she read them, so, possibly, she read her husband's fiction, accepting distress but gratified by images of love and beauty and eager for intimations of ideal truth.

For Hawthorne, however, dreams posed riddles, and he could expect no help from Sophia as he worked out his profound ambivalence about them. He feared that dreams drew him apart from life into a world of shadows and that stories emergent from that world were thin and cold concoctions; at the same time he also affirmed that dreams carry dark knowledge hidden from the waking mind. Recording his dreams, even asking Sophia to help interpret them, he recognized that they were more complex than conventions of the time, and his own wife's conventional mind, declared. He took them seriously, inquiring into their connections with waking experience even when he cautioned Sophia to draw no sombre omens from them and averted his own eyes from their most painful implications. Not only did he conceive of dreams as fictional subjects and structures, but his ambivalence about their truth and value became a central component of his fiction, integral to what critics have called his preternatural ambiguities, and integral to his heroes' dilemmas of belief and behavior.

If he could not come to terms with his uncertainty, he could turn it into a subject for fiction. He could explore the limits and possibilities of inner fantasies and streams of associated images as unstable compounds of subjective, objective, and possibly ideal truth. All the time he was reporting his dreams to Sophia or reflecting on "the real course of a dream" in his notebook, he was seeking a way to witness dreaming in process, to see his own mind reflecting profoundly on itself. His goals as a writer required it.

2. Creative Reverie

Reflecting on his weariness of beautiful scenery in the English Lake District, Hawthorne said, "I am slow to feel— slow, I suppose, to comprehend; and, like the anaconda, I need to lubricate any object a great deal, before I can swallow it and actually make it my own" (EN, 182). This cautious self-judgment suggests the purpose and method of his descriptions of scenery in his notebooks. Observing a scene was the first step toward assimilating it; he then had to "feel" and "comprehend" it and so "swallow it and actually make it my own." Only then would it be available to his imagination. According to Waggoner, Hawthorne rarely transformed his detailed observations of the external world into successful fiction because his sensibility "could respond fully only to moral values. When he could see no moral significance in a fact, he could not ordinarily use the fact creatively."[37] It would be more accurate to say that Hawthorne could respond to any "fact" that he had "lubricated" by thought and feeling, whether or not he saw moral significance in it. The impetus behind his detailed journal records seems to be the accumulation of sharp first impressions for later assimilation and possibly for subsequent incorporation into fiction. Without such a storehouse of recorded impressions, he feared his mind would have only itself to feed upon.

He deliberately paid attention to the real world, assigning his "observant faculty" to record both "characteristics" and "remarkables" of specific scenes; at the same time he tried to steal sidelong glances at his own observing mind. As ideal conditions for such notation, he had to be alone but not lonely and in surroundings that were at once familiar and unusual. "Every new aspect of the mountains, or view from a different position, creates a surprise in the mind," he observed during his trip

37. Hyatt Waggoner, *Hawthorne: A Critical Study* (Cambridge: Harvard University Press, 1963), 44.

through the Berkshires in 1838 (*AN*, 104). Sometimes he tried to trick himself into surprise: if he sat outdoors reading, a casual glance at the landscape would yield a sharp impression; "you seem to catch Nature at unawares" (*AN*, 486). But the unusual aspect of an ordinary New England scene might emerge from his own concentrated attentiveness. Thus he describes a beach ramble where he saw "cocks, with their squad of hens, in the grass-fields, hunting grasshoppers, chasing them eagerly with outspread wings," the beach of "brown sand, with hardly any pebbles," and the beach birds "with gray backs and snow-white breasts." An underlying purpose of the description becomes evident when he retraces his steps along the sand, pleased to make himself conscious of his mind's earlier unconscious wanderings, "the whole mood and occupation of your mind." As he looks at a seaweed, he remembers what he thought when he saw it before; he recalls the moment he felt "the effect of the wide sea"; and when he encounters his own circling footprints, he concludes that "some vagary of mind seems to have bewildered you" (*AN*, 162–64). He realizes how outer experience has generated inner activity, and how his mind in turn affected behavior. As in the sketch he later developed from this episode, "Foot-prints on the Sea-shore," Hawthorne observes the scenes and becomes aware of his role of observer; he sees he is seeing, and he sees how his mind has wandered.

An even longer section of Hawthorne's notebook is devoted to the July day when he deliberately sat down in Sleepy Hollow to "await such little events as may happen, or observe such noticeable points as the eyes fall upon around you." He is pleased by the gradual refinement of his ability to perceive "noticeable points": "And how strange is the gradual process with which we detect objects that are right before the eyes; here now are whortleberries, ripe and black, growing actually within reach of my hand, yet unseen till this moment." His senses respond to animals, birds, and insects; he notices changes in the sun and the wind; he hears a locomotive's whistle; he becomes increasingly aware of flourishing life and also of decay. Nor is he merely passive: he becomes an agent of mischief as he drops sand into an anthill, and in the end he deliberately refuses to let himself think about gathering clouds, or even to "take one of them into our present observations."

His concluding comment on the day's events is especially significant:

And now how narrow, scanty, and meagre, is this record of observation, compared with the immensity that was to be observed, within the bounds which I prescribed to myself. How shallow and scanty a stream of thought, too,—of distinct and expressed thought—compared with the broad tide of dim emotions, ideas, associations, which were flowing through the haunted regions of imagination, intellect, and sentiment, sometimes excited by what was around me, sometimes with no perceptible connection with them. When we see how little we can express, it is a wonder that any man ever takes up a pen a second time. (AN, 245–50)

He began the day by making observations, and these observations generated a "stream of thought," though he denigrated the streams as all too shallow. Meanwhile the observations also generated a broad but often imperceptible "tide of dim emotions, ideas, associations" flowing through his "imagination, intellect, and sentiment." Aware of the "broad tide" within, Hawthorne despaired of what he could achieve as a writer. It was not enough merely to describe what he saw, not even if he could express his stream of thought. He also wanted to convey the tide of emotions, ideas, and associations that flowed through his haunted mind. Sometimes he succeeded, as in his animated description of grape vines near Brook Farm:

The vines had caught hold of maples and alders, and climbed to the top, curling round about and interwreathing their twisted folds in so intimate a manner, that it was not easy to tell the parasite from the supporting tree or shrub. Sometimes the same vine had enveloped several shrubs, and caused a strange tangled confusion, converting all these poor plants to the purposes of its own support.

65

. . . The broad vine-leaves . . . were seen apparently growing on the same stems with the silver maple leaves . . . thus married against their will. (*AN*, 197)

Hawthorne's associations convert the vine into a sexual villain. Two weeks later when revisiting the vine, he consumes its last grapes and perceives its seasonal decay; and he now feels entitled to call it "my grape vine" (*AN*, 213). It has become accessible to his creative imagination. When the vine reappears in *The Blithedale Romance*, the notebook's implicit moral condemnation has become explicit, and it extends to Coverdale, the detached writer who makes the vine-entangled trees his hermitage.

Whenever Hawthorne recorded observations of scenes that were new to him, as he did when visiting Horatio Bridge in Maine in 1837, unfamiliarity sharpened his attention: giant toadstools were "as yellow and about the size of a half boiled yolk of an egg"; a "long flat-bottomed boat" on the Kennebec River had brown sails that "looked like leather, or skins, but were really cloth"; Canadians and Irishmen lived in small shanties made "picturesque" by turf piled against their walls that "becomes covered with grass and white." Sometimes he placed himself in the scene as an observer and pressed beyond visible detail toward moral significance, as in describing "a small Canadian boy, who was in a hollow place, among the ruined logs of an old causeway, picking raspberries—lonely among bushes, and gorges, far up the wild valley—and the lonelier seemed the little boy for the bright sunshine, that showed no one else, in a wide space of view, except him and me" (*AN*, 39, 47, 57).

"On being transported to strange scenes, we feel as if all were unreal," Hawthorne observed, and then extrapolated that feeling to a metaphysical assertion: "This is but the perception of the true unreality of earthly things, made evident by the want of congruity between ourselves and them." His lament about man's accommodation to familiar "earthly things" recalls Wordsworth on the infant's gradual loss of "clouds of glory":

"By and by we become mutually adapted, and the perception is lost" (*AN*, 168). What concerned him was how to find some special point of vantage that would keep perception sharp.

During his years abroad he was often delighted to find himself attaining a double detachment from a scene, observing himself as an observant foreigner, walking as a sharp-eyed stranger among crowds in London or Rome, or exploring country byways. Ancient ruins increased his sense of detachment even further, as he noted after a visit to Furness Abbey: "I believe that one great charm and beauty of antiquity is, that we view it out of the midst of quite another mode of life;—and the more perfectly this can be done, the better" (*EN*, 159). Whenever he traveled, he tried to capture "the sharpness of the first impression" in his notebooks, though often the sharpness was so fleeting that he had to settle for "the sentiment of it" (*EN*, 66).

Whether he was describing people or scenes, he always tried to register "characteristics" and "remarkables," however elusive they might be. He had concluded that his friend George Bradford was "a character to be felt and understood, but almost impossible to describe; for, should you seize upon any characteristic, it would inevitably be altered and distorted in the process of writing it down" (*AN*, 347). In fact, the only person he felt he really understood was Sophia, as he told her through metaphors of mutual assimilation: "The deeper we penetrate into one another, and become mutually interfused—the happier we are" (*AN*, 366). Yet like a squirrel preparing for winter, he kept filling his notebooks with sketches of people he encountered. He could easily spot gross characteristics such as the beefy haunches of English women; but it was far more gratifying to find himself attaining sympathetic insight into the lives of strangers.

Two passages in *The English Notebooks* record his observations of dignified self-restraint yet mutual concern among the poor. One day when he shared the waiting room of the Liver-

pool ferry with a poor Irish family, he found himself empathiz-
ing with the mother's anxiety and her daughter's "expression of
childish endurance." His notebook description was inadequate,
he felt, but somehow or other, "I got into the interior of this
poor family, and understand, through sympathy, more of them
than I can tell" (*EN*, 34–35). Sympathy enabled him to assimilate his observation, though he did not understand it well
enough to translate it into words.

An even more unusual sight more directly challenged his
imagination. One day he saw an English beggar woman "sitting in a small hand-wagon," which he assumed that volunteers
moved from place to place. "There is something in this (I don't
yet well know what) that has impressed me, as if I could make a
romance out of the idea" (*EN*, 38–39). He registered the sight
and stored it for possible future use, but it remained unassim-
ilated; he could not isolate the "something" that so impressed
him. As at Sleepy Hollow years before, Hawthorne was fascinated as an observer yet frustrated as a writer.[38]

Usually what engrossed Hawthorne as an observer was complex human experience; but even buildings could evoke, embody, or suggest such complexity. Thus he enjoyed looking at a
Gothic church, St. Michael's in Coventry: It was "so old, yet so
enduring, so huge, so rich, with such intricate minuteness in its
finish, that, look as long as you will at it, you can always discover

38. Hawthorne had earlier turned a comparable low-keyed description of an
American "remarkable" into a published sketch. A notebook passage describes the
"hopeless, shivering, aspect" of an old apple dealer in the busy Salem railroad station.
Hawthorne interprets his observations (a sigh is construed as symbolic of the chill-
ness and torpor of his old age) and speculates about the old man's earlier existence,
yet feels he has "not expressed the aspect and character of the old man, in anything
like a satisfactory manner" (*AN*, 222–26). The sketch entitled "The Old Apple-
Dealer" achieves a "satisfactory manner" by its focus on the narrator's problems as a
"lover of the moral picturesque" trying to describe a character who remains "feature-
less" even though "he has become a naturalized citizen of my inner world." In the
end, he exultantly interprets a gesture as the key to the man's character: "See! he
folds his lean arms around his lean figure, with that quiet sigh, and that scarcely
perceptible shiver, which are the tokens of his inward state. I have him now." Once
he "has" him, Hawthorne can evolve a moral generalization to conclude the sketch:
the old man has "soundless depths of soul" like all others (*Mosses*, 439–46).

something new directly before your eyes." This pleasure in increasing discovery is comparable to the pleasure of his gradual discoveries at Sleepy Hollow; but he more fully assimilated his perceptions of the church, as he explained through a surprising metaphor: "I admire this in Gothic architecture—that you cannot master it all at once—that it is not a naked outline, but as deep and rich as human nature itself, always revealing new little ideas, and new large ones. It is as if the builder had built himself up in it, and his age, and as if the edifice had life." He admired St. Michael's because the church helped him understand his interest in human nature, and vice versa. He could not completely assimilate his response to this or to other Gothic churches— "there is something much more wonderful in them than I have yet had time to make myself know and experience," he said— but as his reference to time suggests, he thought he might do so eventually (*EN*, 137–38).

His response to another Gothic edifice a few days later offers a crucial contrast. Although he was fascinated by the complexity of the Cathedral of Lichfield, with its "strange, delightful recesses," all "consonant in its intricacy," he was disturbed to find he could not "melt it all into one idea, and comprehend it in that way." When he looked at St. Michael's he knew he could not assimilate the experience "all at once"; but Lichfield Cathedral was more overwhelming. He hated to stop looking at it "and yet I wanted to leave off, because I knew I never should adequately comprehended its beauty and grandeur" (*EN*, 149). His ambivalence about an experience that he could not "melt . . . into one idea" is a key to his ambivalence about any such experience, whether observing mountain scenery, great painting, or the fantastic emanations of his own dreams.

Too much of any experience caused a sense of surfeit that prevented him from assimilating it. Traveling through Scotland, he wrote, "We saw Ben Venue, and a good many other famous Bens, and two or three lochs; and when we reached the Trossachs, we should probably have been very much enraptured, if our eyes had not already been weary with the other mountain-shapes" (*EN*, 333). He was even more explicit about why he could not enjoy the English Lake Country: "I was weary of fine scenery; and it seemed to me that I had eaten a score of mountains, and quaffed down as many lakes, all in the space of two or three days; —and the natural consequence was a surfeit." He could easily spend more time in any of the places they passed through, "but, by flitting so quickly from one point to another, I lost all the more recondite beauties, and had come away without retaining even the surface of much that I had seen" (*EN*, 182). He was exactingly aware of the needs and limits of his imagination. He could not thrive in dull surroundings with a dull routine, as in the Boston or Salem Custom Houses. He required new sights and experiences, but not in great quantity or all at once. An epicure in perception, he needed time to savor and digest.

Predictably, in the British Museum he felt depressed—not only on his own account, but also for future generations: "It quite crushes a person to see so much at once; and I wandered from hall to hall, with a weary and heavy heart, wishing (Heaven forgive me!) that the Elgin marbles and the frieze of the Parthenon were all burnt into lime, and that the granite Egyptian statues were hewn and squared into building stones. . . . We have not time, in our earthly existence, to appreciate what is warm with life. . . . I do not see how future ages are to stagger onward under all this dead weight" (*EN*, 294). He felt the same weary distress as he began his self-imposed course in art appreciation at the Manchester Exhibition of Art in the summer of 1857. Initially he felt crushed by the sheer quantity of art, but he forced himself to concentrate on one group of paintings at a time. He concluded that "a picture cannot be fully enjoyed except by long and intimate acquaintance with it," like the scenery of the English countryside; yet "you must really love a picture, in order to tolerate the sight of it many times" (*EN*, 559, 565). Some paintings—Turner's, for example—he could barely learn to tolerate at all. It was possible to assimilate some experiences that originally seemed overwhelming, but not all of them. This pattern of initial depression that could only partly be allayed would recur, more intensified, in Italy.

Curiously, Hawthorne's comments on the Civil War reveal a similar pattern. The war was too complex and potent a reality for his imagination to assimilate. Although he opposed slavery, he could not accept the arguments of abolitionists such as Emerson or his sister-in-law Elizabeth Peabody, and he dedicated *Our Old Home* to Franklin Pierce, a well-known opponent of abolition. For a time, he felt curiously excited, even elated, by the war. This "excitement had an invigorating effect on me," he wrote Ticknor on May 26, 1861, though he commented with grim self-mockery that "it is rather unreasonable to wish my countrymen to kill one another for the sake of refreshing my palled spirits; so I shall pray for peace." The war never refreshed his spirits enough for him to complete any of his projected romances, however. He concluded that "it is impossible to possess one's mind in the midst of a civil war to such a degree as to make thoughts assume life." As he explained his problem in the preface to *Our Old Home*, "The Present, the Immediate, the Actual, has proved too potent for me. It takes away not only my scanty faculty, but even my desire for imaginative composition" (*OOH*, 4).[39]

Throughout his career, he pursued the present, immediate, and actual, within bounds his mind could assimilate, although frequently he worried that his writing was inadequate to his ex-

---

39. Hawthorne to Ticknor, May 26, 1861, in Berg Collection. Daniel Aaron, in *The Unwritten War: American Writers and the Civil War* (New York: Knopf, 1973), 41–55, sees grim humor in Hawthorne's comment about his excitement; yet Hawthorne really did feel excited even as he deplored the curse of war. By contrast, dull routine was a form of the present, immediate, and actual that deadened his imagination, as suggested by a letter to Longfellow during his employment at the Salem Custom House: "I am trying to resume my pen; but the influences of my situation and customary associates are so anti-literary, that I know not whether I shall succeed"; the mornings in the custom house "undo all that the afternoons and evenings have done."

perience. Any experience too vast for such assimilation, whether majestic scenery, the layered ruins of Rome, or the Civil War, crushed his imagination. All his life he tried to balance inner and outer experience, aware that either extreme was perilous to his creative sensibility, though he often despaired about maintaining that balance. In youth, he condemned himself for subjection to dreams, and in his last years he felt victimized by the unassimilable "Present."

Fusion of actual experience and imaginative vision is as central to Hawthorne's aesthetic theory as to his sensibility. He believed that the artist, whether a writer or a painter, should liberate his audience from the shackles of the material world by suggesting an immanent or spiritual ideal. He should tell "the prosaic truth about Nature" but at the same time "etherealize" it. He thought Turner's misty paintings ignored that prosaic truth and so falsified nature: "I care no more for his light-colored pictures than for so much lacquered ware, or painted gingerbread." The Pre-Raphaelites, he believed, suffered from the opposite problem: their paintings were so cluttered with "truth of detail" that the viewer was never led to "a broader and higher truth."[40] He praised Dutch genre painters because "their life-like representations of cabbages, onions, turnips, cauliflower, and peas" are "more real than reality"; the Dutch "get at the soul of common things, and so make them types and interpreters of the spiritual world" (*EN*, 550, 556). Yet he finally rated such works far below the grand paintings of Raphael or Michelangelo, concluding that although it is good to depict ordinary reality, it is more important to try for the broader truths and higher mysteries, as he himself tried to do in his romances.

Hawthorne's romantic aesthetic was contingent on his idealistic metaphysic, his faith in an eternal world of spiritual perfection beyond this transient world. But in developing that aes-

40. Suzanne Blow cites only Hawthorne's praise of the Pre-Raphaelites in her analysis of "Pre-Raphaelite Allegory in *The Marble Faun*," *American Literature*, XLIV (1972), 122–27.

thetic, he became increasingly aware of the subjective response of the perceiver: in some moods even a Raphael seemed shallow to him, and conversely, he was aware that some devout Catholics saw beauty in ugly prints of martyrs. All his attempts to assess artistic value brought him back to the complexities and mysteries of his own inner experience, particularly as he glimpsed it during perception, meditation, or on the borders of sleep.

On several occasions he tried to record such a glimpse: "A perception, for a moment, of one's eventual and moral self, as if it were another person,—the observant faculty being separated, and looking intently at the qualities of the character. There is a surprise when this happens,—this getting out of one's self,—and then the observer sees how queer a fellow he is" (AN, 178). The third person objectivity of this speculation is typical of Hawthorne: he sees "the observer" as a queer fellow.

Yet he was always reticent about his deepest inner experience. This was no doubt partly out of modesty and a sense of decorum, partly out of fear of acknowledging his darkest secrets, even to himself. But it is also a token of his reverence for the soul's mysteries—or so he believed. He wrote to Sophia in May, 1840, "Lights and shadows are continually flitting across my inward sky, and I know neither whence they come nor whither they go; nor do I inquire too closely into such phenomena. It is apt to create a substance where at first there was a shadow. . . . Words may be a thick and darksome veil of mystery between the soul and the truth which it seeks." He might distort the truths about the soul by examining them too closely, he feared, or even by trying to find words for his intimations. This in turn suggests one reason why his dramatizations of the mind in dream or reverie so often remain abstract. Another letter to Sophia, in February, 1842, is similar both in language and in tone: an "involuntary reserve" leads him to write "what is common to human nature, not what is peculiar to myself"; "a cloudy veil stretches over the abyss" within him, though a sympathetic reader would be "worthy to come into my depths. But he must find his own way there. I can neither guide him nor enlighten him." As he wrote in his preface to *Mosses from an Old Manse*, "So far as I am a man of really individual attributes, I veil my face" (*Mosses*, 33).

Daydreaming was for him a special kind of vision compounded of perception and imagination, a way of gaining access to the "broad tide" within himself without looking intently into his inner abyss, and a way of assimilating the extraordinary complexity to be perceived there without violating its mystery. He understood daydreaming as the Scottish Common Sense philosophers did: the mind is simultaneously aware of its own operations and its experience of the outer world; the imagination can operate freely; but since the will retains control, unpleasant thoughts cannot attain dominion. The mind does not penetrate to its deepest recesses, but it can call into play its own latent knowledge and capacities—recalling the past, rehearsing options for the future, entertaining thoughts, and animating fantasies. Thus Hawthorne valued daydreaming not as a mode of achieving absolute truth, but as a mode of multiple consciousness which might later result in imaginative composition. During daydreams, the real and the imaginary could combine, while the daydreamer could observe and modify their combinations.

He thought of daydreaming as an activity available to everyone and important for the fullest development of each person's inner capacities. As Hawthorne looked at clouds near Williams College one day, he remarked, "It was like a day dream to look at it; and the students ought to be day-dreamers, all of them—when cloud-land is one and the same thing with the substantial earth" (*AN*, 122–23). Common sense recognizes that clouds differ from substantial earth, but daydreamers who imaginatively contemplate their similarities can come to know more about earth, sky, and their own imaginations.

For Hawthorne the writer, daydreaming had a further function. In the course of reverie, he might "dream strange things
and make them look like truth." Such "dreaming" might occur
involuntarily. Near the end of his term in the Salem Custom
House he told Longfellow, "Whenever I sit alone, or walk
alone, I find myself dreaming about stories, as of old," although
he did not have enough energy to write the stories;[41] and "The
Haunted Mind" describes his mind on the threshold of sleep
when "thoughts rise before you in pictures" (*T-t T*, 308). Sometimes he deliberately courted reverie as the condition for such
pictures, hoping they might then take on life of their own. He
would sit down, alone, in a comfortable and dimly lit place, inviting intellect, sensibility, and imagination to interact with the
world about him, and so initiate the process of "dreaming about
stories."

In an early sketch, he described traveling on the Erie Canal
at night among decaying trees, through what seemed a "land
of unsubstantial things, whither dreams might betake themselves, when they quit the slumberer's brain" (*Mosses*, 437).
"Foot-prints on the Sea-shore" describes a day in 1837 when
he deliberately left the "haunts of men," and lay down in a
nook by the sea which became "his": his "musings melted into
its rocky walls and sandy floor, and made them a portion of
myself." Both places are appropriate for fantasies, but because
the nook is familiar, essentially unchanging, and relatively un-
obtrusive, it is more useful to the writer, more conducive to
sustained fantasies. "Dreams haunt its precincts, and flit around
me in broad sunlight, nor require that sleep shall blindfold me
to real objects, ere these be visible." Once dreams become
visible, the imagination can work on them: "Here can I frame
a story of two lovers, and make their shadows live before me,
and be mirrored in the tranquil water, as they tread along the
sand, leaving no foot-prints." The bachelor-writer faces a threat

41. Hawthorne to Longfellow, November 11, 1847, in Houghton Library, Harvard University.

from his own inventions, however. He can easily "summon up a single shade, and be myself her lover," but he would in the process become all the more aware of his own real loneliness (*T-t T*, 458–59).[42] He is aware of how his fantasies and perceptions can interfuse with memories and desires: his mind is at once subject, object, and theater, the perceiver and what is perceived.

Hawthorne's most extensive description of such deliberately initiated creative reverie occurs in "The Custom-House" preface to *The Scarlet Letter*, set in his Salem parlor one evening when his family is asleep. The parlor, like the nook, is a familiar place where fancies, perceptions, and memories can interfuse, but the middle-aged writer sitting there is different from the young writer sprawled on the sand. As husband and father, he now feels immune from the dangers of loneliness. Yet as the complex intermingled lights of moon, fire, and mirrored reflections lead him to speculate about his mind's ministrations, he worries as he did years before that his powers of description are not adequate to his experience. In the notebook entry on which this "Custom-House" passage is based, after describing the sitting room where fire and moonlight invest familiar objects with strangeness appropriate for "ghosts of persons very dear," Hawthorne interrupts himself to express his frustration: "I cannot in any measure express it," he says; and the paragraph ends on a note of surprised complaint: "It is strange how utterly I have failed to give anything of the effect of moonlight in a room." Yet he persists in trying to convey the effect, concluding that the whole scene is "like a dream,

---

42. An earlier notebook entry suggests as a story idea, "A person to be writing a tale, and to find that it shapes itself against his intentions; that the characters act otherwise than he thought; that unforeseen events occur; and a catastrophe comes which he strives in vain to avert. It might shadow forth his own fate,—he having made himself one of the personages" (*AN*, 16). The idea of a writer tyrannized by fantasies he had invoked and finding himself a personage in a plot is crucial to *The Blithesdale Romance*.

and which makes me feel as if I were in a conscious dream" (*AN*, 283–84).

The expanded passage in "The Custom-House" enlarges upon this frustration and doubt about his creative powers. Hawthorne is not merely worried about adequate description but about his imagination itself: if it will not "picture forth imaginary scenes" under ideal conditions, it may never work at all. He begins by referring to his mental torpor and ends by referring to a "class of susceptibilities" that he had lost during his dull round of custom house duties. Within this outer frame of self-denigration is an inner frame of self-doubt. As he begins to describe the moonlit parlor, he says, "If the imaginative faculty refused to act at such an hour, it might well be deemed a hopeless case"; and at the end of the description he expands this warning phrase by phrase: "Then, at such an hour, and with this scene before him, if a man, sitting all alone, cannot dream strange things, and make them look like truth, he need never try to write romances." Within the two frames, he defines the ideal conditions for creative reverie.

Moonlight in the room, "making every object so minutely visible," makes perception and cognition easy and at the same time causes transformations of both. Familiar objects are "so spiritualized . . . that they seem to lose their actual substance, and become things of intellect"; thus doubly assimilated, they can mingle freely with all the writer's "illusive guests." The simultaneous clarity and strangeness of the moonlight transforms the entire room into "a neutral territory, somewhere between the real world and fairy-land, where the Actual and the Imaginary may meet, and each imbue itself with the nature of the other." Two crucial words here are *may* and *imbue*. The process Hawthorne describes is not what always happens but what may happen if the writer has freed himself from material facts and can describe what he has mentally "swallowed," like the anaconda, and made his own. Both Matthiessen and Feidelson suggest that Hawthorne's notion of a "neutral territory" does not represent a conjunction but a disjunction, a drawn battle between Actual and Imaginary; but the word *imbue* indicates that Hawthorne required the Actual and the Imaginary to be not merely contiguous but fused.[43] To this end he conceived his stories in the atmosphere characteristic of dreams.

From the "magic moonshine" in which "ghosts may enter,"[44] Hawthorne moves to a further stage of imaginative assimilation: firelight is metaphorically equivalent to the interfusion of "heart and sensibilities of human tenderness" in "forms which fancy summons up. It converts them from snow-images to men and women." Hawthorne's earlier description of his placing Hester's A on his own breast and feeling its fiery heat expressed the same conviction: unless a writer's passions are excited, his fictions remain lifeless.

After this firelight stage when the mind's fantasies are endowed with life, the narrator looks at the reflection of the room

43. F. O. Matthiessen, in *American Renaissance* (New York: Oxford University Press, 1941), 264–65, says Hawthorne's idea of a neutral territory where "Actual and Imaginary may meet" contrasts with Whitman's idea that "imagination and actuality must be united," and he suggests that Whitman would have interpreted Hawthorne's terms as "suggestive of a drawn battle"; but the key to Hawthorne's intention is the word *imbue*: Actual and Imaginary must each "imbue itself with the nature of the other." Charles Feidelson, Jr., in *Symbolism and American Literature* (Chicago: University of Chicago Press, 1953), 8, asserts that Hawthorne vacillated between two conceptions of the imagination: that it mediated between private and objective vision and that it erected castles in the air. Hawthorne consistently espoused the first conception, and the second is not a separate concept but a value judgment that an attempt at mediation had failed, or that an artist had failed to make the attempt. Feidelson says allegory was Hawthorne's back door out of a dilemma, since allegory is based on a formal correspondence between ideas and things and so avoids the question of whether reality lies in one of the planes or in the interaction between them; but Hawthorne did not face or deliberately avoid such a dilemma. He always tried to imbue substance with spirit and to imbed ideas in vital forms; and in his best writing he succeeded. Only when he fell short of his own goal did he produce mere "fancy pictures" or "castles in the air."

44. That Hawthorne believed in ghosts is suggested by notebook entries both in America and abroad. In one he remarks matter-of-factly, "An apparition haunts our front-yard" and says Sophia has also noticed it; "it always appears to be entering the yard from the street, never going out" (*AN*, 279). "The Ghost of Dr. Harris" is his account of seeing the ghost of an old theologian he used to observe in the reading room of the Boston Athenaeum.

in a mirror. Earlier he had complained, "My imagination was a tarnished mirror. It would not reflect, or only with miserable dimness"; but now a real mirror assists his creative reflections. Now, "glancing at the looking-glass," he can perceive everything he had noticed in "the gleam and shadow" of the parlor as a framed "picture," at "one remove farther from the actual, and nearer to the imaginative."

The sequence of this passage defines a pattern so deeply imprinted on Hawthorne's consciousness that it recurs repeatedly in his fiction. Within a frame of waking consciousness, the mind makes observations and frames thoughts, then passions arise, the will increasingly surrenders its control, and the imagination gradually moves away from the actual scene. In such dream tales as "The Haunted Mind," "Young Goodman Brown," and "My Kinsman, Major Molineux," the central figure proceeds by gradual stages from moonlit thoughts and memories through firelit feelings and imaginative fantasies. The landscape and characters correspond to the landscape and images of his mind as the will gradually surrenders control. He enters a reverie or a dream. The writer who cannot enter this state cannot write romances, cannot make "imaginary scenes . . . flow out on the brightening page" (SL, 34–36).

Not only is the place where reverie occurs symbolically equivalent to the writer's imagination, it is an equivalent to the world Hawthorne tried to create in his fiction. He explained this repeatedly in the prefaces to his romances. The preface to *The House of the Seven Gables* describes his "fancy-pictures" set in "castles in the air," and the personages "really of the Author's own making, or, at all events, of his own mixing" (HSG, 3); the preface to *The Marble Faun* refers to Italy as "a sort of poetic or fairy precinct, where actualities would not be so terribly insisted upon" as in America (MF, 3); and in the preface to *The Blithedale Romance* Hawthorne complains that in America "there is as yet no such Faery Land, so like the real world, that, in a suitable remoteness, one cannot well tell the difference, but with an atmosphere of strange enchantment, beheld through which the inhabitants have a propriety of their own." He explains that he has therefore tried "to establish a theatre, a little removed from the highway of ordinary travel, where the creatures of his brain may play their phantasmagorical antics, without exposing them to too close a comparison with the actual events of real lives" (*BR*, 2, 1). The suitable place for the romancer to dream must be translated into a suitable place for the reader to share those dreams, another kind of "neutral territory, somewhere between the real world and fairy-land."

In that neutral territory of the fictional world, what happened in the theater of the author's mind could be recreated within the mind of the reader, who could then move through the poetic precinct in a state of passive sensibility. Sometimes Hawthorne worried that as a writer, he might be enacting the devil's role, ensnaring the reader and drawing him away from reality into a world of illusions, even delusions. He might be like the storyteller of "An Old Woman's Tale," whose "fiction hid its grotesque extravagance in this garb of truth, like the devil (an appropriate simile, for the old woman supplies it) disguising himself, cloven-foot and all, in mortal attire" (*S-I*, 241). But his career was predicated on the belief that the dreamer— including the fictional dreamer, the reader, and the writer himself—could go beyond the admixture of fantastic extravagance and ordinary experience to find moral significance in both. Thus, he marshaled "the creatures of his brain" into tales and romances calculated to involve his reader as in a dream.

III
The Tales

1. The Dreamers

Hawthorne's self-pitying, self-mocking, yet self-affirming image of himself as an isolated dreamer engendered a variety of fictional dreamers, especially numerous during his bachelor years. If a character is a habitual dreamer, he is an alien, estranged from normal compassion or understanding. His dreams may lead him to truths concealed in the daylight world, but he may become lost in his own fantasies. If the fictional dreamer is himself a writer, he has a special problem: he risks forfeiting the fullness of life on which the fullness of literature depends. He may glimpse truth, yet be unable to communicate it. Hawthorne often mocks the writer-dreamer through metaphor: he is separated from the chain of humanity; his heart is an unwarmed chamber or a cold cavern; he lives amid shadows, mists, and moonshine; his creations are like soap bubbles, icicles, or castles in the air. Yet significant stages of development separate the foolish poets of the early sketches from the writers who follow them.

The disappointed poet of "The Canterbury Pilgrims" (1831) has "an intelligent eye" and speaks with a certain majesty, but his poems have not won the reputation he thinks he deserves. His plan for revenge against "an ungrateful world" is petulant and hypocritical. He will compose one last lyric, then join the Shakers. To get himself in the right mood for composition, he "gave himself up to a sort of vague reverie, which he called thought," during which he regarded the patterns of radiant moonlight changing "like the material of unshaped dreams." We later learn that he sent his "last" lyric off for publication, along with "two or three other little pieces, subsequently written." This "thin and stooping figure, in a black coat, out at elbows," is a vain man who combs his hair to dramatize his forehead. He has "susceptible nerves," "too much of one sort of brain and hardly any of another." The "little pieces" of such a shallow and self-centered man could hardly win great fame (S-I, 123–26).

The poet of "The Great Carbuncle" (1832) is also bright-eyed "but wofully pined away"; he also wears tattered clothing, thinks vague and dainty thoughts, and longs for fame. Hawthorne enjoyed his joke about the poet's intellectual fare: "fog, morning mist, and a slice of the densest cloud within his reach, sauced with moonshine, whenever he could get it. Certain it is, that the poetry, which flowed from him, had a smack of all these dainties." But the poet's ambition makes him not only ridiculous but morally contemptible. If he found the great carbuncle, he would run home to let its radiance "be diffused throughout my intellectual powers, and gleam brightly in every line of poesy that I indite. Thus, long ages after I am gone, the splendor of the Great Carbuncle will blaze around my name!" He is unaware that poetry produced by "intellectual powers" alone can never win such fame. Hawthorne's final joke is his mistaking a chunk of ice for the carbuncle; and with poetic justice, his critics subsequently agree that "if his poetry lacked the splendor of the gem, it retained all the coldness of the ice" (T-t T, 151, 155, 164). Like the cold and self-assured poet who appears briefly in "Sketches from Memory," he is detached from life, limited in sensibility and therefore incapable of producing great art.

The moody and self-critical writer of fiction who appears in 1834 is a more fully developed character, and his problems are central to his tale.[1] He condemns himself for his dreams and suffers both for them and in them; unlike the poets, he is tormented by the phantoms of his mind. He is not the first person narrator—the "I" is his friend—but his autobiographical origins are clear. He is the character Hawthorne partly created, the haunted dreamer of the lonely chamber, and his name, Oberon, is the nickname Hawthorne adopted in corresponding with Horatio Bridge.

In "The Devil in Manuscript," he is the despondent author about to burn the manuscripts that record his dreams, as Hawthorne himself had burned many early tales. He is identified as a law student, but his torment is an intense, melodramatic version of Hawthorne's. "I am surrounding myself with shadows, which bewilder me, by aping the realities of life," he complains. He had been drawn "from the beaten path of the world . . . into a strange sort of solitude." His solitary dreams at first inspired him to write, but he cannot share those dreams since no one will publish his tales. Now his dreams are nightmares or nonsense, and he is their victim. "That scribbled page describes shadows which I summoned to my bedside at midnight," he tells his friend: "they would not depart when I bade them; the gray dawn came, and found me wide awake and feverish, the victim of my own enchantments!"

His ambivalence toward his tales is conveyed through a shocking metaphor suggesting Hawthorne's attitude toward his own destroyed tales: "He drew the tales towards him, with a mixture of natural affection and natural disgust, like a father taking a deformed infant into his arms." They must be de-

1. Millicent Bell, in *Hawthorne's View of the Artist* (Albany: State University of New York Press, 1962), 135–50, discusses the Oberon sketches as "probably the most autobiographical of all Hawthorne's works." I accept the dating of Elizabeth Chandler, in *A Study of the Sources of the Tales and Romances Written by Nathaniel Hawthorne Before 1853*, Smith College Studies in Modern Languages (Northampton, Mass.: Smith College, 1926).

stroyed, though he once thought them precious. Another more familiar metaphor develops his sense of loss: "My treasure of fairy coin is changed to worthless dross." He denigrates the tales and his entire period of lonely creativity: "I have been eloquent and poetical and humorous in a dream—and behold! it is all nonsense, now that I am awake." Only in an ironically literal sense do his dream tales reach the public: one of his burning pages flies up the chimney to "set the town on fire" (S-I, 170–78).

In "Fragments from the Journal of a Solitary Man," the writer's efforts are even more futile. All Oberon's manuscripts were destroyed at his own request; only a few journal fragments remain. His fictional distance from Hawthorne is clearly defined: "his disease was pulmonary"; he wasted away, and he is dead. Yet the pathos and pessimism of his journal echo Hawthorne's own worst fears. Oberon was an isolated dreamer who hoped to "muster sufficient energy of will to return into the world. . . . But life never called the dreamer forth; it was Death that whispered him," before he could experience life's "deep and warm realities." The metaphor of unattainable fairy gold again expresses Oberon's sad recognition of an opportunity forever lost: "There has been a mighty treasure within my reach, a mine of gold beneath my feet, worthless because I have never known how to seek for it." This Oberon is young and pathetic, but he seems a forerunner of James's Marcher in "The Beast in the Jungle."

He is obsessed by a "dreary thought that haunted me,— the terrible necessity imposed on mortals to grow old or die," and his "morbid fancies" erupt in the only dream narrated in this group of tales, a realistic if melodramatic articulation of his despair. He is walking on Broadway, and passersby shun him in horror; he looks in a mirror and sees he is in his shroud; then he "awoke, with a horrible sensation of self-terror and self-loathing" (S-I, 312–28). The mournful Oberon, trapped in his imagination and his mortality, tantalized by treasures and terrorized by demons, embodies Hawthorne's most intense self-pity and self-contempt.

Hawthorne's most whimsical version of the haunted dreamer appears in "Graves and Goblins," another 1834 tale. Here the narrator is a ghost whose life had been wasted in dreams, and who is now responsible for what the lonely writer in the tale writes, including this tale. He moves through the writer's dreams and reveries: "I steal into his sleep, and play my part among the figures of his dream. I glide through the moonlight of his waking fancy, and whisper conceptions, which, with a strange thrill of fear, he writes down as his own. I stand beside him now, at midnight, telling these dreamy truths with a voice so dream-like, that he mistakes them for fictions of a brain too prone to such." The ghost takes credit for any "mysteries of truth and reality" in the tale "now" written. Paradoxically, this validates the experience of dreams, especially when the ghost abandons the obtuse writer in the end: "Farewell, dreamer—waking or sleeping! Your brightest dreams are fled; your mind grows too hard and cold for a spiritual guest to enter" (*S-I*, 297). Hawthorne ridicules the author and himself by this Pirandellesque farewell: the author deserves no credit for what he "wrote," and his "spiritual guest" has now fled.

"The Village Uncle" (1833) proposes a radical solution for the problems of a writer-dreamer. The old "Uncle" tells how he emerged from his dream-haunted youth and found fulfillment as husband, father, and fisherman—but at the cost of his career as a writer. Using terms that recur in the Oberon tales and anticipate Hawthorne's 1837 letter to Longfellow, he recalls his youth as "a hermit in the depths of my own mind . . . a man who had wandered out of the real world and got into its shadow, where his troubles, joys and vicissitudes were of such slight stuff, that he hardly knew whether he lived, or only dreamed of living." A woman's love had enabled him to leave the shadows; he renounced his "scribbling" and even the alphabet itself, "the key to a fatal treasure." Yet the contradictory morals he proposes for his tale suggest a fundamental ambivalence. "Since fancy can create so bright a dream of happiness, it were better to dream on from youth to age, than to awake and strive doubtfully for something real," he suggests; but he immediately rejects this thesis to urge a life of "warm affections" and "honest toil" (*T-t T*, 311–23).

Equivocations in the tale express the same ambivalence. The "Uncle" insists he is no longer a writer, but he is nevertheless a storyteller. He insists he does not make up tales, but he hopes to make men wise by recounting true adventures, including this tale. Then in the last paragraph, he calls the entire tale only "the slight tissue of a dream," finally justifying the story's subtitle, "An Imaginary Retrospect." Yet even if a fictional writer invented the village uncle, he is the first of Hawthorne's first-person author-dreamers to manage a workable compromise with life.

Early in 1838, right after *Twice-told Tales* publicly established Hawthorne's identity as an author, a more complex writer appears as the narrator of several discursive sketches. This relatively self-confident writer, careful to balance his experience of dreams and reality, displaces the emotionally tempestuous and dream-haunted Oberon. The author of "Night Sketches" has enjoyed a day of indulging in fancy, but at the end of the day his fantasies will no longer do his bidding. Since he knows "a dreamer may dwell so long among fantasies, that the things without him will seem as unreal as those within," he deliberately goes out for a walk, paying attention to the dark, wet streets, to other people he sees walking, and to "mortal affairs" he glimpses through lighted windows. Unpleasant thoughts about his loneliness emerge, but he can control them. He imagines returning to his fireside and "fancying a strangeness in such sights as all may see." Then, after observing a stranger carrying a lantern, he frames a comforting moral: all men are night wanderers, but "if we bear the lamp of Faith, enkindled at a celestial fire, it will surely lead us home to that Heaven whence its radiance was borrowed" (*T-t T*, 427, 432).[2] Both the fancied "fancying" and the actual moralizing firmly identify him with all mankind; he can return to write this very sketch, his dreams put in their place.

The narrator's immediate purpose in "Foot-prints on the Sea-shore" is different, but his ultimate purpose is the same. He periodically leaves "the sultry sunshine of the world, to plunge into the cool bath of solitude," to commune with nature and his own "fantasies, and recollections, or anticipated realities." The change of setting and activity is again part of a deliberate program; and again he enjoys the pleasures and endures the pains of solitude: "I shall think my own thoughts, and feel my own emotions, and possess my individuality unviolated." (The poet-dreamer Coverdale later gives the same explanation for his retreats from Blithedale.) Like "Night Sketches," this sketch ends optimistically, this time in the real world rather than in moral speculation. Three girls invite him to a picnic, and "this is the sweetest moment of a Day by the Sea-Shore" (*T-t T*, 451–62). The daydreamer in these dispassionate sketches is a modest man who can understand and control his moods and fantasies and later write about them. He can enjoy them, and they help preserve his individuality.

In two tales of 1842, the year of his marriage, Hawthorne praised the imagination more forcefully: it can "lessen those iron fetters, which we call truth and reality," he said in "The New Adam and Eve"; in "The Hall of Fantasy" he said, "There

2. Hyatt Waggoner, in *Hawthorne: A Critical Study* (Cambridge: Harvard University Press, 1963), 266, says "'Night Sketches' begins with mind triumphant in daydream, moves to the shock of the initial confrontation with the impenetrable void of meaningless nature, and ends with the darkness illuminated with the true light, meaninglessness shaped into sufficient meaning by the true dream"; but these distinctions do not suggest that the sketch is a dramatic representation of the two ways Hawthorne marshaled his imagination. When the narrator is outdoors, he invests perceptions with imagination, and he returns to muse and doze in his familiar chamber and also to write this sketch. He is never certain he has attained a "true dream"; he uses the "lamp of Faith" for his moral "for lack of a more appropriate one" (*T-t T*, 432).

is but a half of life—the meaner and earthlier half—for those who never find their way into the hall." In "The Hall of Fantasy," some writers are called "rulers and demi-gods in the realms of imagination": statues in the hall honor Homer, Aesop, Dante, Ariosto, Rabelais, Cervantes, Shakespeare, Spenser, Milton, Bunyan, Fielding, Richardson, Scott, and Brockden Brown. And although the narrator says he has no desire to meet the "techy, wayward, shy . . . laurel-gatherers" conversing among the statues, his host dismisses this "old prejudice" that "men of genius" lack "social qualities"; present-day writers like being "on equal terms with their fellow-men." The "honest citizen" still wonders whether authors who "penetrate the universal heart" are fit for ordinary life, but his host simply ridicules the question (*Mosses*, 247, 172–76). Thus Hawthorne insists, as always, that for successful writers the imagination does not preclude ordinary experience. Further, the tale affirms what he so often doubted: the author whose dreams "penetrate the universal heart" is an important member of society, and he may win undying fame.

"The Great Stone Face" (1848) makes this point more strongly through a wise and humble poet, Hawthorne's most idealized embodiment of the writer-dreamer. Unlike the self-centered poets of the early sketches, he pours "out his sweet music amid the bustle and din of cities," revealing spiritual truths few could perceive for themselves. "The world assumed another and a better aspect from the hour that the poet . . . came to interpret, and so complete it"; he showed "the golden links of the great chain" that binds men together on earth and leads them to heaven. Yet he is dissatisfied: "I have had grand dreams, but they have been only dreams, because I have lived . . . among poor and mean realities." His dreams have been translated into poetry but not into his own life (*S-I*, 43–48). Despite this self-denigration, however, his dreams are not "only dreams." He has accomplished what all Hawthorne's writer-dreamers attempt: living among "realities," he could give life to his spiritual visions, and consequently readers can share his dreams. Hawthorne never praised a writer more highly.

Hawthorne's changing attitudes toward himself determined his conceptions of fictional writers; conversely, changes in the characters indicate changes of self-judgment. By the time of "The Great Stone Face," he had moved past detached mockery of cold poets, beyond sympathy with disconsolate storytellers, and beyond the disinterested self-display of the first-person narrators. During his early years as husband and father, Hawthorne had reached a stage of tentative self-approbation.

More than ten years earlier, during the years of the Oberon tales and the first-person sketches, he had written five tales about habitual dreamers who are not writers, projecting at a slightly greater distance the problems that always anguished him. Three tales—"The Vision of the Fountain," "The Three-fold Destiny," and "Sylph Etherege"—treat dreaming as a problem of youth; "Peter Goldthwaite's Treasure" and "Old Esther Dudley" consider it a problem of old age. Sylph and Esther are women; the others are men. Hawthorne had read in Dugald Stewart and surely he observed for himself that youthful desires and senile frustrations often find outlets in daydreams. All these tales are about individuals whose dreams are for a time an alternative to waking life, and all are treated sympathetically. But in an important sense, the highly imaginative women prove weaker than the men: they cannot survive the loss of their dreams.

In "The Vision of the Fountain" (1834), the narrator recalls the time he was fifteen and fell in love with a girl's face reflected in a spring. At first he spent "a dreamy and delicious hour" hoping for the vision to return, and he comments, "Thus have I often started from a pleasant dream, and then kept quiet, in hopes to wile it back." But as months passed, and he could not be sure if his imagination or a real girl had produced the image, he became gloomy: "I withdrew into an inner world, where my thoughts lived and breathed, and the Vision in the midst of them." Seduced by his "burning fancy," he lived only in the world it created. "I became at once the author and hero of a romance, conjuring up rivals, imagining events . . . till jealousy and despair had their end in bliss" (*T-t T*, 215–17). The bliss is his meeting with the real girl whose reflection he had seen, and he can thus abandon his dreams. The greatest energy in the slender tale emerges from the boy's daydreams as they take on their own life, and the tale's charm comes from its sympathy with the bittersweet fantasies of adolescence.

A girl also helps a dreamer return to reality in "The Three-fold Destiny" (1837). Ralph, a young man obsessed by recurring dreams of a lovely maid, buried treasure, and the "gift of extended empire," has been away from home for ten years, seeking the destiny the dreams foretold. The search itself had been like a dream, as if he "had gone forth that very morning, and dreamed a day-dream till the twilight, and then turned back again." Back in his own bedroom, the familiar dreams "thronged riotously around to welcome his return. In the well-remembered chamber . . . he had passed a wilder night than ever in an Arab tent, or when he had reposed his head in the ghastly shades of a haunted forest." Even when he is awake, the dream phantoms persist, "though fainter in the daylight," and he looks at the real world through the "misty romance that pervaded his mental world." Finally he realizes that his old friend Faith is the maiden of his dreams, and he can then interpret his other riddling dream images; "The wild dreamer was awake at last." Ralph can marry his maiden, cultivate the "buried treasure" of his garden, and rule the "extended empire" of a schoolhouse (*T-t T*, 475–81). The tale condemns subjection to dreams but not dreams themselves; rightly understood, they can lead to a full life.

But in "Sylph Etherege" (1837), there is no reconciliation between the dream world and reality: when reality forces its way in, the dreams are forced out, taking the dreamer with them. Young Sylph has so insulated herself from the real world that return is impossible. She is Hawthorne's fragile fairy-tale princess wooed by a fairy prince who turns out to be a demon lover. Like Oberon, Sylph is shy, fanciful, sensitive, and frail. She lives in seclusion, "left to seek associates and friends for herself, in the haunts of imagination, and to converse with them, sometimes in the language of dead poets, oftener in the poetry of her own mind." Her most constant imaginary companion is the "airy presence" of the fiancé she has never seen, Edgar Vaughan.

Vaughan plans to free Sylph from "the haunts of imagination." This ugly man, pretending he is Vaughan's friend, gives her a beautiful miniature portrait, ostensibly of her fiancé. But by lending "a brighter semblance of reality" to her daydreams, the portrait commits her more deeply to "the realm of fantasy and moonlight where dwelt his dreamy kindred!" She is "happy, yet hapless." Hawthorne laments, "Many, in their youth, have visited that land of dreams, and wandered so long in its enchanted groves, that, when banished thence, they feel like exiles everywhere." Sylph increasingly becomes such an exile; "Her loveliness seemed the creation of a delicate and dreamy fancy."

Vaughan destroys the miniature and presents himself as the reality, like the gloating villains of Gothic romance. "Your dream is rudely broken," he announces; but Sylph's life is broken with it. Hawthorne does not condemn the gentle dreamer whose visions were too good to be true. If Vaughan represents reality, dreams are a better alternative, though this is the only story to reach this conclusion (S-I, 111–19).

"Old Esther Dudley" (1838) explains why an old woman might want to take refuge in dreams, but does not consider that refuge a happy alternative. Esther is a royalist who refuses to accept the fact of American independence. She stays in the Province House after the British rulers leave, certain they will return. She inhabits a self-contained world of dreams and endures the penalties Dugald Stewart had warned about: "Living so continually in her own circle of ideas, and never regulating her mind by a proper reference to present things, Esther Dudley appears to have gone partially crazed." She lives with "the ghosts" that haunted "the chambers of her own desolate heart." When reality breaks in, when the man she welcomes as the new British governor turns out to be an elected American official, she looks at him "dimly and doubtfully, as if suddenly awakened from a dream" (*T-t T*, 297–301). Sylph dreamed of love and beauty, Esther of the past; but neither the young girl nor the old woman can stand the shock of awakening. Esther dies with her dreams.

Only one habitual dreamer is conceived in the spirit of comedy. Peter of "Peter Goldthwaite's Treasure" (1837) does not have youth to excuse his hopeful dreams, yet Hawthorne treats him indulgently. He is an elderly variant of the early poet-dreamer: "Gray-headed, hollow-eyed, pale-cheeked, and lean-bodied, he was the perfect picture of a man who had fed on windy schemes and empty hopes, till he could neither live on such unwholesome trash, nor stomach more substantial food." The food metaphor signals Hawthorne's comic distance, as does his ironic suggestion that Peter's imagination might have earned him success as a poet.

The story follows Peter as he destroys his house searching for his family's legendary buried treasure. Hawthorne mocks him yet admires his "aspiring soul"; he can forget his troubles and enjoy "the sunshine of a bright futurity." In a comic variant of the American dream, the old man plans to get the treasure and then "go a wooing, and win the love of the fairest maid in town." Suppressing fears that his dreams may be delusory, he pursues what "might possibly be a phantasm, by a method which most people would call madness." Yet he is not completely mad. When his dream collapses he does not go under with it; from the ashes of his old dream a new one rises, and Peter's spirits with it (*T-t T*, 386–400). The moral Hawthorne had rejected for his other tale about an elderly dreamer, "The Village Uncle," seems applicable here: "Since fancy can create so bright a dream of happiness, it were better to dream on from youth to age, than to awake and strive doubtfully for something real." Peter survives his dream and his dreams help him survive.

A tale requiring special attention is one written in the early years of Hawthorne's marriage, in which a habitual dreamer creates a valuable work of art. Owen Warland of "The Artist of the Beautiful" (1844) is a sensitive artist who dreams of winning Annie Hovenden's sympathy and love, and that dream becomes connected to "all his dreams of artistical success." But as a special case of the dreamer, he is punished when he abandons his "dreams of artistical success." At such periods he dismisses his idea of creating a "spiritualized mechanism" as an idle thought of his "idle and dreamy days"; it is "a dream, such as young men are always mystifying themselves with." Later, his imagination revives despite Annie's marriage to the blacksmith, and he can impart life to his dream. In the end, Owen knows the butterfly he created is superior to any he imagined "in the day-dreams of my youth."

Nevertheless, Hawthorne is profoundly ambiguous about this achievement. Owen is a small man who has produced one small but marvelous artifact, necessarily inferior to his envisioned ideal. If his heart had been warmed by reciprocated love, he "might have wrought the Beautiful into many a worthier type than he had toiled for." Yet such as he is, like all Hawthorne's fictional dreamers, Owen is defined by his dreams: they express his anxieties and his ambitions, and his daydreams not only enable him to understand this world, but propel him beyond to the realm of the beautiful (*Mosses*, 447–75). He is not lost in fantasies but maintains a precarious sanity because his creative imagination requires clear-eyed knowledge of the world about him; since he is satisfied with his limited achievement, he retains self-esteem.

Most of Hawthorne's dreamers long for the shared identity of love, fame, or social approval. Further, they require it, to sustain emotional balance and to generate psychic energy, whether or not they are artists. Through Owen, but only through Owen, Hawthorne says it is possible for a dreamer to survive and to incorporate his dreams in works of significant merit even if there is no one to approve but himself.

The number and range of Hawthorne's habitual dreamers, particularly those who are writers, is a measure of the intimate connections between his self-image and his fictions at each stage of his career. All of these habitual dreamers are assessed in the same way: each is admired or condemned in exact proportion to his ability to integrate his dream visions with the "warm realities" of life. Hawthorne construes his problem as a more extreme form of the problem all men share. It is finally a measure of Hawthorne's ability to go beyond his unique problems and his unique identity that in his most successful fiction the protagonist is rarely a writer or a habitual dreamer. Like most of us, he is an individual who intermittently attains fleeting or tormenting insights into himself and the world he inhabits through the mode of the dream and the daydream.

2. Dreaming

Repeatedly in the tales, a protagonist's mind moves from outer to inner reality and within its own interior world, intermixing perceptions with memories and emotions and generating its own fantasies. The tales are often suffused with a glimmering half-light in which characters move back and forth across the threshold of daydream, or drift from one level of surrendered consciousness to another. A dream may take shape as a spectral procession, a preternatural hallucination, or simply a mystifying episode imperfectly recalled when awake. But always, dreaming in the fiction invites and requires penetration beyond material surfaces: the dreamer moves unsteadily toward an enlarged understanding of himself and the natural universe, sometimes confronting his own buried secrets of guilt and desire. Dreaming is at once the activity of the protagonist and an invitation to the reader to enter the dream world, an invitation to grasp a story's "leading idea" and to ponder broader questions about the limits of mortal understanding.

Repeatedly Hawthorne created in his stories the kind of atmosphere that encouraged him to daydream, the half-light stimulating to the imagination and symbolic of it, the light that could make any place the neutral territory of romance. That Hawthorne's imagination required half-light has often been observed, but it must be stressed that the half-light provokes imagination by evoking a dreamlike state. The adjectives "glimmering" and "wavering" are recurrent: when light is "glimmering," a character's mind starts "wavering" between fantasy and reality. Such light does not encourage sentimental fantasies, as in the magazines or Ik Marvel's *Reveries*; it loosens what Hawthorne called the iron fetters of truth and reality, inviting the imagination to cope with reality in its own way.

As the narrator of *Grandfather's Chair* puts it, the "glimmer and pleasant gloom" of twilight assists the imagination more than "vulgar daylight": anything viewed through such a glimmer seems transmuted. Thus the "glimmering shadows" on the footpath to the Old Manse are a "kind of spiritual medium" transforming the house into an object of imagination without "quite the aspect of belonging to the material world." Mist, rain, and snow can also effect such transformations; but moonlight is the most magical and mysterious light, creating the "beautiful strangeness in familiar objects" that elicits a viewer's imaginative participation. Many of Hawthorne's tales begin at twilight and proceed as the light fades, including "Young Goodman Brown," "The Hollow of the Three Hills," "Ethan Brand," "The Wives of the Dead," and "Alice Doane's Appeal"; in many, including "My Kinsman, Major Molineux," "The White

Old Maid," and "An Old Woman's Tale," the main events occur in moonlight. Repeatedly in the dim and glimmering light of the tales, characters drift into a dreamlike state and begin to see beyond material surfaces.

"The White Old Maid" opens with two women mourning at the moonlit deathbed of the man both had loved and ends years later when the dying women meet again in the moonlit bedroom. In both scenes, moonlight makes the dead seem alive and the living seem ghosts, and in a sense that appearance is the truth: the women have been sustained only by their love for the dead man. The old clergyman who enters the room nearly pierces their secret of guilt, but the story ends as he says, "It glimmers to-and-fro in my mind, like the light and shadow across the Old Maid's face. And now, 'tis gone!" (*T-t T*, 382). Yet the knowledge is not all gone, since he had not before suspected there was a shameful secret; and the story invites the reader to speculate about it.

Lantern light can also stir imaginative thought and serve as its analogue, usually inviting understanding. Thus, the swinging lantern in "The Wives of the Dead" brings "to view indistinct shapes of things, and the fragments of a world, like order glimmering through chaos, or memory roaming over the past" (*S-I*, 196). And the narrator of "Night Sketches," observing that a stranger's tin lantern allows him to walk fearlessly in the dark, then thinks about a different kind of guiding light, the lamp of Faith. But few of Hawthorne's protagonists carry lanterns or walk purposefully in the dark; instead they wander through it, trying to make sense of "indistinct shapes of things, and the fragments of a world."

Because a window, a veil, or a reflecting surface can make familiar objects seem strange, they too can stimulate the imagination and serve as its analogues. Dreamers in "The Hall of Fantasy" view the world through stained glass windows which subsequently color their dreams; each pane of frosted glass "presents something like a frozen dream" in "The Haunted Mind"; and a veil provokes the villagers to dark thoughts about what lies behind it in "The Minister's Black Veil." Usually reflections in a stream invite pleasant speculations about ideal truths. Hawthorne describes reflections in the Concord River as "dream-pictures," wonders whether "objects palpable to our grosser senses, or their apotheosis in the stream beneath" are more real, and concludes that "the disembodied images stand in closer relation to the soul" (*Mosses*, 22). If a character looks at himself in a mirror, however, he is invited to contemplate his own "eventual and moral self," to pierce his own "impenetrable mystery." This is the subject of "Monsieur du Miroir," a sketch that begins whimsically, but moves to terrified self-awareness (anticipating Dimmesdale staring into his looking glass). The narrator confronts his epistemological uncertainties in a way that makes Hawthorne seem an ancestor of Borges: he wonders "which of us is the visionary form, or whether each be not the other's mystery" (*Mosses*, 171).

Firelight evokes knowledge of the heart. A man may sit by the fire remembering those who have died, as in "The Village Uncle," "Grandfather's Dream," and "John Inglefield's Thanksgiving," and affection can bring them back for a time. But more often, fire evokes nightmare images of suppressed guilt and searing passions, demons of the inner hell, as in "Ethan Brand," "Young Goodman Brown," and "My Kinsman, Major Molineux."

The unsteadiness of vision that excites the imagination in Hawthorne's tales may be directly attributed to the mind of the perceiver. Drowsiness or illness can interpose their own veils between the protagonist and the external world. He can then drift easily back and forth across the shifting borders between sleep and waking, and his mind can become partly aware of its own involuntary processes. Like Poe, Hawthorne dramatized the mind's unsteady oscillations from waking perceptions to illusory images; but he always represented such oscillations as part of normal experience. And in the course of a character's drift in and out of dream or reverie, he may find that at some point he involuntarily confronts his own repressed fears and desires. That kind of drift and confrontation is explored and exhibited in one of Hawthorne's most powerful sketches, "The Haunted Mind."

It begins at the strange moment when you wake up and "seem to have surprised the personages of your dream in full convocation round your bed. . . . Or, to vary the metaphor, you find yourself, for a single instant, wide awake in that realm of illusions, whither sleep has been the passport, and behold its ghostly inhabitants and wondrous scenery, with a perception of their strangeness, such as you never attain while the dream is undisturbed." The narrator can enjoy the perspective of a traveler in a strange land, but it is not Hawthorne's purpose to conduct us through its "wondrous scenery." Like Hawthorne telling Sophia about his dreams, the dreamer is poised on the threshold between illusion and reality and looks both ways.

As always when the conscious mind glimpses the subconscious, the narrator becomes more fully aware of the present moment. Most of the sketch occupies the "intermediate space" between sleep and waking where the mind can observe its own activities. With his "mind's eye" half shut, he looks through the "frozen dream" of his frosted window to the icy street beyond, shivering at the "idea of a polar atmosphere." His stream of associated ideas becomes increasingly distressing: he meditates about spending his life in bed, "like an oyster in its shell, content with the sluggish ecstasy of inaction"; then that simile evokes a similar yet contrasting image of dead men shivering "in their cold shrouds and narrow coffins." He knows his mind well enough to anticipate that this "gloomy thought will collect a gloomy multitude," and he now passively awaits the waking nightmare which is the heart of the tale, the funeral train of sorrow followed by demons of guilt.

These images emerge in procession within the haunted mind, one succeeding another until finally all disappear. Behind them, we can trace the long line of allegorical processions that wind from medieval poems and paintings through Spenserian narrative and Miltonic masques into eighteenth-century didactic tales; and these figures who mock the helpless dreamer adopt the melodramatic postures of Gothic romance. Further, their sequence conforms to Scottish associationism: figures succeed one another according to the principles of cause and effect, similarity, and contrast. The way Hawthorne shaped the nightmare also owes something to his fear of looking too closely into his inmost self, and his fear that verbalizing insights might distort them. But he personified and costumed his anxieties; they emerge in single file, conventional figures on parade.

Each figure is characterized by a few abstract details, perhaps in part because Hawthorne only dimly remembered his own dreams; but the selectivity is artful. First, two sad young women appear, then two stern old men. The second figure of each pair causes more pain than the first, and the men cause more pain than the women. Sorrow is the first and most traditional figure—a pale and beautiful mourner in a sable robe. Next comes a more pathetic figure of "ruined loveliness, with dust among her golden hair, and her bright garments all faded and defaced"; she had once been Hope but is now Disappointment. After these young victims, the stern authority figure of fatality appears, not one who is ruined but one who ruins, "a demon to whom you subjected yourself by some error . . . and were bound his slave forever." An exclamation introduces the last of this group: "See! those fiendish lineaments." This mocking demon, who anticipates Chillingworth, touches "the sore place in your heart"; as in the later tales, Shame makes the dreamer suffer most of all. The passage contains suggestions of sexual guilt, especially in the figure of ruined loveliness, but the narrator's memory of an "act of enormous folly" is all the more enormous because it is never specified.[3]

The terrorized dreamer now fearfully awaits a "fiercer tribe" of embodied remorse, "devils of a guilty heart, that holds its hell within itself," emerging when the will has lost control. Their metamorphoses conform to real dream experience, yet they are Gothic stereotypes, introduced by the distancing hypothetical introduction, "What if . . . ?" Like the earlier apparitions, these demons cause increasing distress. Remorse may appear in the guise of "an injured friend"; the fiend may lie beside him in a woman's dress; or he may appear as the epitome of Gothic terror, "a corpse, with a bloody stain upon the shroud." These spectres of guilt do not betray the protagonist's unique anguish but the "nightmare of the soul" all dreamers sometimes endure. The dream pageant is essentially an artificial device, yet it serves to convey the mysterious torments of the inner life.

It takes "desperate effort" to tear his attention from these fiends; only by deliberately concentrating on his firelit bedroom can he exorcise them. Then he can deliberately change the tone of his fantasies. Instead of thinking the fiend might lie beside him, he imagines the pleasure of sharing his bed with a woman. This turns the threshold between sleep and waking into "a flowery spot . . . while your thoughts rise before you in pictures, all disconnected, yet all assimilated by a pervading gladsomeness and beauty." As the diction of this passage suggests, these culminating visions—composite images of generally shared pleasure—are as conventional as the specters that preceded them. "Gorgeous squadrons" of wheeling birds are followed by another image of innocent joy, merry children by a rustic schoolhouse. A splendid traditional image of natural har-

3. See Barton Levi St. Armand's analysis of the sequence of the sketch, and his conclusion that Hawthorne substituted "sentimental and easy images of the sublime and the beautiful for the archetypal forms which might have composed the denouement of his intense drama of the self" ("Hawthorne's 'Haunted Mind': A Subterranean Drama of the Self," *Criticism*, XIII [1971], 25).

mony then appears: a rainbow over Niagara Falls. Next, the "mind struggles pleasantly between" two contrasting images of domestic joy: a newlywed couple by their hearth, and birds flying "about their newmade nest." Two metonymic images follow: the "merry bounding of a ship," then girls' feet dancing at a splendid ball. This leads to a finale appropriate both to the sketch and to Hawthorne's recurrent image of the mind: you "find yourself in the brilliant circle of a crowded theatre, as the curtain falls." None of these visions departs from the sentimental realism characteristic of nineteenth-century gift books; but they go beyond sentimentality in conforming to principles of mental association and in conveying the lonely bachelor's desires for the ordinary pleasures of domesticity.

After waking involuntarily from his pleasant visions, he says, you "prove yourself but half awake, by running a doubtful parallel between human life and the hour which has now elapsed. In both you emerge from mystery, pass through a vicissitude that you can but imperfectly control, and are borne onward to another mystery." Then as both dreamer and theorist, he describes his plunge back into "the wilderness of sleep" from which he had emerged as the sketch began; there his spirit moves "like a free citizen, among the people of a shadowy world, beholding strange sights, yet without wonder or dismay." Such calm may prevail in the afterlife, he says, a curious suggestion from an author whose protagonists are rarely calm in "the wilderness of sleep" (*T-t T*, 304–309).

The dream processions in the sketch can all be explained by the dreamer's physical and emotional state and his prior experience, as can other such processions in Hawthorne's fiction. The device of a dreamer observing his own spectral ideas is recurrent, in the novels as well as the tales. The reveries of Hester and Dimmesdale present each dreamer with a version of problems he has yet to solve; in *The Blithedale Romance*, Coverdale confronts masqueraders who seem embodiments of his worried dreams; and Robin in "My Kinsman, Major Molineux" tries to

101

make sense of a dreamlike midnight parade. But even the many fictional pageants not explicitly associated with dreams have fundamental dreamlike characteristics. They are linear and open-ended dramatized extensions of the "life is a dream" metaphor near the end of "The Haunted Mind," or of the similar statement in "A Toll-Gatherer's Day" that life is "a flitting show of phantoms for [a] thoughtful soul to muse upon." The "soul" can muse on the phantoms themselves and the connections their sequence suggests. Thus, in "The Procession of Life," Death arranges the marchers according to what has dominated their lives, whether grief, guilt, disease, or intelligence; in "Earth's Holocaust," groups advance in patterns of shared misery; and the guests of "A Select Party" and "The Christmas Banquet" are ordered by affinities of their secret selves. "Main-Street" presents a different sort of spectacle: the reader attends a kind of puppet show and contemplates a chronologically ordered panorama of scenes from Salem's past. In all these sketches, the reader is vicariously the audience of a dreamlike procession of unbidden and often distressing guests.

But in three early tales, Hawthorne tried a different mode of representing and provoking the mind's entry into itself. All three of these tales establish tenuous connections with ordinary reality through hints that what seems supernatural might actually be a dream. They are all set in twilight or moonlight in the legendary past; all the protagonists are emotionally unsettled; and they all confront mystifying spectral processions. The tales are apprentice work of varying success, yet all succeed in generating an atmosphere of enchantment.[4]

"An Old Woman's Tale" is a relatively simple dream vision,

4. Elizabeth Hawthorne recalled that the "Seven Tales of My Native Land" were written soon after Hawthorne left Bowdoin and included "two witch stories" (Randall Stewart [ed.], "Recollections of Hawthorne by His Sister Elizabeth," in *American Literature*, XVI [1945], 323). Chandler assumes that "The Hollow of the Three Hills," "An Old Woman's Tale," and "Alice Doane's Appeal" were three of the "Seven Tales" and concludes that they were written in 1824 or by June, 1825—that is, while Hawthorne was still at college. Chandler, *Study of the Sources*, 55.

unusual because it is shared by a poor young man and the girl he wants to marry. From the start, the tale is set at a distance from ordinary reality. It was told to the narrator by an old woman whose plots were "seldom within the widest scope of probability," and who says someone else told it to her. It is set in her native village whose inhabitants, she says, were "periodically subject to a simultaneous slumber, continuing one hour's space"; and the old woman further qualifies the truth of her narrative by saying it "perhaps" happened when David and Esther sat down together one moonlit evening. "Perhaps they fell asleep together, and, united as their spirits were by close and tender sympathies, the same strange dream might have wrapped them both in its shadowy arms." Thinking themselves awake, though with "a sort of mistiness over their minds," they watch a crowd of people garbed in ancient clothing emerge in the moonlit street, looking like "shadows flickering in the moonshine." As "the dream (if such it were)" unrolls before them, a lame old lady appears and seems to dig for treasure, then seems to look fondly at David and Esther. Eventually, "like cloudy fantasies," the spectral figures disappear. David exclaims to Esther, "I have had such a dream!" and she replies "And I such another!" To test their vision they proceed to dig a hole where the old lady was digging, using a shovel that perhaps is the dream shovel. But the story ends irresolutely with David's unanswered question, "Oho!—What have we here!" The story claims special privilege as an old wives' tale, but its irresolute plot is unsatisfying, and the shared dream is devoid of psychological probability. The charming idea that poor lovers may receive a gift from the past through a dream is not strong enough to redeem it (S-I, 240–50).

In "The Hollow of the Three Hills," structurally the tightest of these three tales and the only one Hawthorne chose for book publication, a witch summons "news from the ends of the Earth" at the behest of a pale lady. The tale takes place between twilight and midnight "in those strange old times,

103

when fantastic dreams and madmen's reveries were realized among the actual circumstances of life." The old witch's smile in the fading autumn twilight is another kind of unsteady light: it "glimmered on her countenance, like lamplight on the wall of a sepulchre." The lady is frightened but requests information about those she has abandoned.

Kneeling before the old woman, her face covered by the old woman's cloak, she hears words "resembling the dim pages of a book, which we strive to read by an imperfect and gradually brightening light." Her despairing parents talk of their shamed daughter and some "more recent woe," then their voices melt into the sound of the wind. The lady lifts her eyes in humiliation, confronting the old woman's smile, then covers her face again. She now hears the sounds of the second scene, set in a madhouse. Among the shrieks and "dreamy" noises, she hears a man complain of his perfidious wife, his madness a form of nightmare within a nightmare. Again the illusive words merge with the wind, the lady lifts her head, and the old woman smiles. In the final and most melancholy scene, the lady hears sounds of her child's funeral. This time as the wind moans, she does not raise her head; but the old crone now laughs.

These episodes are cast as demoniacally summoned auditory hallucinations; but they make sense as eruptions of a guilty imagination. Such fantasies might torment a sinner whose will is surrendered in dreams, the crone being an instrument of her desire to know the worst. The narrative is consistent with Hawthorne's later comment about an alleged spiritual communication: "It resembles a dream, in that the whole material is, from the first, in the dreamer's mind, though concealed at various depths beneath the surface" (X, 395–96). The woman's fantasies have the compulsiveness of nightmare, fulfilling her self-punishing desire to confront the consequences of her guilt. From these fantasies, it is easy to piece together the melodramatic narrative of a sinful wife and mother; despite its obtrusive artifice, the tale effectively conveys her increasing and finally self-destroying guilt (*T-t T*, 199–204).[5]

The most tangled of these weird tales is "Alice Doane's Appeal." Despite its disjunctions, it has all the qualities of the dream as Hawthorne described it, with "its strange transformations . . . its eccentricities and aimlessness—with nevertheless a leading idea running through the whole." Further, "Alice Doane" makes extensive use of devices recurrent in Hawthorne's dream tales—glimmering light, wavering minds, and spectral processions. And as in many of Hawthorne's fictional dreams, it offers knowledge so terrifying that it is not wholly understood.[6]

The tale has a densely detailed frame: the narrator reads his manuscript to two young ladies as they sit in fading light on Gallows Hill, where the Salem witches had died. He moves in and out of his own grim story of murder, commenting on his narrative devices and on the witchcraft frenzy. He begins with a tale of murder set over a hundred and fifty years before, as Leonard Doane, a young man of "diseased imagination," confesses his guilt to a wizard. Doane's sister had become fond of the evil Walter Brome, who seemed his "very counterpart." After Brome claimed he had "shamed" her, Leonard killed him, feeling afterward like "one who struggles through a dream" and imagining he had performed the deed "in madness or a dream."

Looking at his dead "counterpart," he remembered his father, killed by Indians: "Methought I stood a weeping infant by my father's hearth; by the cold and blood-stained hearth where he lay dead. I heard the childish wail of Alice, and my own cry arose with hers, as we beheld the features of our parent." Now

5. This tale, which Poe praised for its auditory imagery, is the only one in which the dreamer's existence terminates with the unbearable dream.

6. Both Waggoner (*Hawthorne*, 48–56), and Frederick C. Crews (*The Sins of the Fathers: Hawthorne's Psychological Themes* [New York: Oxford University Press, 1966], 44–60) suggest that this complicated narrative of fratricide, parricide, and incest invites, even demands, psychoanalytic interpretation.

the face of the man he killed "still wore a likeness of my father."[7] The terrifying childhood scene explains Leonard's dependence on Alice, his horrified fascination with violent death, and his identification with, yet rejection of, the man he subconsciously recognizes as his brother. Through the wizard who hears Leonard's confession, Hawthorne casts the narrative as a supernatural tale: the wizard says he had arranged the fateful encounter of Walter, Alice, and Leonard. Yet, like the old woman in "The Hollow of the Three Hills," he can be taken as a projection of the sinner's guilty imagination.

To introduce the climactic scene of this story, the narrator self-consciously describes moonlight turning the familiar world of Salem into "the creation of a wizard power." Hawthorne was never more explicit about his own purpose in using moonlight: the young writer intends to "throw a ghostly glimmer round the reader, so that his imagination might view the town through a medium that should take off its every day aspect, and make it a proper theatre for so wild a scene as the final one." This wild Gothic scene is set in a cemetery, an expanded variant of the bedroom of "The Haunted Mind," where the guilt-stained brother stands beside his sister to confront a "company of devils and condemned souls" emerging from their graves "to revel in the discovery of a complicated crime."

The narrator now invites his audience to a more distressing effort of imagination, to think about real deeds of sin and real sinners. As night falls on Gallows Hill, he evokes a second dreamlike pageant, this one an imaginative version of historical fact. In a scene comparable to the climax of "My Kinsman, Major Molineux," he describes victims of the witchcraft trials mounting the hill, their accusers behind them, with the fiend-

---

7. The word "still" is curious, since he did not mention the likeness earlier. This is not irrelevant "to the rest of the fragments," as Waggoner suggests (*Hawthorne*, 52), since it extends the moment of Leonard's shock by overlaying on it the moment after the Indian massacre when he first realized he and Alice were fatherless, presumably the only other time he had seen a murdered man; its climax is Leonard's identification of the two dead men.

like figure of Cotton Mather looming at the procession's end. This proud man on horseback had been able to "madden the whole surrounding multitude" in that time when "feverish dreams were remembered as realities."

Yet Hawthorne was certain that feverish dreams, whether real or fictional, individual or communal, contain hidden truths. The storyteller, the young ladies who hear his tale, Alice and her brothers, the Puritans of Salem, and even the readers of the tale are implicated in this disjunctive narrative of deceit, jealousy, and violent death. Although in the central tale Walter's ghost proclaims Alice's innocence and the evil spirits flee, neither that tale nor the broader narrative effectively exorcise nightmares, but rather dramatize their recurrent terror. The figures of the wizard, the murdered brother, the massacred father, the hanged witches, and the triumphant Cotton Mather together suggest the guilt of destructive malice latent in every haunted mind (S-I, 266–80).

In these three early tales—as in the far more successful "Young Goodman Brown," which requires separate analysis—Hawthorne questions whether we should believe the visions of dreams and fictions, or whether we should discount them as in some sense the devil's work. In "An Old Woman's Tale," the question of deception is relatively unimportant, although fiction garbed as truth is compared to the devil himself, disguised in mortal attire, and so—presumably—leading men astray. Yet in the tale the lovers are not penalized but rewarded when they behold a spectral procession of long-dead townspeople. The elderly lady who is the last of the illusory figures moves them to compassion, and she shows them where to dig for some unspecified buried treasure.

The question of demoniac deception is more urgent in "The Hollow of the Three Hills" and "Alice Doane's Appeal." Since the devil is the author of lies, he can evoke hallucinations to deceive his victims and muster evil spirits to masquerade as real individuals. The old crone and the wizard in these tales serve as the devil's surrogates: they apparently delight in their victims' torment. They are masters of illusory revels, like the writer of romance, manipulating lights and shadows for maximum emotional effect. Yet, though the spectral processions have no objective validity, they are not to be taken as false inventions. Hawthorne indicates that they have the same validity as feverish dreams in which guilt gives shape to memory and fantasy; they are at once explanations and projections of the victims' guilt, and they cause further torment. Thus, the storyteller of "Alice Doane's Appeal" seems to be playing the devil's role when he torments his listeners by marshaling before their imaginations a procession of the villains and victims of Salem's witchcraft delusions; he plunges into his own imagination "for a blacker horror, and a deeper woe" until the ladies can bear no more. At the same time that Hawthorne sees the romancer as a devil, however, he tacitly distinguishes between them, praising the one and condemning the other for their purposes and final effects. The crone and the wizard provoke their victims into morbid states of self-regarding despair; but the storyteller feels triumphant when his truth-based fictions reach the secret places of his listeners' hearts, evoking tears of compassion and deeper understanding of our common nature. Clearly, Hawthorne considered this the proper function of dreams and fictions alike.

Unlike the spectral analogues in the weird tales, most of the dreams in Hawthorne's fiction are closer to those of ordinary experience, brief episodes that erupt in the midst of sleep. Hawthorne always used such episodes to make the dreamer confront unresolved problems that trouble his waking existence, though the dreams are not equally convincing in all the tales. "The Threefold Destiny" and "Peter Goldthwaite's Treasure," for example, both contain dreams of cognition that are well-crafted but simplistic, like the tales themselves; they express the dreamer's immediate concerns without exploring his latent anxieties. Nevertheless, they are appropriate to the dreamer, they provide the "tinge of the wild and wonderful" Hawthorne always tried to achieve, and they give structural unity to each tale.

In "The Threefold Destiny," Hawthorne explains at the outset, he combined "the spirit and mechanism of faëry legend . . . with the characters and manners of familiar life," and the hero's three dreams provide that spirit and mechanism. Each would be appropriate in a fairy tale: Ralph dreams repeatedly of winning a young girl who wears a jeweled heart, of discovering buried treasure, and of entertaining three visitors who offer him a position of power. Yet it is not incredible that such dreams should obsess Ralph throughout his ten-year search for their fulfillment, or that they persist even when he is awake; and Hawthorne ties them firmly to "familiar life." The girl turns out to be Ralph's childhood playmate, he will dig for treasure by cultivating his garden, and finally, three townsmen offer him the post of schoolmaster. The tale is atypical in several ways: the three reiterated dreams are deliberately crafted as the tale's unifying structural device, they are all happy wish-fulfillments, and they all come true, if not in the romantic form Ralph expected. Yet like all Hawthorne's fictional dreams, they derive from ordinary waking life; and they affect it in the end (*T-t T*, 472–84).

In the comic fable of "Peter Goldthwaite's Treasure," dreams also offer prophetic conundrums. Here they are shaped not only by experience and desire, but also by repressed fears, though the repression is not far beneath the level of waking consciousness. Yet like Ralph's, Peter's dreams reveal truths about the present and the imminent future without probing dark secrets of past or present guilt.

Peter Goldthwaite decides to tear down his house to find a treasure reputedly hidden by an ancestor; then he has a night of gorgeous dreams intermixed with peculiar moments of gloom. He opens a door, but it is "not unlike the door of a sepulchre." He discovers a vault filled with all the gold men had ever lost, but in the dream he returns home "as poor as ever, and was received at the door, by the gaunt and grizzled figure of a man, whom he might have taken for himself, only that his garments were of a much elder fashion." The dream house seems transmuted into a palace of gold and silver; yet Peter's happiness is troubled by "a certain ocular deception, which, whenever he glanced backward, caused the house to darken from its glittering magnificence into the sordid gloom of yesterday." Peter's repressed doubts interrupt his wish-fulfilling dreams.

As the story continues, treasure-hunting days are followed by nights of wish-fulfilling dreams, always undercut by doubts. Finally, as the dreams had foretold, Peter finds the buried treasure, but remains "as poor as ever." The treasure is a box of worthless provincial currency. His dream has further ironic validation: he learns he looks exactly like the earlier Peter Goldthwaite, who was also an optimistic but unsuccessful treasure-seeker. In a sense the dream image of the house transmuted into gold comes true, but as a result of Hawthorne's design rather than Peter's insight: a buyer wants the house because its site is valuable. Yet dreams are more effective and less obtrusive as a structural device than in "The Threefold Destiny," and more psychologically credible. They manifest Peter's obsessive hopes qualified by his healthy skepticism (*T-t T*, 383–406). But in both tales the dreams are relatively transparent, their "strange transformations" readily understood.

In Hawthorne's most successful fiction, the knowledge that forces its way through fictional dreams is usually darker and more perplexing, as in "Rappaccini's Daughter" and "The Birthmark." In each of these tales, a single dream conveys terrifying truths important to the dreamer's waking life, and his response to the dream defines his moral limitations. Each dream is a riddling extension of waking perceptions and thoughts, and curiously, each propels the dreamer to morally equivocal behavior.

A brief riddling dream is central to "Rappaccini's Daughter," but the story implicitly argues that dreams may tell only half-truths. Since Giovanni is a shallow youth, his dream gives him only superficial knowledge. The story is not only a criticism of ruthless scientific experimentation, not only a study of ambivalence about female sexuality, but a commentary on the limited truths accessible to a man of "quick fancy" whose heart is not quickened by trustful love.[8]

As Giovanni looks down into a garden from his chamber, "it was strangely frightful to the young man's imagination" to see an emaciated man in scholar's garb cautiously tending his plants, then relinquishing care of the most magnificent flower to a girl of splendid beauty. "Giovanni's fancy must have grown morbid," but he fancied girl and flower were sisters, both "to be touched only with a glove." The same fancy recurs as he watches Beatrice tend the flower: he "almost doubted whether it were a girl tending her favorite flower, or one sister performing the duties of affection to another." When he goes to sleep, his "wonder-working" fancy pursues the identification: he "dreamed of a rich flower and beautiful girl. Flower and maiden were different and yet the same, and fraught with some strange peril in either shape."

Giovanni is now confused by his "wild vagaries" of imagination about Beatrice and the "terrible attributes" she seems to possess. He is so absorbed by his fantasies that when the practical scientist Baglioni speaks to him, "he stared forth wildly from his inner world into the outer one, and spoke like a man in a dream." This confusion continues when he actually enters Rappaccini's garden: now it seems that his "dreams have condensed their misty substance into tangible realities."

He becomes even more distressed after he meets Beatrice, the girl "who had so wrought upon his imagination—whom he

8. For divergent readings of the story, see Roy R. Male, *Hawthorne's Tragic Vision* (Austin: University of Texas Press, 1957), 54–70; Richard Harter Fogle, *Hawthorne's Fiction: The Light and the Dark* (Norman: University of Oklahoma Press, 1952), 91–103; Waggoner, *Hawthorne*, 111–24; and Crews, *Sins of the Fathers*, 116–35.

had idealized in such hues of terror," and who now seems pure of soul. Beatrice gives him the clue to her mystery when she warns him that fancy tested only by "the outward senses . . . may be false in its essence"; but he is incapable of understanding her essence. He tries to repress the ugly fancies his outward senses tested. Now each repressed suspicion about her "stole away and hid itself among those shapeless half-ideas, which throng the dim region beyond the daylight of our perfect consciousness." When Baglioni says Beatrice is poisonous, Giovanni protests, "It is a dream! . . . surely it is a dream!" Both the reality and the dream convey the identical false truth.

Giovanni has desperately tried to deny the message of his dream, but it can no longer stay confined. His faith in Beatrice is now displaced by distrust and horror. She tells him the magnificent flower "has qualities that you little dream of," but he did dream of them. His dream had told him that "flower and maiden were different and yet the same, and fraught with some strange peril." He had tried not to think about the peril, but now that thought obsesses him. This immature young man can neither accept the mixture of good and evil in mortal existence, nor value spirit above material fact. His dream had told him that "flower and maiden were different" though the same; but the difference forever escaped him (*Mosses*, 91–128).

Aylmer's dream in "The Birth-mark" resembles Giovanni's in several obvious and important ways: both are recognitions of the mortal imperfections of a lovely woman, and both are concise summaries of waking anxieties.[9] Aylmer's dream is a more complex symbolic action, however, in which he is the chief agent; it provokes Hawthorne's most extensive comments about

9. Crews (*Sins of the Fathers*, 125, 156) distorts Hawthorne's complexity when he says Aylmer's dream "reveals a fantasy of sadistic revenge and a scarcely less obvious fantasy of sexual consummation," and when he argues that Aylmer's "magic show is a prelude to murder, a distraction covering psychopathic intentions." Through Georgiana, Hawthorne praises Aylmer's desire for perfection; Aylmer recognizes what he cannot acknowledge, that his operation will kill his wife, but he does not intend "sadistic revenge" or murder.

the self-protective strategies of dreams. Whether he is asleep or awake, Aylmer's "sombre imagination" is obsessed by his beautiful wife's birthmark, "the visible mark of earthly imperfection." Hawthorne explains this obsession in terms Dugald Stewart might have used. Although the husband tried not to think about the birthmark, "it so connected itself with innumerable trains of thoughts, and modes of feeling, that it became the central point of all."

The plot complication begins after Aylmer's obsession has erupted in a dream that he cannot at first bring to consciousness, even when Georgiana asks if he recollects "a dream, last night, about this odious Hand." He comments, "I might well dream of it; for before I fell asleep, it had taken a pretty firm hold of my fancy." Georgiana now repeats the words he spoke in his sleep: "It is in her heart now—we must have it out!" By urging him to recall the dream, to become conscious of what had been repressed, Georgiana is an agent in her own destruction. Hawthorne suggests that remembering the nightmare might bring further distress to Aylmer's waking life: "The mind is in a sad note, when Sleep, the all-involving, cannot confine her spectres within the dim region of her sway, but suffers them to break forth, affrighting this actual life with secrets that perchance belong to a deeper one." Perhaps these spectres and secrets should remain interred.

In his dream, he is operating to remove the birthmark: "But the deeper went the knife, the deeper sank the Hand, until at length its tiny grasp appeared to have caught hold of Georgiana's heart; whence, however, her husband was inexorably resolved to cut or wrench it away." The dream is clear and concise, yet it hides a guilty secret. Aylmer wants to perform radical surgery to make his wife physically perfect. He can readily unravel this strand of his dream, but another remains tightly knotted: he cannot admit that he knows the operation will prove fatal.

When his will was relaxed in sleep, his obsessive desire

113

emerged unchecked. As Hawthorne explains, "Truth often finds its way to the mind close-muffled in robes of sleep, and then speaks with uncompromising directness of matters in regard to which we practise an unconscious self-deception, during our waking moments. Until now, he had not been aware of the tyrannizing influence acquired by one idea over his mind, and of the lengths which he might find in his heart to go, for the sake of giving himself peace." His dream informs Aylmer of his selfish motive: to ease his mind, he can "find it in his heart" to cut into Georgiana's heart. His dream resembles the prophecies of biblical dreams: it anticipates the fatal results of the operation; but its terms are appropriate to the scientist's imagination. The dream also differs from biblical prophecy in its attention to the dreamer's state of mind both in the dream and after waking. Aylmer has "a guilty feeling," though he assures his wife that the operation has "perfect practicability." Mortal perfection is a self-contradiction, the story asserts; but Aylmer will not, perhaps can not, comprehend what he is telling himself through his dream (*Mosses*, 36–56).

Some of Hawthorne's tales make lighter use of dreams. A few tales draw on the romantic cliché that dreams are sources of artistic inspiration: the writer of "The Antique Ring" "had the good fortune to possess himself of an available idea in a dream," Hawthorne says; "Graves and Goblins" is a comic version of such inspiration; and the sculptor of "Drowne's Wooden Image" says he achieved his single splendid work of art in a kind of dream. In "The Hall of Fantasy," Hawthorne observes that some dreams can console sufferers: Sylph Etherege finds such consolation in dreams of an ideal love, and Esther Dudley escapes in dreams of days long past. A striking simile in "The Wives of the Dead" suggests another way the dreamer may be protected from his own distress: a grieving wife's "heart, like a deep lake, had grown calm because its dead had sunk down so far within. Happy is it, and strange, that the lighter sorrows are those from which dreams are chiefly fabricated" (*S-I*, 196). But more characteristic of Hawthorne's fiction and more fully reflecting his own insights and irresolutions is the brief dream of cognition in "The Birth-mark," fabricated from heavy sorrow. Aylmer feels guilty when his dream reaches consciousness, and his uneasiness proves justified. Hawthorne had instructed Sophia to interpret his dream of falling asleep for a year, but not to draw any sombre omens from it; in "The Birth-mark" he intimates that it may be best not to know the darkest secrets of the inner life.

3. *The Real Course of a Dream*

Three of Hawthorne's most successful stories fulfill his ambition "to write a dream"—two written when he was still a young bachelor and the other a few years after his marriage.[10] In each, the atmosphere and setting, as well as the protagonist's state of mind and his strange adventures are all associated with dreams, and together determine meaning. The stories subordinate plot to psychological and moral truth, and the reader is invited to respond to each story's detail as a dreamer responds to his dream, accepting inconsistencies and transformations, apparent "eccentricities and aimlessness," sensing "a leading idea running through the whole."

"The Celestial Rail-road," "Young Goodman Brown," and "My Kinsman, Major Molineux" are all parabolic stories of self-discovery, of bewilderment only partly dispelled, of night journeys terminated but not completed. In each, a protagonist tries to understand what happens as he moves from perception to understanding; he is soon adrift on his memories, desires, and submerged feelings of guilt, carried toward horrifying vortices of self-knowledge. Moral confrontation is also self-betrayal. At

10. According to Chandler, *Study of the Sources*, Hawthorne wrote "My Kinsman, Major Molineux" and "Young Goodman Brown" in 1828 or 1829 and "The Celestial Rail-road" in 1843.

once agent and observer, he confronts demonic figures in a dark place illuminated by infernal fires, a place symbolically equivalent to the depths of his own mind. Like Hawthorne himself, the central figure avoids acknowledging the horrors within, but he acknowledges that he harbors them. He ends no longer the self-confident individual who set off on a quest at the beginning of his tale.

The earliest of these three dream tales, and the one whose "everyman" hero is youngest, is in some ways the most complex. At only one point does Robin drift into a dream, yet dreams permeate "My Kinsman, Major Molineux."[11] It is dreamlike in its transformations, condensations, and elliptical communications; like a dream it takes place in a series of curious half-lights; and as in a dream the central figure is a perplexed individual who tries to make sense of his strange visions. The story's dense pattern of extrinsic events corresponds to the protagonist's inner drama. Robin's moonlit adventures take him deep into his own unconscious mind, urging him to imagine what he cannot consciously formulate. He is on a quest, and the town is as much a symbolic equivalent of his inner labyrinth as the forest in "Young Goodman Brown."

Critics have long recognized that "My Kinsman" can be read as a historical and a political fable, with the resonance of poetry, centering on a young boy's passage from adolescence into the fallen world of adults. And psychiatrists have praised Hawthorne's psychological acuity in rendering Robin's problems and the implied consequence of his *rites de passage*. Writing in *Fiction and the Unconscious* of how fiction shapes our fancies and "lays claim to the vaster and less accessible

11. Neal Frank Doubleday says, "The tale is a sinister Midsummer Night's dream; Robin is ill met by moonlight." He adds, "The moonlit scene of the tale for the most part does not seem to be this time that 'neutral territory' of romance, where the Actual and the Imaginary may meet, but a territory of lunacy, where nothing seems actual, and the imaginary a nightmare" (*Hawthorne's Early Tales, A Critical Study* [Durham: Duke University Press, 1972], 231–32). Yet for Hawthorne the neutral territory has room for lunacy and nightmare.

realm of our fantasies and dreams," Simon O. Lesser reaches provocative if sometimes inexact conclusions about the tale.[12]

Lesser says Robin does not really want to find his kinsman, who represents paternal authority, but is "searching for sexual adventure" and economic independence. However, Lesser does not adequately recognize Robin's ambivalence: the boy resists the girl in the red petticoat, though with an assist from the night watchman; and until the end he hopes for help from his kinsman. Surely it is misleading to say that "the Major symbolizes just those aspects of the father from which the youth so urgently desires to be free": Robin likes being helped. He is seeking new experiences, but within limits. His approach to the sepulchral citizen makes it clear that he expects to stay within the established order. At the end of the story, he is on the verge of accepting a freedom greater than he had sought. External circumstances as well as dream and reverie have prepared him for this independence, and the nightmare conclusion of his adventure has brought grim self-knowledge. Although Lesser argues that "My Kinsman" is the "story of the youth's hostile and rebellious feelings for the relative—and for the father—and his wish to be free of adult domination," this is an oversimplification of the story.

Robin's adventure into self-knowledge has two main movements, both dreamlike—one culminating in a dream of isolation, the other in a waking nightmare of communion. Waggoner says that "we begin to feel the tale taking on the texture of a dream" after the barbers laugh at Robin, but actually that "texture" begins earlier.[13] We see Robin as an isolated and confused figure from the moment the ferryman examines him by the lantern beneath the moon; from that point on we look through Robin's eyes as he moves as if in a dream, trying to

12. Simon O. Lesser, *Fiction and the Unconscious* (Boston: Beacon Press, 1957), 212–24. Lesser believes fiction is important because it "gives shape and substance to the most incorporeal and fleeting fancies of our infinitely fecund minds" (60).

13. Waggoner, *Hawthorne*, 57.

make sense of a night town unsteadily illuminated by the moon and artificial light. The dreamlike atmosphere is intensified by his humiliating encounters with townspeople from the barbershop episode until the final torchlit parade.

Increasingly he feels bewildered as he wanders through town, as if "a spell was on him," until his second encounter with the two-faced man, who advises him to await his kinsman at the church where they stand. Here "the moon, 'creating, like the imaginative power, a beautiful strangeness in familiar objects,'" gives the street "something of romance"; and Robin's reveries begin. His will relaxes and his imagination becomes increasingly active. Despite his sleepiness he tries to concentrate on the moonlit street, but finds "distant objects, starting away with almost ghostly indistinctness, just as his eye appeared to grasp them." Then a glance at the church graveyard gives rise to a terrifying thought: his kinsman might be dead; he might be a ghostly figure who could "glide through yonder gate, and nod and smile to him in passing dimly by." The derivative fantasy is appropriate for the lonely boy; it expresses a submerged fear that proves ironically prophetic.

At this point, Robin is awake enough to dispel his disturbing thought. Like the narrator of "The Haunted Mind," he deliberately chooses something pleasant to think about, to divert his attention: he invokes images of the beloved family he has just left. As in dreams, his thoughts rise as pictures. He had noticed a moonlit Bible in the church, and by clear patterns of association he now envisages his father conducting family services at sunset that day. But almost immediately, he finds himself involuntarily immersed in a dream whose message is too distressing for conscious acknowledgment. The fantasy of his family united in worship only confirms his lonely sorrow. By the logic of dreams, he attributes his sorrow to them, imagining them grieving at his absence. "Then he saw them go in at the door; and when Robin would have entered also, the latch tinkled into its place, and he was excluded from his home." Until that moment he was the spectator of a reverie calculated to give him comfort, but suddenly he entered a dream state that peremptorily denied that comfort: he was locked out of his old home.

So disturbing are the sight and sound of the latched door that Robin immediately wakens, as commonly happens when a nightmare proves intolerable. But he remains confused by his dream and its relation to his present plight. " 'Am I here, or there?' cried Robin, starting; for all at once, when his thoughts had become visible and audible in a dream, the long, wide, solitary street shone out before him." His question is crucial. As Lesser recognizes, in a sense the drama he is involved in takes place simultaneously "there—at home—as well as in the town where bodily he happens to be."[14] To say he can no longer join his family at home is another way of saying he is alone in the town. The dream says he has left childhood behind and can never return; at the crossroads of maturity, he has already made choices whose implications he has not understood. His question "Am I here, or there?" sums up his confusion: he cannot distinguish the dream from the waking reality, nor can he see how each explains the other. Excluded from "there," he is necessarily "here," though he can travel home by imagination. Sunset is long past, and he must try to make sense of the moonlit town.

But his confusion persists as his mind intermixes perception, memory, and imagination, trying to reconcile the intolerable dichotomy between "here" and "there." He deliberately turns his attention to a building, but "still his mind kept vibrating between fancy and reality; by turns, the pillars of the balcony lengthened into the tall, bare stems of pines, dwindled down to human figures, settled again in their true shape and size, and then commenced a new succession of changes." Although he is on a town street, his imagination presents the pine

14. Lesser, *Fiction and the Unconscious*, 120.

woods of the country; he is alone, but imagines he has company; and his mind cannot keep hold of "true shape and size." Recent past and uncertain present intermingle in ambiguous and shifting images as Robin struggles to locate himself in time and space.

As in a dream, his role as spectator merges into the roles of victim and participant. Robin's dream of home was the climax of his isolation; the story now moves steadily to his nightmare of communion. He thinks he sees a face, perhaps his kinsman's, observing him from across the street. Then his mind moves deeper into itself as "a deeper sleep wrestled with, and nearly overcame him, but fled at the sound of footsteps." This introduces his first gratifying exchange with another human being, a kind gentleman who volunteers help. Robin's conversation with this gentleman is at once an interlude before the culminating dreamlike scene and a bridge to it. If the kind gentleman can survive in the night town despite revolutionary conspiracy, perhaps Robin can too.

Now in the final scene, as in the deepest moments of dreams, the story's suspense reaches new intensity. With Robin and the gentleman, we wait for something to happen. From the beginning, the story has raised questions. Will Robin find his kinsman? What place in the world would he then have? Will the threats and mockery of the adult world overwhelm him? Can he emerge from his state of confusion where he cannot tell fancy from reality? The story answers these questions in a thoroughly surprising way. By the mixed light of moon and torches, confused by drowsiness and anxiety, Robin now takes part in a scene explicitly likened to nightmare. It seems "as if a dream had broken forth from some feverish brain, and were sweeping visibly through the midnight streets." As in a dream, Robin is a spectator yet a central figure who can affect the final direction and meaning of the adventure. Yet this is no dream.

The parade that moves toward Robin is itself confusion compounded. Its musical accompaniment is a discordant "band of fearful wind-instruments," and its torches "disturbed the moonbeams . . . by their glare concealing whatever object they illuminated." The fierce leader is a demoniac embodiment of complex passion: his eyes glow "like fire in a cave," and in his "infernal visage," half red and half black, apparently "a fiend of fire and a fiend of darkness, had united." The crowd is a confused mass of "wild figures in the Indian dress, and many fantastic shapes without a model, giving the whole march a visionary air," comparable to the congregants of "Young Goodman Brown," the infernal fiends of "The Celestial Rail-road," and the masqueraders near the end of *The Blithedale Romance.* From the moment when the "double-faced leader" fixes his mesmeric hold on the boy's eyes, the scene moves steadily toward its two moments of climax: Robin's recognition of his kinsman and his orgiastic participation in ritual mockery.

When the parade had first approached, Robin could not penetrate its "veil" of unsteady torchlight; for a time his perception remains uncertain as "confused traces of a human form appeared at intervals, and then melted into the vivid light." The word "melted" conveys the dreamlike evanescence of the entire procession. As in a dream, sounds also emerge suddenly and become transformed; they rise to a crescendo in the leader's thunderous shout and the trumpets' horrid vomit, then die away to "a universal hum, nearly allied to silence." In this still moment the parade halts, and suddenly Robin sees on an uncovered cart the man he has been seeking: "There the torches blazed the brightest, there the moon shone out like day, and there, in tar-and-feathery dignity, sate his kinsman, Major Molineux!"

In the central moment of recognition, Robin suffers "pity and terror" like a spectator at Greek tragedy. But catharsis comes quickly. His kinsman continues to suffer, but not Robin. Immediately and involuntarily he transfers the townspeople's ridicule of himself to the Major; he frees himself from anguish, but only by repudiating part of himself. He pays the fearful

121

price of initiation into the sinful human race by acting the part of a sinner.

He moves toward this role as in a dream, while sounds which had erupted separately before are repeated and take on new meaning. Robin hears once more the mocking laughter of the watchman, the girl in the red petticoat, the innkeeper, the sepulchral citizen—"all who had made sport of him that night." The laughter erupts like a contagion until it seizes him, "and he sent forth a shout of laughter that echoed through the street." He has involuntarily asserted membership with the anarchic crowd, abandoning his separate identity to join a community of shame. His laughter is directed toward his kinsman, but it also suggests involuntary self-mockery and a surprised farewell to innocence.

This condensed moment takes place at the level of experience removed from ordinary life, and in a sense the whole tale has operated at such a remove following its introductory paragraph. The dreamlike atmosphere of the story is sustained throughout by metaphors of labyrinths and enchantments, by repeated references to sleep and yawning, and by such verbs as *slip*, *slide*, *melt*, and *quiver*, all conveying a sense of ontological uncertainty and change. All these devices relate to the imperative question of what is dream and what is reality. In the middle of the tale, Robin had emerged from his dream of home wondering whether he was still dreaming, and before the parade appears, Robin asks the kind gentleman if there really is a Major Molineux, "or am I dreaming?" The gentleman does not answer, but after the parade passes he redirects the question to the boy: "Well, Robin, are you dreaming?" The answer is literally no, but in a sense yes; as in "Young Goodman Brown," the literal question is not of central importance.

Earlier Robin had a dream that seemed real, but in the end he has a real experience as compelling, vivid, and laden with disturbing significance as a dream. Both experiences have forced him to acknowledge his present predicament, though not at the conscious level. Both have taught him that his childhood is over and he must be prepared to stand alone. Ironically, he has found the kinsman he was looking for, and he can be ironic about his discovery. Most horrifying is his recognition of an unexpected kinship with the wild rioters of the midnight street. For the brief moment when he laughs with the mob, Robin becomes as much a fiend of the haunted mind as a victimized dreamer, joining the crowd of "fiends that throng in mockery round some dead potentate, mighty no more, but majestic still in his agony." The nightmare scene has involved him in its destructive mockery, leading him to enact his own latent guilt. The question "are you dreaming?" reestablishes the literal reality of the fantastic scene that has just ended; but that scene, like a bad dream, has taken Robin into dark places within himself that he would rather not have seen. Nonetheless, he has learned that he can survive such traumas and perhaps even rise in the world. He has completed the archetypal rhythm of all dreams: withdrawal, but then return (S-I, 208–31).

"Young Goodman Brown" is the story of a literal journey into the forest, yet Hawthorne has so contrived the journey that it must also be read as a journey into the self, into the interior world of dreams. The story relates the night adventures of a young man who, despite his wife's protests, enters the forest on some evil mission. By prearrangement, he meets an old man who will conduct an impious ceremony later that night. He then observes ostensibly pious villagers apparently headed for the forest meeting, perhaps his wife Faith among them. He arrives in despair at the unholy altar where the fiendish old man, in the presence of his congregants, is prepared to initiate him and his wife as converts to evil. Brown urges Faith to resist, then immediately finds himself alone in the forest. He returns to Salem the next morning to begin a long life of gloomy distrust.

But from the beginning of the story, when Faith urges him to sleep that night in his own bed, we know there is much more at stake. "A lone woman is troubled with such dreams and such thoughts, that she's afeard of herself, sometimes," Faith says. Her plea implies that the story may be a shared dream (as in "An Old Woman's Tale"); but Hawthorne sustains it as Goodman Brown's interior quest. What Faith's importunity clearly establishes is that his quest is not necessarily unique to this one man.

In refusing her, he says, "My journey, as thou callest it, forth and back again, must needs be done 'twixt now and sunrise." The phrase "as thou callest it" suggests it might be called something else. As he leaves, he thinks of her troubled face, "as if a dream had warned her what work is to be done tonight"; but he firmly concludes, "'twould kill her to think it." He is about to think it, and in a sense the thought destroys him. The way to understand his forest "errand" is through his dreaming mind.

As daylight fades, Goodman Brown enters the road "darkened by all the gloomiest trees of the forest" which seem to make way for him and then close behind him; his mind begins to waver between what it dimly perceives and what it intensely fears yet desires to encounter. Hawthorne might have remembered the observation of the Scottish philosopher Thomas Brown that superstitious men "incorporate their fears with the objects which they dimly perceive, till the whole, thus compounded, assumes the appearance of external reality." As he wonders if the devil might be nearby, he sees "the figure of a man" whose staff seems to be a living serpent. Inviting the reader to determine the locus of reality, Hawthorne says this "must have been an ocular deception, assisted by the uncertain light." We have entered a neutral territory where actual and imaginary meet and interfuse, and the mind tries to come to terms with its visions.

In this uncertain light, unsure of what he sees and hears, Brown's mind wavers between pursuing or evading his "evil purpose." Hiding when the woman who had taught him catechism comes along, he hears her recognize the devil and talk about the young man to be initiated that night. Although her "friend" cannot now accompany her, he offers her his staff, "if you will." Hawthorne says "perhaps it assumed life," though Brown in his astonishment "could not take cognizance" of it. Her will is resolved, but not his. He is ready to turn back: if Goody Cloyse should "choose to go to the devil," he does not have to follow her. At this point the devil vanishes, and for a short time Brown can think pleasant thoughts about returning home to sleep "in the arms of Faith."

Yet he is still "conscious of the guilty purpose that had brought him thither." After that thought, he hears the minister and Deacon Gookin talk of a young woman about to join their communion; his confusion is expressed in his inability to see them. He wonders if there is a heaven, and for a moment he has a reassuring glimpse of blue sky. But a black cloud obscures the stars, and from its depths comes "a confused and doubtful sound of voices." He "fancied" he heard his townspeople, a sad young woman among them, though perhaps he heard merely the sounds of the forest. At this moment he calls for Faith; but the confused voices only get louder, something flutters from the sky, and he beholds "a pink ribbon." This illusive object makes him assume all his fancies have been real perceptions, and he becomes "demoniac." Propelled not by will but by the instinct to evil, he rushes into the "haunted forest" where all paths disappear, a place "peopled with frightful sounds." In his despair, he thinks nature is mocking him, but "he was himself the chief horror of the scene."[15] He is now committed to the encounter he dreads.

15. David Levin in "Shadows of Doubt: Specter Evidence in Hawthorne's 'Young Goodman Brown,'" *American Literature*, XXXIV (1962), 344–52, points out that if the devil is not merely a fantasy figure, he can conjure a pink ribbon. It is also important to observe that Hawthorne says Brown beheld a pink ribbon, not that such a ribbon in fact was there. Michael J. Colacurcio in "Visible Sanctity and Specter Evidence: The Moral World of Hawthorne's 'Young Goodman Brown,'" *Essex Institute Historical Collections*, CX (1974), 259–99, argues that spectral evi-

The climactic scene takes Goodman Brown to the center of the forest and the center of his horrible vision. In the "lurid blaze" of four pine trees, amid "the sounds of the benighted wilderness," he approaches a rude altar. By fitful light, he sees an amorphous congregation, resembling the dream processions of earlier tales, that sometimes seems to disappear in shadow, then grow out of the darkness. Among the "shapes and visages of horror on the smoke-wreaths, above the impious assembly," he sees the figures of present villagers and those long dead, "quivering to-and-fro," known sinners together with those reputedly virtuous, perhaps his parents among them. When he wonders where Faith is, she is brought forth beside him. The fiend now emerges to celebrate the communion, proclaiming that they shall exult to behold the whole earth one stain of guilt. Husband and wife had hoped "virtue were not all a dream," but they are now "undeceived," he says. By dream logic, if he is telling the truth and "evil is the nature of mankind," faith in virtue must be relegated to the status of a dream.

For a time, Brown has been involuntarily observing the dreadful scene he had first thought up and then envisioned. But as he and Faith are about to be baptized with blood or "liquid flame," standing poised "on the verge of wickedness, in this dark world," Goodman Brown is at the furthest point of his journey into darkness. He can endure no more. Determined to leave Faith for this one night, he had been horrified to think she might be in the forest; but he cannot bear thinking she might be committed to evil. He cries out, urging Faith to resist the devil, and this terminates the scene of torment.

Like other dreamers in Hawthorne's fiction who wake from nightmares, he carefully observes the real physical world around him: he listens to the wind, feels the damp rock, and is sprinkled by dew from a "twig, that had been all on fire." But he remains "bewildered" even when he returns to the daylight of Salem

---

dence, a Puritan "figure" for guilty fantasies, is a central issue in Hawthorne's fiction, starting with "Alice Doane's Appeal."

village. Like the haunted dreamers of the Oberon tales, like Giovanni, and like Aylmer, he will now endure the torments of nightmare in his waking life.

The story must be approached through Hawthorne's rhetorical question near the end: "Had Goodman Brown fallen asleep in the forest, and only dreamed a wild dream of a witch-meeting?" But the immediate answer is equally important: "Be it so, if you will." The reader must commit his own mind. One critic reads the tale as a dream of self-punishment, another as a wish fulfillment; but it can clearly be read as a dream exposing deep inner fears.[16] Goodman Brown wants to know what he is afraid to know. As Hawthorne had said in "The Birth-mark," the dreaming mind can penetrate "unconscious self-deception." Brown persistently tries to deflect his compulsive desire to know the worst about himself, but his fear that all men are evil gives rise to a dream enacting that fear.

The story is plausible as a daydream that merges into nightmare, beginning in fading light as Brown walks into the dark forest. His path is intermittently lit by stars and obscured by clouds until at midnight he reaches the "hell-kindled" pines, and he continues to be uncertain about the reality of the sights and sounds that seem to emerge from the forest, even at the central point when he beholds the fiendish congregation. The

16. Reginald Cook in "The Forest of Goodman Brown's Night: A Reading of Hawthorne's 'Young Goodman Brown,'" *New England Quarterly*, XLIII (1970), 473–81, says Brown willfully mistakes illusion for reality because of his desire for punishment, his psychological masochism. Taylor Stoehr, in " 'Young Goodman Brown' and Hawthorne's Theory of Mimesis," *Nineteenth Century Fiction*, XXIII (1969), 393–412, interprets Brown's loss of faith as a kind of wish fulfillment; he imagines the worst and then believes it. Donald Ringe, in "Hawthorne's Night Journeys," *American Transcendental Quarterly*, X (1971), 27–32, discusses "Young Goodman Brown," "My Kinsman, Major Molineux," and "Ethan Brand" as deliberate journeys into the outer and inner darkness, all ending in some resumption of light. What Hawthorne stresses, however, is how the seeker in these tales and in other dream tales is harrowed by his terrifying visions. "Ethan Brand" offers an interesting comparison with "The Threefold Destiny": in both a seeker returns home, but Ethan's questions were answered before his return. Unlike the dreamers who struggle cognitively with their fantasies and perceptions, he willfully ends his nightmare of self-damnation.

figures of this nightmare vision—devil, witches, and unholy communicants—are credible embodiments of a young Puritan's obsession with evil: figures that loomed so large in pulpit rhetoric might well invade men's dreams. Hawthorne had understood Cotton Mather's belief in witchcraft in such terms; Mather was so obsessed with the demons of his imagination that he was convinced they had objective existence. Repeatedly Brown's thoughts give rise to fantasies, and since most of the thoughts are about his "evil purpose," most of the visions embody that purpose.

At each stage of his progress through the forest, Goodman Brown's problem is one many readers have: he wants simple answers. But Hawthorne never gives simple answers. Brown's journey is real whether or not it was dreamed: it conveys the tormenting knowledge all men confront in dreams, knowledge that produces the fiends of the haunted mind. Whether he has dreamed or really participated in evil rites, Goodman Brown has confronted evil as one—though only one—inevitable fact of life. The burden of his midnight vision is that evil exists; but Brown's mistake is to confuse partial knowledge with absolute truth. His nightmare knowledge of evil in all men obliterates his ability to believe in human virtue. The narrator of "The Celestial Rail-road" tries to believe his dream was only a dream; by contrast, Brown becomes trapped by what Hawthorne finally unequivocally calls his "fearful dream" (*Mosses*, 74–90).

"The Celestial Rail-road" is a story of a dream journey with heaven the goal but hell the possible destination. It is a peculiar journey: once he boards the train, the curious but self-satisfied narrator is carried without willed effort through the Valley of the Shadow, to Vanity Fair, and to the land of Beulah; he can see the Celestial City but cannot reach it. He has not earned heaven, though he is not finally consigned to hell. At times he becomes aware of his sins and his mortal danger, but at no point does he openly reckon with his guilt. Waking, he remembers his dream, but he does not recognize it as a self-indictment. The story presents his increasing anxiety and his effort to discredit the inner knowledge that will not stay hidden.

The tale is obviously modeled on Hawthorne's favorite dream vision, *Pilgrim's Progress*.[17] Of all his stories, it most closely approximates the traditional dream vision, and like Bunyan, Hawthorne uses the dream to introduce an allegory satirizing spiritual hypocrisy and moral complacency. But Hawthorne is more interested than Bunyan in man's elusive inner experience, particularly the mind's tactical self-evasions.

As the story begins, the narrator is at ease with himself, a genial traveler accompanied by a gentleman called Mr. Smooth-it-away. "Not a great while ago, passing through the gate of dreams, I visited that region of the earth in which lies the famous city of Destruction," he announces. His determined complacency while addressing his "benevolent reader" sounds suspect, and we soon detect doubt beneath his certainty. Like Coverdale later, he dissembles to himself and the reader, claiming he decided on a journey to the Celestial City merely "to gratify a liberal curiosity."

His complacency is soon shaken. At the station, he sees the train's engine looking as if it "would hurry us to the infernal regions" and then the engineer, Apollyon, emitting smoke and flame. He asks, "Do my eyes deceive me?" But such evidence

17. Randall Stewart, in his edition of *The American Notebooks* (New Haven: Yale University Press, 1932), 297, suggests that "this tale may have been Hawthorne's attempt to carry out the plan suggested in his journal" in the passage beginning "To write a dream." Clearly, there were other such attempts. David E. Smith in *John Bunyan in America* (Bloomington: Indiana University Press, 1968), 47–89, discussing Bunyan's influence on Hawthorne, points out that the narrators of both dream visions are self-confident and optimistic but essentially ignorant men. Jospeh C. Pattison in "'The Celestial Railroad' as Dream-Tale," *American Quarterly*, XX (1968), 224–36, reads the story as "a study in rationalization and self-evasion," as I do, though he believes the narrator rejects his dream whereas I contend Hawthorne's subject is a not wholly successful attempt to reject it.

cannot readily be dismissed. The dreamer suspects what he cannot admit: the train has an infernal destination.

The train speeds as it enters the Valley of the Shadow, an approach to death but also an analogue of descent into the deeper regions of the self. His sudden entry into that "doleful region" frightens him, giving him "palpitations of the heart"; but he evades his anxiety by praising the engineering of the causeway. Fearful sights and sounds displace the discrete imagery characteristic of didactic allegory, but the dreamer deliberately distracts himself from them. Observing the gas lamps along the tracks in this valley where sunlight never penetrates, he protests he is grateful for any light at all, "if not from the sky above, then from the blasted soil beneath." Yet he admits the gaslight is "hurtful . . . to the eyes, and somewhat bewildering, as I discovered by the changes which it wrought in the visages of my companions." It is not clear what those changes are, and the narrator seems too disturbed to tell us. The journey seems increasingly threatening. The gas lamps "appeared to build walls of fire," and again the narrator suffers a pang of moral knowledge: it "made my heart quake" to fear "the bottomless pit," he says, but he then quickly adds, "if there be any such place." He tries to retain such skepticism, but his fear grows. Hell may exist.

When the engine stops to refuel, he finds new cause for fear and needs new effort to dispel it. "There came a tremendous shriek . . . as if a thousand devils had burst their lungs." The images announce that the train has reached the Inferno, the place Bunyan had "designated, in terms plainer than I like to repeat, as the mouth of the infernal region." But where Bunyan was distressingly plain, Mr. Smooth-it-away is comfortingly duplicitous: he "took occasion to prove that Tophet has not even a metaphorical existence. The place, he assured us, is no other than the crater of a half-extinct volcano." The narrator's eager acquiescence in this theory, denying his own dark knowledge and the story's metaphorical base, is testimony to his increasing terror.[18] Immediately, new infernal images refute Mr. Smooth-it-away. As "huge tongues of dusky flame" dart from the cavern, the dreamer sees "strange, half-shaped monsters, and visions of faces horribly grotesque, into which the smoke seemed to wreathe itself," and he hears "the awful murmurs, and shrieks, and deep shuddering whispers of the blast, sometimes forming itself into words almost inarticulate." Within the dream as on the border of dreams, remnants of sense perception interfuse with the mind's fantasies in half-shaped visions and almost inarticulate sounds, emotionally intensified by their inchoate and changing forms.

Again the train resumes its journey, the gaslight more "fierce" than ever, enabling the traveler to see frightening images of tantalizing familiarity. In a variant of the dream procession, the dreamer moves past portentous apparitions. "Sometimes, in the dark of intense brightness, grim faces, that bore the aspect and expression of individual sins, or evil passions, seemed to thrust themselves through the veil of light, glaring upon us, and stretching forth a great dusky hand, as if to impede our progress." By the logic of dreams, apparitions of "individual sins" condense and coalesce into a single image of antagonistic power—a great, dusky hand. The narrator immediately proposes yet simultaneously denies the insight he cannot tolerate even in the dream: "I almost thought, that they were my own sins that appalled me there." Absorbing the role of Mr. Smooth-it-away, he tries to mock himself by calling the apparitions "mere delusions, which I ought to be heartily ashamed of." This is true, but in a sense he did not intend. His "freaks of imagination," like the apparitions of "The Haunted Mind," embody his shame. In a last effort to dispel the "waking

18. Pattison says the narrator "implicitly sees himself as finally earning his right to Christian's role not so much by rejecting the dream upon its completion . . . as by realizing . . . that Mr. Smooth-it-away is an 'impudent fiend' " who carries Tophet within him. The narrator never does see himself as earning Christian's role, however, and although he recognizes his companion as a fiend, he never realizes that Mr. Smooth-it-away also carries Tophet within him.

dreams" of the valley, he attributes them to a simple physical cause, the mephitic gas lamps.

As the train moves out of the valley into the sunlight, the dreamer moves to a stage of more conscious control where he can more easily evade his subconscious knowledge. He can now dismiss the apparitions of sin as "vain imaginations" which "lost their vividness" in daylight. The entire passage through the valley is sealed off as a dream within a dream by the sentence that ends this paragraph: "Ere we had gone a mile beyond it, I could well nigh have taken my oath that this whole gloomy passage was a dream." Freud's contention that an attempt within a dream to call only part of it a dream is the strongest confirmation of its importance seems applicable here:[19] the narrator betrays his guilt and shame by his earnest attempts to deny them.

The rest of the dream vision conforms to what we know about alternating stages of dream activity. For a time in Vanity Fair, the narrative resumes its original dispassionate satirical tone. When the narrator reboards the train, he enters a stage of deep and dreamless sleep, and his brief passage through the pleasant land of Beulah, with its fountains and fruit trees, recalls the pleasant dreams near the end of "The Haunted Mind." Abruptly, the engine stops with a last "infernal uproar," mixing sounds of woe, wrath, and "the wild laughter of a devil or a madman." Now the narrator boards a ferry for the last stage of his journey, but Mr. Smooth-it-away stays behind, and as he laughs, "a smoke-wreath issued from his mouth and nostrils; while a twinkle of lurid flame darted out of either eye, proving indubitably that his heart was all of a red blaze. The impudent Fiend! To deny the existence of Tophet, when he felt its fiery tortures raging within his breast!" Ironically, the narrator's accusation applies also to himself.

19. Sigmund Freud, *The Interpretation of Dreams*, Vols. IV and V of *The Complete Psychological Works of Sigmund Freud*, trans. James Strachey (23 vols.; London: Hogarth Press, 1962), IV, 338; V, 488–89.

As in the other dream tales, the dreamer reaches the end awake and alone. He is about to jump off the ferry he knows is not bound for heaven; but in the tale's penultimate and most terrifying moment, "the wheels . . . threw a dash of spray over me, so cold—so deadly cold . . . that with a shiver and a heart-quake, I awoke." Only infernal cold is more fearful than infernal heat. He then dismisses the dream, the journey, and the story with a last comment: "Thank Heaven, it was a Dream!" That final dismissal is the story's final irony. Especially in the gaslit valley with its craters of hell, the dream enacts the narrator's recognition of his own sinful nature, which he tries to suppress to the very end. Like most men, he has passed through the Valley of the Shadow; but whereas "The Haunted Mind" ended on a note of hope, this more complex and devious tale ends with an evasion. Within the dream of "The Celestial Rail-road," the narrator can get no farther than the land of Beulah; the self-deluding man has no chance of reaching heaven. Hawthorne is finally more pessimistic than Bunyan.

Although the story's ending seems simple, it is as open and ambiguous as the endings of "Young Goodman Brown" and "My Kinsman, Major Molineux." The dreamer emerges from his nightmare when its truths prove intolerable; he cannot admit that he is fit for hell. His Dantesque infernal journey across a landscape of his own inner space has changed but not transformed him. He has glimpsed the monsters of hell, but to the last moment tries to persuade himself they are delusions. He has become aware that Tophet is in the heart of Mr. Smooth-it-away, but not that Mr. Smooth-it-away is in himself. His mind is not mediating between dream and reality but between accepting and rejecting the truths urged in his dream. His equanimity is restored by his waking up, enabling him to thank heaven and narrate his vision to the "benevolent reader"; yet he cannot altogether forget his "heart-quake." He had been frightened by the fiery abyss, the apparitions of sin, and the final spray of deadly cold, and that fright disrupts his complacency, if only intermittently, as he tells his tale (*Mosses*, 186–206).

These three narratives have different thematic centers and reach different resolutions, yet all follow essentially the same dream pattern. Initially, the dreamer—a representative human being, regardless of his age—deliberately undertakes a journey which is also a quest. He is not after power, material profit, or even love, the usual objects of quest. He is impelled by curiosity or a desire for self-fulfillment, and the ultimate direction of each journey is inward. Whether he is the curious narrator boarding the carriage in "The Celestial Rail-road," the young husband striding into the forest in "Young Goodman Brown," or Robin taking the ferry to town in "My Kinsman, Major Molineux," he feels in control of his journey at the start.

But soon he has some disturbing experiences which suggest that his traveling might be unpleasant or even dangerous: the railroad engineer emits smoke and flame; the staff of the man in the forest may be a serpent; Robin does not know where to find his kinsman and is mocked when he asks. Illumination is dim or unsteady in these early experiences, and the protagonist's mind wavers. Memories intermingle with perceptions; thoughts and images succeed one another according to readily discernible principles of association (most frequently, similarity and contrast). The dreamer is on the threshold between waking consciousness and dream.

This stage leads imperceptibly to a further "moonlit" stage when the imagination becomes more active and "ghosts" may enter, as Robin imagines his kinsman gliding in ghostly form at the churchyard. The protagonist's will becomes increasingly impotent as inner compulsions take over. The self is bewildered by its acts and discoveries, especially its visions of hellfire: at the refueling stop in "The Celestial Rail-road," at the unholy altar in "Young Goodman Brown," and at the torchlit parade in "My Kinsman, Major Molineux," suppressed guilt and desires in the guise of infernal fiends mock and terrify the dreamer. He looks in horror, trying to dispel his suspicion that he is both the source and the object of the horror. Like Milton's Satan, he is in hell and hell is in him. But with a terrified shriek, he terminates the intolerable adventure, and returns to waking consciousness.

Each of these stories gives a new twist to the old tradition of the helpful dream guide. In "The Celestial Rail-road" and "Young Goodman Brown," the guide at first seems benevolent, but he turns out to be the devil. In "My Kinsman, Major Molineux," the role is split: the kind gentleman is benevolent, but the two-faced man is a devil. In each story, the guide is a projection of the self as it is or as it may become. This is most explicit in "Young Goodman Brown": Goody Cloyse observes that the devil resembles Brown, and Brown looks like the devil as he runs into the heart of the forest. The demoniac is in ourselves.

Entry into the interior life is a liberation only from the fetters of material fact. The interior is never an open space but a wilderness that confuses the dreamer, and where he feels victimized by his own guilty memories and desires that have emerged while his will is relaxed. His inner journey gratifies his curiosity, but that gratification is itself a penalty. Finally, what he learns is incomplete: with an involuntary shout, he extricates himself before uncovering all his dark secrets.

He never reaches the stage of delight Hawthorne predicated in his image of the heart as a cavern. Beyond the entry is "a terrible gloom, and monsters of divers kinds; it seems like Hell itself," he wrote. But after a period of bewildered and hopeless wandering, you see a light, "press towards it," and reach a sunny region in "the depths of the heart, or of human nature, bright and peaceful; the gloom and terror may lie deep; but deeper still is this eternal beauty" (AN, 237). Hawthorne's dreamers do not reach this ultimate light, peace, and eternal beauty. After a period of gloom and bewilderment, they emerge from the hellish interior and return to the ordinary social order.

Despite the differences between them, all the dreamers—a young boy, a young man, and a man who seems middle-aged—are adept at rationalization and self-evasion. They are typical and representative human beings, seeking only limited understanding of themselves and their relations with other men. They are not overreachers like Ethan Brand, but within-reachers, seekers of their own subjective consciousness. They take risks and face dangers. Yet like Hawthorne and most of his readers, they avert their eyes from what they find most disturbing. Although they do not reject their dreams as false or foolish, none of them can decipher the entire dream message. They all move toward shocking recognitions; but at the climactic moments, the precise nature of their distress is simultaneously veiled and revealed. By involuntary strategies of self-preservation, they protect their conscious selves from knowledge that might prove catastrophic.

Each dreamer is changed by his trip, though he is not necessarily improved. Robin has become more resilient and self-aware, but Brown is embittered and inflexible. Each dreamer partially surrenders his will before recovering it at the end. His initial predicament can be understood in relatively simple terms, but his adventures soon go beyond the reach of reason, until eventually he feels overwhelmed and longs to escape. In some sense he has found what he was looking for, though he is surprised and distressed by the form in which he finds it. As he acts and reacts, his increasing horror extends beyond his individual predicament to predicaments all men share.

A similar dream pattern recurs in stories that are not explicitly dream visions. In "Rappaccini's Daughter," for example, the central figure deliberately risks entry into a situation that provokes his curiosity; he is both distressed and gratified by his encounter with Beatrice, yet he feels compelled to continue his adventure until eventually he becomes a participant in evil as well as an observer of it, revealing his own moral imperfection. And a similar pattern controls episodes of reverie, whether brief, like Hester's on the scaffold, or more protracted, as in "Foot-prints on the Sea-shore." But the three tales that Hawthorne apparently conceived as dream visions most fully articulate the dream pattern as he understood it, and each is dominated by the same leading idea: the dreamer's limited recognition of his own nature, and the tendency to sin we all harbor within us.

Yet some distinctions must be made. All three are successful and tightly developed stories, but "My Kinsman, Major Molineux" and "Young Goodman Brown" are better than "The Celestial Rail-road," and not only because in the early years of his career Hawthorne was passionately concerned about problems of the American past, particularly as expressed in terms of a dilemma troubling an eager but confused young man. In even earlier tales he had introduced preternatural figures who seem to control guilt-ridden minds, and in "My Kinsman, Major Molineux" and "Young Goodman Brown" he introduced other demoniac figures more deeply rooted in American communal beliefs and experiences. As he wrote the tales, uncertain about his future career, Hawthorne was particularly vulnerable to worries about whether some perverse purpose might mislead him; that anguish gives resonance to the plights of Robin and Goodman Brown. Further, these two stories succeed because their narrative density accommodates questions about an individual's complicity in his own torment. Neither Robin nor Goodman Brown can clearly separate their dreams and daydreams from waking experience, nor can they wholly understand their motives or the journeys they feel compelled to undertake; yet they move toward distressing insights into their own nature and all men's.

If the success of "The Celestial Rail-road" seems more limited, it is in part because its narrative line is thinner and the episodes more fantastic than in the earlier dream visions. The story is not immersed in the real world of social intercourse even when Hawthorne satirizes the optimistic simplifications of Unitarians and Transcendentalists. More important, we have no clue to any particular guilt the self-protective narrator has incurred. The spectral shapes of sin, for example, are merely that; they have no alternative "real" identities. And despite the narrator's moments of anxiety, the dominant tone is more complacent than in the earlier dream stories, suggesting that when he wrote it, Hawthorne was managing to live with his knowledge of the demons all men harbor within them. The narrator takes his journey more out of curiosity than necessity or some incomprehensible compulsion.

These discriminations help account for the varying success of Hawthorne's other dream fictions. In those that succeed best, the protagonist draws in and out of a densely specified waking reality, moved by fears and desires he can only partly understand. His dreams and daydreams express his immediate problems, and the reader shares his concern about them. Thus, "The Haunted Mind" is a more absorbing and consequential sketch than the relatively even-toned "Foot-prints on the Seashore." And it is an indication of the limits of "Peter Goldthwaite's Treasure" that Peter's dreams are wholly explicable, with no residue of mystery to perplex him and the reader. At each stage of his career, Hawthorne used dreams and dreamlike perceptions to explore mysteries of motive and action, particularly mysteries of guilt; but when he could not account for a dreamer's involvement in the mystifying events of his dreams, as in the unfinished romances, the fictions falter.

This is not to suggest that all Hawthorne's stories are about dreams, but rather that he used dreams with remarkable frequency to fathom the unconscious mind as it copes with memory and desire and struggles toward self-knowledge. Even when the

stories ask if the apparitions of dreams, daydreams, and beyond them the fictions themselves should be construed as foolish fantasies or infernal deceptions, Hawthorne most strongly
suggests a third possibility, that dreams are a mode of knowledge, a necessary complement to—but not a substitute for—
awareness of the waking world.

IV
The Romances

In his romances, Hawthorne is more continuously concerned with the waking world than in his short stories. Most of the characters in his long fictions pay more attention to each other and to the consequences of their actions than to their own inner mysteries. The complex formal requirements of a sustained fiction probably imposed on Hawthorne a wariness of concentrating too exclusively on any individual's fantasies. Even so, dreams, daydreams, and dreamlike states of consciousness recur frequently in the romances.

It is hardly surprising that Hawthorne drew on the rich resources of dreams and reverie for these long fictions. Dreams serve to establish and develop character, and daydreams trace the interrelations of fantasies with external reality, particularly during moments of crisis. Repeatedly, the narrative dream pattern developed in the short stories recurs in the romances, even though only within particular episodes: central characters move from perceptions to fantasies, then return to waking consciousness when the fantasies prove intolerable. Further, dreamlike pageants occur in all the romances, though usually as real events—notably, the masquerade in *The Blithedale Romance*, and the carnival in *The Marble Faun*. And the devil of the earlier dream visions appears in the form of the villain in each romance—Chillingworth, Judge Pyncheon, Westervelt, and Miriam's Model—men who do not dream but haunt the dreams of their victims. Particularly in *The House of the Seven Gables*, *The Marble Faun*, and the Grimshawe narrative, the past haunts the present like a dream, and erupts in dreams and daydreams. The haunting effect of a dream so enigmatic and overwhelming that it reduces the dreamer to despair is pervasive in all the novels, but especially in *The Marble Faun* and the Grimshawe narrative; this accounts for much of the confusion in these two romances, but also for their suggestive resonance. Whether as metaphor or event, dreams give entry into the vast ranges of human experience beyond conscious control, inviting the reader to follow their course and solve their riddles. In each work, their substance, their tone, and their importance differ; yet dreams are calculated to support the central concerns and themes of the romance.

1. *The Mirror and the Labyrinth:* The Scarlet Letter

In *The Scarlet Letter* there are no dreams at all; but daydreams bring the reader into intimacy with the two main characters as they try to come to terms with the consequences of their sexual encounter. Hester's daydream takes place at the outset of the novel as she stands on the scaffold, her baby in her arms and the A on her breast. Dimmesdale's takes place midway in the novel, in his study, in a torrent of guilt that later drives him out to the same scaffold. Hester's daydream establishes her character, and Dimmesdale's explores his dilemma. Both are integral to the novel's central problem—the causes and (more important) the effects of sin on the two sinners. The reveries are deliberately initiated acts of introspection that implicitly explain their public behavior.

Daydreaming is psychologically necessary for them both, since each is essentially alone in the Puritan community. The narrator of "Foot-prints on the Sea-shore" can go from daydreaming to a picnic, but easy social gratification is not available to Hester or Dimmesdale. With the single exception of

141

the forest interlude, they can share intimate thoughts with no one.

Structurally, the two episodes of daydreaming are integral to two of the novel's three major scaffold scenes. The first introduces Hester as she takes inner refuge from her public shame; the second reveals Dimmesdale's inner mortification and leads to his midnight travesty of public shame on the scaffold. Only in the final scaffold scene when the hidden relationship is publicly revealed are we not granted privileged entry into the sinner's mind.

By placing Hester's reverie near the beginning of the novel, Hawthorne deftly establishes the expository background of her predicament while accomplishing another important task. The reader approaching Hester through her inner consciousness necessarily sympathizes with her. The occasion of her reverie is psychologically convincing: standing on the scaffold, weighted by grief while her punishment is still new, she has no other hope of relief. She is not temperamentally a habitual dreamer; but like the sufferers in "The Hall of Fantasy," she takes brief refuge from "the gloom and chilliness of actual life." At the same time, her recollections implicitly explain how she came to violate the Puritan code.

The discursive structure of the reverie expresses Hawthorne's understanding of how the mind drifts along its levels of consciousness, one idea drawing another in its wake, while a single strong emotion dominates the stream of association. As Hester moves from active perception to semipassive consciousness, the reader follows the inward spiral of her thoughts. From her stance on the scaffold, the marketplace sometimes seems blurred: "There were intervals when the whole scene . . . seemed to vanish from her eyes, or at least, glimmered indistinctly before them, like a mass of imperfectly shaped and spectral images." The familiar word "glimmered" serves its usual purpose of suggesting the threshold stage when perceptions and imagined forms fleetingly intermingle: Hester's consciousness of the marketplace fades as her inner visions intensify.

The scaffold now becomes a neutral territory: she sees "other faces than were lowering upon her from beneath the brims of those steeple-crowned hats" as spectral memories emerge in rapid sequence. "Reminiscences, the most trifling and immaterial, passages of infancy and school-days, sports, childish quarrels, and the little domestic traits of her maiden years, came swarming back upon her, intermingled with recollections of whatever was gravest in her subsequent life; one picture precisely as vivid as another; as if all were of similar importance, or all alike a play." In keeping with the principles of association, the visual swarm is roughly ordered by chronology, but interpenetrated by recollections associated with her present gloom. Her will virtually in abeyance, she becomes the observer of thoughts that appear before her as a changing spectacle, a pageant emerging from "memory's picture-gallery." Here Hawthorne speculates about the daydreamer's involuntary strategies of self-protection: "Possibly, it was an instinctive device of her spirit, to relieve itself, by the exhibition of these phantasmagoric forms, from the cruel weight and hardness of the reality."

The chief narrative function of the "phantasmagoric forms," however, is to suggest the causes of her predicament, more than she consciously comprehends. The scaffold not only defines her physical separation as an emotional and moral isolation, but it provides "a point of view that revealed to Hester Prynne the entire track along which she had been treading, since her happy infancy."

Although she tries to take refuge in happy memories, like Robin in "My Kinsman, Major Molineux," sorrow immediately obtrudes. Thoughts of "happy infancy" lead to thoughts of the "poverty-stricken aspect" of her family home, with its "half-obliterated shield of arms" (implicitly suggesting why Chillingworth might have been welcomed as a suitor). She recalls the faces of her loving parents and her dead mother's disturbing "look of heedful and anxious love." Next an even more detailed image implicitly explains her eventual moral vulnerability: she recalls her own "girlish beauty," her face "illuminating all the interior of the dusky mirror in which she had been wont to gaze at it." The mirror of Hester's imagination reflects a memory of a real mirror, revealing both her beauty and her vanity.

She then immediately envisions in the same mirror the misshapen individual who became her husband. This second reflected image is more detailed and disturbing than anything else in the daydream; it emphatically establishes Hester's narcissism and her physical distaste for Chillingworth. She recalls him as a pale and thin old man, with eyes "dim and bleared" by study, yet able to "read the human soul." The next sentence describes his physical deformity and Hester's awareness of it: her "womanly fancy failed not to recall" that one shoulder was higher than the other. The curious negative phrase "failed not to recall" emphasizes Hester's forthright nature: even in the refuge of memory, she does not avert her attention from unpleasantness. The mirror separates and frames Beauty and the Beast in a monstrous marriage portrait, suggesting why Chillingworth desired her and why she could not be happy with him.

Her last "shifting scene" is set in an ancient "Continental city," her "new life" there likened to "a tuft of green moss on a crumbling wall," thus pointing to the incongruity of her marriage and the sense of disjunction and futility that later made her vulnerable to sin. An emphatic inversion of subject and verb signals Hester's abrupt return from "memory's picture-gallery" to the present: "In lieu of these shifting scenes, came back the rude market-place of the Puritan settlement." The hiatus between memory and perception invites sympathy and asserts that Hester knows where she is. Imagination offered only momentary escape (SL, 57–59).

This passage colors the reader's subsequent views of Hester. It is her only reverie, but Hawthorne later draws on imagery he usually reserved for dreams to define the two preoccupations of her inner life. The first is her passion for Dimmesdale. In a brief passage near the beginning, that passion is likened to a monster imprisoned within her (like the dream phantoms of "The Haunted Mind"). It emerges from time to time "like a serpent from its hole," and she must then struggle to reimprison it (*SL*, 80).

Her second preoccupation is with moral speculation, established in three passages which use almost identical words and images. In all three, Hester wanders through a labyrinthine wilderness, a terrain more dangerous and terrifying than the forest of "Young Goodman Brown," and as in that tale, the metaphor has a literal equivalent. The first of these passages asserts that Hester's heart is not in harmony with her mind, envisaging her mind as a confusing and dangerous place: "Thus, Hester Prynne, whose heart had lost its regular and healthy throb, wandered without a clew in the dark labyrinth of mind; now turned aside by an insurmountable precipice; now starting back from a deep chasm. There was wild and ghastly scenery all around her, and a home and comfort nowhere" (*SL*, 166). Her journey through this landscape links her to the heroines of Gothic romance; but unlike them, Hester is no tremulous figure in flight. She is a seeker, though with no specific goal; a challenger of the social order, though with no alternative program.

Next, in a brief passage, the metaphor of wilderness emerges in Hester's own mind as she enters the real forest, suggesting how readily she assimilates experience. The path she takes into the "primeval forest" where she expects to encounter Dimmesdale offers "such imperfect glimpses of the sky above, that, to Hester's mind, it imaged not amiss the moral wilderness in which she had so long been wandering" (*SL*, 183). On the real path and the metaphorical one, Hester has gone beyond the frontiers of civilization; and as in Goodman Brown's forest or in the Valley of the Shadow, there is no hope of celestial illumination.

The last and longest of these passages offers a retrospective summary of Hester's inner life during her years of punishment, paradoxically establishing her strength of character despite her moral uncertainty. While Dimmesdale had remained confined by the social order, "she had wandered, without rule or guidance, in a moral wilderness; as vast, as intricate and shadowy, as the untamed forest. . . . Her intellect and heart had their home, as it were, in desert places, where she roamed as freely as the wild Indian in his woods." In these gloomy regions "where other women dared not tread," her teachers are "Shame, Despair, Solitude," familiar demons of "The Haunted Mind." They taught her much "amiss," yet they strengthened her (*SL*, 199–200).

Hester is the only woman comparable to the central figure of the Oberon tales or the major dream stories, alone in her dark mind. Like theirs, her inner life becomes more absorbing than her outer experience, although unlike the earlier dreamers and unlike Dimmesdale, she is never confused about what is real. Her character develops as her initial reverie suggested it would: she is a figure of fortitude. But at the end of the novel Hawthorne suggests that she did not have to wander forever in a moral wilderness: near the end of her life she "had no selfish ends," but gave comfort and counsel to wretched women, assuring them she believed in a brighter future when man and woman might join together "on a surer ground of mutual happiness" (*SL*, 263). The mirror of self had been put away.

Dimmesdale's long reverie in the middle of the novel is more an attempt to recover than to discover self. Significantly, it is not a particular reverie but an abstraction and compendium of all his reveries, a credible expression of his continual spiritual probing, self-torment, and irresolution. Dimmesdale is no ordinary dreamer adrift in a sombre dream world, but a man out of tune with himself. Chillingworth, an agent of malevolence, had stirred up demons of thought to trouble the minister's mind; in Dimmesdale's reverie, spiritual aspiration and guilt struggle for mastery. Yet he learns nothing new: his reverie can only restate his problem, not resolve it. Because he is an "untrue man, the whole universe is false"; and he is too cowardly to become "true."

The reader does not accompany him in and out of his reverie, as with Hester's; yet Hawthorne describes how Dimmesdale's usually begin, and how they end. His nightly vigils, "sometimes with a glimmering lamp; and sometimes, viewing his own face in a looking-glass, by the most powerful light which he could throw upon it," not only induce his reveries, but are emblematic of them: "He thus typified the constant introspection wherewith he tortured, but could not purify, himself" (SL, 145).

However abstracted, the reverie is psychologically credible. The glimmering lamp and the mirror create an atmosphere that invites dreams. Dimmesdale's brain "reeled, and visions seemed to flit before him; perhaps seen doubtfully, and by a faint light of their own, in the remote dimness of the chamber, or more vividly, and close beside him, within the looking-glass." Fantasies mingle with memories, and by an act of imaginative projection, he can see them "vividly" in the mirror. By contrast with the mirror Hester remembers, envisaging herself with Chillingworth, Dimmesdale looks not at but into himself with the aid of a real mirror which then seems to reflect his fantasies.

In the next stage, the images become more specific, arranged as in a morality play: "Now it was a herd of diabolic shapes, that grinned and mocked at the pale minister, and beckoned him away with them; now a group of shining angels, who flew upward heavily, as sorrow-laden, but grew more ethereal as they rose." The chapter in which the reverie is set

147

is called "The Interior of a Heart," but the word "mind" would be equally appropriate, since within that interior theater the vices and virtues engage in a struggle for Dimmesdale's soul. The moral conflict is appropriate to the mind of a conventional minister trying to come to terms with a sin he can neither publicly acknowledge nor expiate.

The rest of the paragraph is given to more realistic visions, figures of memory who pass in brief parade, notably his father "with a saint-like frown, and his mother, turning her face away as she passed by," embodiments of his own self-loathing. Hawthorne as narrator invites pity for Dimmesdale with curious indirection, saying the fantasy mother "might yet have thrown a pitying glance towards her son!" But in his self-contempt, Dimmesdale cannot imagine such pity. In the final and most psychologically convincing sentence, Hester glides in with Pearl, pointing like the embodiment of Shame at her own scarlet letter and then at the minister's breast. With the compression of dreams, this composite image dramatizes the bond between the sinners, his obsession with his guilt, and his urge to confession.

The silent figures dominating the minister's guilty imagination seem to have real existence in his "ghastly" chamber, like the nightmare figures of "The Haunted Mind." They are also a direct link to the crucial scenes that soon follow, Dimmesdale's midnight vigil on the scaffold and the forest meeting with Hester. In both he is uncertain whether Hester and Pearl are real or imagined. Dimmesdale is like Dugald Stewart's man of disordered imagination whose thoughts are dominated by creatures of his mind.

At the conclusion of the passage, Hawthorne distances us from the reverie by speaking of "those ugly nights, which we have faintly hinted at, but forborne to picture forth," as if further specification would be indecorous (SL, 145–46). The dream images of "The Haunted Mind" and "The Celestial Railroad" are equally abstract, but the first person narrators more fully involve the reader in their "heart-quake." In most of Hawthorne's fictional reveries, the protagonist reaches some unbearable knowledge; but Dimmesdale is only a passive witness to familiar images of distress. One night is much like another on this treadmill of self-abasement; Dimmesdale is too cowardly to move forward into an inner forest like Hester's. Yet these self-punishing vigils have more reality for Dimmesdale than his daily duties as minister.

His moral perturbation is best understood by comparing his tormented visions with those of Hester's noontime reverie. The visions of Hester's reverie emerge in continuous linear order, each adding onto the earlier ones; Dimmesdale's are disjunctive, dialectically ordered as a tug-of-war. Hester is informed and Dimmesdale threatened by their separate fantasies. She remains essentially an observer, but he is also the focus of the conflict he envisages, tormented by its imperatives for action. Hester's daydream confronts the initial cause of her guilt and leads her to accept the realities she must live by; Dimmesdale's articulates his continuing anxiety and shows his inability to reconcile his conscience with his public behavior. Hester moves toward knowledge of her heart; Dimmesdale is paralyzed by knowledge of his soul.

Dimmesdale's midnight vigil on the scaffold immediately follows his reverie. Without artifice or melodrama, the scene unfolds as a nightmare. The chapter opens with Dimmesdale no longer transfixed in his chamber but "walking in the shadow of a dream, as it were, and perhaps actually under the influence of a species of somnambulism" (SL, 147), without full control of his behavior. Chillingworth later reinforces the idea that Dimmesdale is neither fully awake nor fully asleep when he says that studious men dream even when awake, then walk in their sleep.

As he stands on the scaffold where Hester had stood seven years before, Dimmesdale's horror erupts in a shriek; then his mind makes another "involuntary effort to relieve itself" in a grimly humorous vision intermixed with "solemn phantoms" of thought. He imagines the townsfolk, "with the disorder of a nightmare in their aspects," discovering him in the morning, frozen on the scaffold in his posture of shame. He involuntarily responds to his own fantasy as Robin had responded to real mockery: with "a great peal of laughter" (SL, 151–52).

As with Robin, the laugh returns him from fantastic nightmare to the nightmare of his real distress. Instead of his fantasy, he sees Hester and Pearl, who join him on the scaffold. Now a strange red meteor appears, and its light agitates his imagination more powerfully than moonlight: the familiar street takes on "a singularity of aspect that seemed to give another moral interpretation to the things of this world than they had ever borne before" (SL, 154). His guilty imagination reads the meteor as a celestial accusation in the form of the scarlet A. Then he sees Chillingworth, whose malevolent expression remains "painted on the darkness" after the meteor vanishes. This is almost too horrifying to endure. When Chillingworth urges him to return home, Dimmesdale responds "like one awaking, all nerveless, from an ugly dream" (SL, 156–57).

Dimmesdale's continuing inability to distinguish what he imagines from what is real explains his vacillation about Hester's plan of escape when they meet in the forest. At first he thinks she is a spectre that stole out of his thoughts, and when she suggests that they escape from Boston, he reacts to her suggestion as an impotent dreamer: "'It cannot be!' answered the minister, listening as if he were called upon to realize a dream. 'I am powerless to go'" (SL, 197). Only when he accepts her plan can he escape "from the dungeon of his own heart"; but that escape is brief (SL, 201). Leaving the forest, he again wonders whether Hester is real; he must look back to reassure himself that he "had not fallen asleep, and dreamed!" (SL, 214).

His temporary acquiescence to Hester's plan generates even greater perplexity in the chapter called "The Minister in a Maze." As he looks at his own church, his perceptions are so strange that his "mind vibrated between two ideas; either that he had seen it only in a dream hitherto, or that he was merely dreaming about it now" (SL, 217). Up to this point, his inner visions had seemed as vivid as reality; now both the town and the townspeople seem as mutable as dreams. Hawthorne then explains this delusion: "Tempted by a dream of happiness, he had yielded himself with deliberate choice . . . to what he knew was deadly sin" (SL, 222). Only Dimmesdale's knowledge enables him to put the tempting dream behind him and seek salvation through confession on the scaffold.

Dimmesdale finally stands on the scaffold in public, leaning on Hester and holding Pearl's hand, "doubt and anxiety in his eyes" yet "a feeble smile upon his lips." His question to Hester conveys both his anxiety and his hope: "Is not this better . . . than what we dreamed of in the forest?" (SL, 254). The question is crucial, but it remains unanswered. Whether he found salvation also remains an open question, though waking from his dreamlike confusion does bring Dimmesdale to a height of spiritual exaltation before he dies. Through his death, however, Hawthorne suggests what he had already asserted through the dreamers of such minor fictions as "Sylph Etherege" and "Old Esther Dudley": man's inner and outer lives are continuous, and abandoning one destroys them both.

2. *The Tyranny of Dreams:* The House of the Seven Gables

When Hawthorne announces in the preface to *The House of the Seven Gables* that he "has provided himself with a moral;—the truth, namely, that the wrong-doing of one generation lives into the successive ones" (*HSG*, 2), the word "provided" exhibits self-mockery, but he proposes this truth seriously. The "legendary mist" of the distant past intermingles with memories of the recent past throughout the novel, especially in the troubled minds of the house's inhabitants. The novel gives local habitation to fantasies. Hawthorne's convictions about the continuum of history and the interdependence of person and place combine in his complex idea of a self extended in time, in space, and through its own layered awareness. Within that self, the past intrudes on the present as the subconscious on the conscious.

In this sense, the novel presents the dream of the house, haunted by the guilt of its founder and the ghost of his victim. From the start, Hawthorne describes the house as if it were human: "The aspect of the venerable mansion has always affected me like a human countenance, bearing the traces not merely of outward storm and sunshine, but expressive also of the long lapse of mortal life, and accompanying vicissitudes, that have passed within" (*SL*, 5). Personification continues in later descriptions of the house as "a great human heart, with a life of its own, and full of rich and sombre reminiscences," its "meditative look" suggesting "that it had secrets to keep, and an eventful history to moralize upon" (*HSG*, 27). It is at once the collective consciousness of a single family, a domesticated American version of the European Gothic castle, and an extensive development of the bedchamber of "The Haunted Mind," where remembered guilt and grief emerge from secret recesses during nightmare.

The house, itself old and haunted, permeates the minds of its aging inhabitants. Hepzibah has lived alone there for thirty years, isolated in her fantasies, "until her very brain was impregnated with the dry-rot of its timbers" (*HSG*, 59). She cannot get away from it even during her brief flight with Clifford. The house haunts her vision: as the train passes through "miles of varied scenery . . . there was no scene for her" but the seven-gabled house; "This one old house was everywhere! It transported its great, lumbering bulk, with more than railroad speed, and set itself phlegmatically down on whatever spot she glanced at" (*HSG*, 258). It seems to have a will of its own. Hepzibah is in that half-crazed state Hawthorne often described, when inner visions are so compelling that they displace perceived reality. During that same train ride, Clifford also carries within him the "rusty, crazy, creaky, dry-rotted, damp-rotted, dingy, dark, and miserable old dungeon" of a house (*HSG*, 261).

The evil spirit that haunts the house is fixed in the portrait of its founder, Colonel Pyncheon, the man who had denounced Matthew Maule to get hold of his property. The old portrait is the demon of guilt within the haunted mind. Its resemblance to Judge Pyncheon, the present villain of the tale, continues the past into the present, as the Judge recapitulates the criminal greed of his ancestry. Although Hepzibah feels reverence for the portrait, she senses its spiritual ugliness; then she identifies Judge Pyncheon as "the very man." Phoebe has seen the portrait and learned its legend; then as she looks at the Judge, she recalls Maule's curse that Colonel Pyncheon would drink blood. The gurgling in the Judge's throat "chimed in so oddly with her previous fancies about the Colonel and the Judge, that, for the moment, it seemed quite to mingle their identity" (*HSG*, 124). Like the dreamers in Hawthorne's earlier fiction who cannot face their dreams, Clifford is so disturbed by the portrait that he asks Hepzibah to curtain it.

The demoniac portrait literally covers a hidden recess behind it, as in Hawthorne's earlier dream fiction figurative demons guard the mind's recesses. Clifford responds to the portrait as to a dream that conceals a secret: "Whenever I look at it, there is an old, dreamy recollection haunting me, but keeping just beyond the grasp of my mind. Wealth, it seems to say! . . . What could this dream have been!" (*HSG*, 315). Then, finally, Holgrave presses a hidden spring, and the portrait tumbles down to reveal the hiding place of a worthless Indian deed "the Pyncheons sought in vain, while it was valuable" (*HSG*, 316). Like other hidden objects in Hawthorne's fiction, the deed is itself evidence of past evil persisting into the present. Holgrave now reveals that he is a descendant of the executed Maule, whose son had built the house and had taken his own

153

revenge on the Pyncheons by building the recess to conceal the valued document. The document itself—like the paper currency in Peter Goldthwaite's treasure chest— is now worthless; but at least Clifford (like Peter) will no longer be haunted by a "dreamy recollection" of wealth.

The mirror in the Pyncheon parlor is another object that figures forth the past, though not literally. In fact, no one in the story even looks into it. Near the beginning of the romance, Hawthorne describes the "large, dim looking-glass . . . fabled to contain within its depths all the shapes that had ever been reflected there"; and he reports a legend that the Maules retain a mysterious power to summon back the dead, and "make its inner region all alive with the departed Pyncheons," who are like obsessed dreamers "doing over again some deed of sin, or in the crisis of life's bitterest sorrow" (*HSG*, 20–21). This is a darker version of the mirror in "Old Esther Dudley," within whose "inner world" Esther reputedly could envision past guests of the Province House.

As the narrator and thus a kind of dreamer, Hawthorne lays claim to a similar power to recall the dead. A second mirror passage, set near the end of the novel after Judge Pyncheon's death, contains a strange dream pageant reminiscent of the one in "An Old Woman's Tale." After reporting a "ridiculous legend" that the dead Pyncheons assemble in the parlor at midnight, Hawthorne imagines them entering in a jostling parade, marching past the Colonel's portrait to confirm that it is still hanging and looking for the secret behind it. He mocks his own conceit as a freak of fancy, but nonetheless suggests that like a dream, it has a life and a truth of its own. He had begun by indulging his fancy as "a little sport," but soon found he had "partly lost the power of restraint and guidance." The "visionary scene" also draws on older dream conventions by conveying information otherwise unknown: the Judge's sole surviving child has died; therefore, all the Pyncheon property will devolve on Clifford, Hepzibah, and Phoebe.

Hawthorne cautions his reader not to think of the episode as "an actual portion of our story" but merely as an extravagance initiated by moonbeams and shadows "reflected in the looking-glass"; however, he then restores its special credibility by saying that such a reflection, "you are aware, is always a kind of window or door-way into the spiritual world." His irresolution about the significance of dreams makes the passage irresolute. He tries to dismiss his fantasy only to find himself caught within it.

Describing the dark parlor containing the Judge's dead body, he finds himself "looking" into the Pyncheons' mirror, then protesting that its reflections had "betrayed" his imagination into creating the pageant. Although the phrase "you are aware" invites belief that the ghostly Pyncheons may exist in a "spiritual world," the invitation is itself qualified by the word "betrayed." The whole bravura interlude is a trick the magician is a little ashamed of, but it is not only a trick. He needed relief from "too long and exclusive contemplation of that figure in the chair," Hawthorne explains; the wild windstorm had confused his thoughts without deflecting them "from their one determined center." The Judge's corpse sits "immoveably" on the narrator's soul, part of his own intolerable nightmare. The "little sport" of the pageant was intended to signal his imaginative distance from the scene of death; but the imagined looking-glass reflections move him from legend into his own distress, making him a participant in his own fantasy. An older Oberon, he is his own victim. He can "breathe more freely" only when morning comes and he can rejoin the "living world" (*HSG*, 279–83).

Although Maule's well is separated from the house, it is symbolically the soul of the house, and it also serves incidentally to define Clifford's imagination. Like the fountains in "Rappaccini's Daughter" and "Egotism, or the Bosom Serpent," and like the ancient spring in *The Marble Faun*, it exists outside the story's temporal limits. Hawthorne stresses that its waters can be contaminated: the first Maule had built his cottage beside its sweet spring, but Colonel Pyncheon's house befouled it. Yet the last paragraph of the novel identifies the well as a reservoir of knowledge, a form of the dreaming mind, "throwing up a succession of kaleidoscopic pictures" only the "gifted eye" can see. Like the biblical dreams, these are prophetic pictures, foreshadowing the future lives of Hepzibah, Clifford, Phoebe, and Holgrave (*HSG*, 319).

The Pyncheons are described as a race of dreamers, and Clifford is the most melancholy and ineffectual of Hawthorne's long line of wasted and delicate dreamers. As the novel opens, he has just emerged from thirty years in jail, but he remains in mental and emotional bondage, victimized by a past he himself perpetuates. His mind is a prison, permeated by images of imprisonment.

We are told that he had been a dreamer before imprisonment: his "whole poor and impalpable enjoyment of existence, heretofore, and until both his heart and fancy died within him, had been a dream—whose images of women had more and more lost their warmth and substance, and been frozen, like the pictures of secluded artists, into the chillest ideality" (*HSG*, 140). Hepzibah recalls that in his youth, Clifford "was always dreaming hither and thither about the house" (*HSG*, 316). In prison even his minimal life of chilly dreams could not survive, and we meet him as a torpid creature, barely alive. His facial expression "seemed to waver, and glimmer, and nearly to die away" as he sat at the breakfast table his first morning home (*HSG*, 104). Hawthorne explains his threshold condition in terms consistent with faculty psychology: "His mind and consciousness took their departure, leaving his wasted, gray, and melancholy figure—a substantial emptiness"; then intermittently his spirit returned to rekindle lights of the heart and intellect "in the dark and ruinous mansion" of self (*HSG*, 105). He dreads that his return may prove to be only a dream even as he enjoys it "with a dreamy delight." Without dreams to sustain him in prison, he had been conscious only of the terrible reality of confinement, and now he cannot trust his awareness of a different reality: "Ah; this must all be a dream! A dream! A dream! But it has quite hidden the four stone-walls!" (*HSG*, 109–10). His uncertainty continues during his convalescence; but frequently when he sits happily in the garden, he pricks himself with a rose thorn to prove to himself that he is awake.

Yet dreaming is essential to his sanity. In the early days of his return to the family house, he often retreated behind a "slumberous veil" that made him seem "almost cloddish" (*HSG*, 111). By returning to childhood through his dreams, as Dugald Stewart points out old men often do, he recovers part of his youthful grace and charm. Hawthorne offers an additional justification of his return to childhood, one he would expand on in the Grimshawe narrative: it was "just as, after the torpor of a heavy blow, the sufferer's reviving consciousness goes back to a moment considerably behind the accident that stupefied him" (*HSG*, 170)—in this case, the "accident" of imprisonment.

He spends so much time in innocent dreams that they readily cross the boundaries of sleep: "He sometimes told Phoebe and Hepzibah his dreams, in which he invariably played the part of a child, or a very young man." Reliving his childhood through dreams, he can even correctly remember the pattern of his mother's dress.[1] In this delicate state of "second growth," dreams insulate him from reality like a robe "he hugged about his person, and seldom let realities pierce through; he was not often quite awake, but slept open-eyed, and perhaps fancied himself most dreaming, then" (*HSG*, 170). Lingering close to childhood, he enjoys "brilliant fantasies"; he went to sleep

1. Frederick C. Crews, in *The Sins of the Fathers: Hawthorne's Psychological Themes* (New York: Oxford University Press, 1966), says "Clifford's mother is his dream" (184); but she is simply a figure who recurs in his dreams. Crews is also mistaken when he reads the fact that the Judge is called Clifford's nightmare to mean that the Judge is a dream version of his father.

"early, as other children do, and dreamed of childhood" (*HSG*, 171–74).

The recollections and fantasies that occupy Clifford's mind are a token and effect of his imbalance even as he advances in his second growth. Looking into Maule's well at water flowing over colored pebbles, he saw beautiful smiling faces; but sometimes the shadow of a tree branch seemed to be a terrifying face. "His fancy—reviving faster than his will and judgement, and always stronger than they" created both the "shapes of loveliness" and the image of grief (*HSG*, 154). His imagination, like the house itself, is haunted by an ominous face; when Phoebe looks into the fountain she sees only the colored pebbles and the tree's shadow. Hawthorne traces the stages of Clifford's mental recovery in terms consistent with faculty psychology: from vegetative greed he has advanced to a stage of lively fancy, and to some degree his passions, intellect, and will later revive.

His will is at full strength only for his brief period of exhilaration after the Judge has died. When Hepzibah asks on the train, "Is not this a dream?" he replies, "A dream, Hepzibah! . . . On the contrary, I have never been awake before!" (*HSG*, 256). This surge of vital energy continues throughout his fantasy-filled conversation with a strange gentleman about the constraints of the past and the advances of material progress. "For the first time in thirty years, my thoughts gush up and find words ready for them," he says to Hepzibah (*HSG*, 262); but the vivacity soon ends and he lapses again into passivity. Yet he has survived his trauma of rebirth, and his faculties are more invigorated by the end of the book than at the beginning or during his dream-filled youth. For a time he had thought of himself and Hepzibah as ghosts, doomed to haunt their accursed house. Hawthorne says, however, that they protracted their own anguish: their hearts have been dungeons with each his own inexorable jailer, and their house is a larger equivalent of that dungeon. As the novel ends Clifford is no longer an isolated dreamer, no longer a tormented prisoner; he can leave the gloomy Pyncheon house and its counterpart, the dungeon of his heart.

During the thirty years Hepzibah lived alone in the confines of the house, she bewildered herself with "fantasies of the old time. . . . She needed a walk along the noonday street, to keep her sane" (*HSG*, 59). David Halliburton's comment on Roderick and Madeline Usher applies to Hepzibah and her brother: they "face a future that is also, strangely, the past, for they can only become, in a manner of speaking, what they already were. Prisoners of time, they are equally prisoners of space; in this work the hermetic space of the chamber is expanded into an entire house and its environs."[2] But unlike Clifford, Hepzibah is sustained by a strong passion, love for her brother. For his sake she begins her venture as a shopkeeper, though her fantasies reveal how she dreads it. No "flattering dream" that her shop might help the community sustains her; her despair increases when "some malevolent spirit" unrolls a panoramic vision of magnificent stores throughout the city; and later she takes refuge in fantasies of sudden wealth (*HSG*, 40, 48, 65). When Clifford returns home, the joy long chained "in the dungeon of her heart" uneasily finds release, and intermittently a black "spectral sorrow" replaces it. These emotions disturb her yet make her flexible enough to act as Clifford's protector.

After the Judge's death, she wanders around the house, wondering if she is dreaming. Then, during the brief interval on the train when Clifford's will is strong, she relinquishes hers, "like a person in a dream, when the will always sleeps" (*HSG*, 251). She feels impotently adrift in a nightmare throughout the train ride, yet that feeling is a curious safeguard: if she

2. David Halliburton, *Edgar Allan Poe: A Phenomenological View* (Princeton: Princeton University Press, 1973), 369–70. Halliburton goes on to say, "More fully embodied than other living-spaces in Poe, the House is also more human (it shares its being with its occupants) and more self-sufficient (it is a complete microcosmic world with its own laws."

were certain she was awake, she might go completely mad. For a time she endures the dreamer's worst penalties: loss of will, loss of sanity, loss even of identity. Nonetheless her sense of responsibility remains intact; and when Clifford again becomes torpid, she can conduct him home. It is as if they share a single power of will, and their identities are interdependent.

As a Pyncheon, Phoebe is also a dreamer, though of a far different kind. During her first night in the house, her dreams, "being such cheerful ones, had exorcised the gloom, and now haunted the chamber in its stead" (*HSG*, 72). She is a force of physical and emotional health, though she is sensitive to Judge Pyncheon's evil from the start. "Through the thin veil of a dream" she becomes conscious of Clifford's fragile presence, recognizing his erratic footsteps the next day as those she had heard "as through her dream" (*HSG*, 96, 103). The gloomy house modifies her gay spirits in the course of the novel, but with increasing maturity she can give Clifford the warm understanding his recovery requires, and she can maintain her own health by the "moral medicines" Hawthorne frequently prescribed. She regularly leaves the confines of the house for seashore walks, lectures, and concerts, and she distracts herself by reading the Bible and thinking about her village home. She is never confused about reality, never absorbed by fantasy. Only for the moment when she drowsily listens to Holgrave's story of Alice Pyncheon is her moral balance in real danger: "A veil was beginning to be muffled about her, in which she could behold only him, and live only in his thoughts and emotions" (*HSG*, 211). She almost becomes, like Alice, a prototype of the impotent dreamer, with no will of her own; but Holgrave's self-control preserves her integrity.

Judge Pyncheon, the hypocritical and greedy man who had unjustly incriminated Clifford, is the incarnation of a bad dream. Hawthorne says unequivocally, "That strong and ponderous man had been Clifford's nightmare" (*HSG*, 313). In death he is described as a grotesque incubus, "a defunct nightmare, which had perished in the midst of its wickedness, and left its flabby corpse on the breast of the tormented one" (*HSG*, 252). When Hepzibah responds to his statement that Clifford knows the secret of hidden wealth in the house by saying, "You are dreaming, Cousin Jaffrey," he replies, "I do not belong to the dreaming class of men"; and we believe him (*HSG*, 235). Earlier Holgrave had complained that the past lies on "the Present like a giant's dead body!" (*HSG*, 182). When the Judge dies, the nightmare of the Pyncheon past nears its end, and the corpse can be removed.

An extended metaphor of disgust establishes the Judge's true character, a variant of Hawthorne's recurrent metaphor for the persistence of repressed ideas. After commenting on the Judge's assumed respectability, Hawthorne makes a qualified suggestion: "Hidden from mankind—forgotten by himself, or buried so deeply under a sculptured and ornamented pile of ostentatious deeds, that his daily life could take no note of it— there may have lurked some evil and unsightly thing" (*HSG*, 229). He then expands this hypothesis in an elaborate image of a splendid palace with marble floors, gilded cornices, and a lofty dome. "Ah; but in some low and obscure nook—some narrow closet on the ground floor, shut, locked, and bolted, and the key flung away—or beneath the marble pavement, in a stagnant water-puddle, with the richest pattern of mosaic-work above—may lie a corpse, half-decayed, and still decaying, and diffusing its death-scent all through the palace!" He concludes the *allegoria* by equating the corpse with "man's miserable soul," then applies the indictment to Judge Pyncheon (*HSG*, 229–30). The conceit is consistent: the Judge is a nightmare whose "unsightly" evil causes distress no matter how well it is concealed.

Holgrave is not a Pyncheon but a Maule, and Hawthorne establishes early in the novel that the Maules were believed to have "an influence over people's dreams" (*HSG*, 26). He is essentially an observer, though even in his daguerreotypes he tries to go beyond external appearances. He says to Phoebe in Melvillean language, "Had I your opportunities, no scruples would prevent me from fathoming Clifford to the full depth of my plummet-line!" (*HSG*, 178). But he is not fair to himself: he has strong moral scruples. Hawthorne describes him as a strong and ambitious young man, though he is for a time slightly imbalanced by his obsessed involvement in the lives of the Pyncheons. Yet he finds practical outlet for that obsession by writing for magazine publication the story of Alice Pyncheon, whose ghost purportedly still haunts the house. Like Hawthorne, Holgrave is fascinated by the inner life of the house and of its occupants, past and present; and he can shape their dreamlike qualities into fiction, which in turn exerts a dreamlike effect on his audience—in his case, on Phoebe, an audience of one.

His ancestor, Matthew Maule, is the villain of Holgrave's story, a man fabled "to have a strange power of getting into people's dreams, and regulating matters there according to his own fancy, pretty much like the stage-manager of a theatre" (*HSG*, 189). Because the aristocratic Gervayse Pyncheon was anxious to find the valuable document hidden in the house, he allowed Matthew to mesmerize his daughter Alice. She did not find the document; but worse, when she awoke from what seemed "a momentary reverie," a power "she little dreamed of" constrained her, and her will was no longer her own (*HSG*, 208). Whenever Maule demands it, her spirit must yield to his. The tale expresses Hawthorne's abhorrence of loss of will in mesmerism: Alice's abasement can only end in death. Holgrave as a Maule becomes aware that he can exert a similar power over Phoebe; but he has too much integrity, too much "reverence for another's individuality," to press his advantage. Phoebe emerges from her dreamlike trance to a beautiful moonlit evening and a new interest in Holgrave which will soon grow into love.

Rarely is the atmosphere of romance sustained by moonlight in the novel, though a dreamlike atmosphere is frequently suggested by metaphor and allusion. As Hepzibah eagerly awaits Clifford's return, Hawthorne says, "Remote and dusky, and with no sunshine on all the intervening space, was that region of the Past, whence her only guest might be expected to arrive!" (*HSG*, 68). One real place is equally remote and dusky, at once a preserve of the past and of romance: the house of the seven gables itself.

Hawthorne said in his preface that he wanted his tale to present the marvelous mingled with the commonplace and "to connect a by-gone time with the very Present that is flitting away from us" (*HSG*, 2). In his earlier fiction, dreams had established such connections. *The House of the Seven Gables* includes no full dreams and relatively few reveries; yet dream allusions weave continually on and beneath the surface of its narrative. The "legendary mist" of the past is repeatedly likened to dreams, and the mistiness is sustained through dreamlike states of mind.

The novel as a whole is thus a kind of dream narrative; and as in a dream, individual characters and even the narrator confront repressed secrets, but then return to waking reality. The bloodstained corpse in the parlor of the gloomy house at midnight can be considered their collective nightmare. And when the Judge lies dead, the long chain of Pyncheon guilt and punishment terminates. It is time for the portrait embodying the family's evil destiny to fall, and time for the hidden secrets— Holgrave's identity, the recess with its worthless treasure, and the Judge's responsibility for Clifford's imprisonment—to be revealed. The Pyncheon crimes finally avenged, the house's ghosts can rest.

In the end, the four main characters prepare to leave the house. Earlier, Holgrave had passionately declared his desire to get rid of the past. This no one can do; but he need not repeat it or live in it. In the last chapter, the "long drama of wrong and retribution is concluded," and the characters can put the house and its burdened past behind them. The communal dream is over.

3. *Living in a Daydream:* The Blithedale Romance

Those who complain that *The Blithedale Romance* is confused and irresolute, its events removed from the real world and its characters insubstantial, have not understood Hawthorne's method and purposes.[3] The novel is about the very problems that trouble its ineffectual narrator as he wavers between regarding life at Blithedale as "dream-work" (*BR,* 206) and committing himself to the community's real existence. It is about Coverdale's curious condition of mind as he recalls life at Blithedale (as Hawthorne recalled life at Brook Farm), "essentially a day-dream, and yet a fact—and thus offering an available foothold between fiction and reality" (*BR,* 2). Finally, it is about Coverdale's dreams and daydreams during his utopian adventure.

The metaphor that controls Hawthorne's preface and recurs in Coverdale's opening chapters is that life at Brook Farm— Blithedale in the novel—was a daydream. The community deliberately separated from the rest of the world to pursue its vision of a nobler and more fulfilling way of life. Imagination is "the great spring of human activity and the principle source of human improvement," Dugald Stewart had said, and the Blithedalers committed themselves to such improvement. For a time Coverdale shared the utopian vision, even though he soon began "to lose the sense of what kind of a world it was,

---

3. See Crews, *Sins of the Fathers,* 194–212, and Hyatt Waggoner, *Hawthorne: A Critical Study* (Cambridge: Harvard University Press, 1963), 188–208. Frank Davidson in "Toward a Re-evaluation of *The Blithedale Romance,*" *New England Quarterly,* XXV (1952), 374–83, discusses the critical opinions of G. E. Woodbury, A. H. Quinn, Matthiessen, and others. Nina Baym recognizes that Coverdale is "represented . . . to some extent as the dreaming mind passively observing the images of its own creating (as in 'The Haunted Mind')." *The Shape of Hawthorne's Career* (Ithaca: Cornell University Press, 1976), 187.

among innumerable schemes of what it might or ought to be"
(*BR*, 140). The community's quest for "a better life" might now
seem absurd, Coverdale says, "Yet, after all, let us acknowledge it wiser, if not more sagacious, to follow out one's daydream to its natural consummation, although, if the vision
have been worth the having, it is certain never to be consum-
mated otherwise than by a failure. And what of that! Its airiest
fragments, impalpable as they may be, will possess a value
that lurks not in the most ponderous realities of any practicable
scheme. They are not the rubbish of the mind" (*BR*, 10–11).
His tone at once apologetic and defensive, Coverdale praises
himself and the brotherhood of Blithedale:

If ever men might lawfully dream awake, and give utterance to their
wildest visions, without dread of laughter or scorn on the part of the
audience—yes, and speak of earthly happiness, for themselves and
mankind, as an object to be hopefully striven for, and probably attained—we, who made that little semi-circle round the blazing fire,
were those very men. . . . Therefore, if we built splendid castles
. . . and pictured beautiful scenes, among the fervid coals of the
hearth around which we were clustering . . . let us take to ourselves no shame. In my own behalf, I rejoice that I could once
think better of the world's improvability than it deserved. (*BR*, 19–
20).

This is Hawthorne's fullest and most fervent tribute to his own
visionary venture into utopia, his elegy for a bygone dream of
the future. His qualified praise is further qualified by the example of Hollingsworth, who had his own "castle in the air,"
his "philanthropic dream" (*BR*, 56), his own "glorious, if im-
practicable dream" (*BR*, 101). But Hollingsworth's dream was
system-bound and ultimately destructive, like the Fourierist
utopian scheme that ultimately ruined both Brook Farm and
Blithedale. In contrast, the Blithedale community's shared daydream was lofty and ennobling.

From the start, Coverdale presents himself as an individual
given to ordinary reverie. *The Blithedale Romance* opens as he

walks on "an obscure part of the street," returning from a mystifying mesmeric performance, "the wonderful exhibition of the Veiled Lady"; he is musing upon the lady's riddling response to his question about Blithedale's success (*BR*, 5). Characteristically, Coverdale struggles in dim light toward an elusive truth.

In the second chapter, Coverdale more deliberately invokes memories of Blithedale by recalling the cheerful fire that first greeted him there. He recreates the fire by stirring embers of memory, but the metaphor is cheerless: "Vividly does that fireside re-create itself, as I rake away the ashes from the embers in my memory, and blow them up with a sigh, for lack of more inspiring breath. Vividly, for an instant, but, anon, with the dimmest gleam, and with just as little fervency for my heart as for my finger-ends!" The metaphor is immediately elaborated. As he sadly reminds himself that the logs he remembers were "long ago burnt out," his imagination transforms the fire into a phosphoric glimmer exuding from "decayed trees, deluding the benighted wanderer"; he fancifully speculates, "Around such chill mockery of a fire, some few of us might sit on the withered leaves, spreading out each a palm towards the imaginary warmth, and talk over our exploded scheme for beginning the life of Paradise anew" (*BR*, 9). Like Coverdale's imaginative fervor, the warm and cheerful Blithedale fire has gone out. The only dynamic word in the passage, "exploded," defines the irreversible destruction of the utopian dream of regeneration. With this metaphorical fantasy of imaginary fire turned to phosphoric glimmering, and the absurd image of his former companions reaching out to its "imaginary warmth," Coverdale introduces his adventure at Blithedale.

In the third chapter, called "A Knot of Dreamers," Coverdale recalls his companions at Blithedale. Even the stalwart Silas Foster "looked vaporous and spectre-like" at one point (*BR*, 18); but Coverdale concentrates on the figures of Zenobia and Priscilla as they first excited his imagination, where they still abide. For each he reports his original perception, his intermingled imagination, and his subsequent fantasy. That first night he sees the gorgeous Zenobia wearing an exotic flower in her hair and fancies it is the image of her luxuriant character. When she later speaks of donning "the garb of Eden," Coverdale is shocked at himself: "Zenobia could not have intended it—the fault must have been entirely in my imagination—but these last words, together with something in her manner, irresistibly brought up a picture of the fine, perfectly developed figure, in Eve's earliest garment." Hawthorne deleted the next line in the manuscript, perhaps because of its prurience: "I almost fancied myself actually beholding it" (BR, 17).[4]

When Priscilla enters, Coverdale perceives her as an entirely different kind of creature. She is enervated, virtually sexless, and he pities her. "The fantasy occurred to me, that she was some desolate kind of a creature, doomed to wander about in snow-storms, and that, though the ruddiness of our window-panes had tempted her into a human dwelling, she would not remain long enough to melt the icicles out of her hair" (BR, 27). This vision of Priscilla as a snow maiden is even more appropriate to the sensibility of a minor poet than his self-censored "picture" of Zenobia. His perceptions have readily intermingled with fancies to produce the wistful fantasy; but it is essentially derivative and neither embodies nor invites deep understanding. Zenobia's later accusation that Coverdale is "turning this whole affair into a ballad" (BR, 223) is partly true: his insights about both Priscilla and Zenobia terminate in fanciful conceits.

After his feverish illness, Coverdale indulges in more elaborate fantasies about his companions, beginning to worry about

4. Donald Ross in "Dreams and Sexual Repression in *The Blithedale Romance*," *PMLA*, LXXXVI (1971), 1014–17, says that Coverdale's reaction to Zenobia's sensuality and his suppression of his sexual desire for her are central to the plot; Claire Sprague in "Dream and Disguise in *The Blithedale Romance*," *PMLA*, LXXXIV (1969), 596–97, argues that Coverdale's dreams reveal him as an eavesdropper on Zenobia's emotionally active and thus dangerous life.

their truthfulness. A passive and impressionable invalid, he comments that "there is a species of intuition—either a spiritual lie, or the subtle recognition of a fact—which comes to us in a reduced state of the corporeal system. . . . Vapors then rise up to the brain, and take shapes that often image falsehood, but sometimes truth" (*BR*, 46). One such intuition concerns Zenobia's sexuality: "Zenobia is a wife! Zenobia has lived, and loved! There is no folded petal, no latent dew-drop, in this perfectly developed rose!" (*BR*, 47). Although Coverdale acknowledges that fantasies may "image falsehood," his image of her as a full-blown rose extends his earlier conceit. Yet he refrains from validating his intuition. Zenobia lets him "look into her eyes, as if challenging me to drop a plummet-line down into the depths of her consciousness"; but he sees only "the face of a sprite, laughing at me from the bottom of a deep well." He then closes his eyes (*BR*, 48). While convalescing, Coverdale becomes more responsive to Zenobia's strong "sphere," but he nervously wishes she would let him alone.

As he lies in bed like a dreaming Oberon, his bodily functions reduced and his will impotent, he seems almost as weak as Priscilla. Hearing a knock at his door, he is so susceptible to her "sphere" that he says, "Come in, Priscilla!" Priscilla then enters, holding a letter from Margaret Fuller that somehow makes her seem to resemble Margaret Fuller (*BR*, 50–52). She is even more impotent than Coverdale, less in control of her life; she is Hawthorne's most extreme version of the will-less dreamer. This pale maiden had spent years subject to Westervelt's mesmeric influence; recalling that thralldom, she asks Coverdale, "Do we dream the same dream twice? There is nothing else that I am afraid of" (*BR*, 76).

She continues to be far more impotent than Coverdale as the story advances. Westervelt could influence her moods and behavior even when she was in the refuge of Blithedale, and near the end of the novel he again exhibits her on the stage as the Veiled Lady. As Matthew Maule had controlled Alice

Pyncheon's will, Westervelt controls Priscilla's. Sitting in the audience, Coverdale recoils in horror from the theological implications of such domination, as Hawthorne did when Sophia planned to be mesmerized. If one individual could control the will and emotions of another, Coverdale says, "the individual soul was virtually annihilated . . . the idea of man's eternal responsibility was made ridiculous, and immortality rendered, at once, impossible, and not worth acceptance" (*BR*, 198). He resists this intolerable hypothesis, believing "religiously" that Priscilla has retained her "sanctity of soul"; yet he feels relieved when Hollingsworth breaks the spell by calling to her. Dreamers waken when their hearts are touched, Hawthorne believed, and love now liberates Priscilla from her trance. Until this point, she has seemed almost disembodied; but her love for Hollingsworth gives her an identity and a hold on reality.

Coverdale's hold on his individuality and on reality are uncertain to begin with; life at Blithedale only makes him more uncertain. To separate his own thoughts and feelings from the stronger "spheres" of his companions, he retreats to his "hermitage" high up in a grape-entwined pine tree, "my one exclusive possession, while I counted myself a brother of the socialists. It symbolized my individuality, and aided me in keeping it inviolate." Above his companions and hidden from them, he can observe them, judge them, and daydream about them. From this vantage, he can "make verses," "meditate an essay," or muse about the world below. Yet he continues to be vulnerable despite his detachment: his fantasies are sometimes so convincing that he thinks they are real. He flings an affectionate message for Priscilla to a passing bird, then realizes he cares not "for her realities . . . but for the fancy-work with which I have idly decked her out!" (*BR*, 98–100). This realization makes the last line of the novel, his blurted confession of love for Priscilla, seem at once suspect and pathetic.

Coverdale retreats from Blithedale to Boston in a more desperate attempt to ascertain "what kind of a world it was." But as he sits before his hotel fire, the dingy room "appeared far off and intangible. The next instant, Blithedale looked vague, as if it were at a distance both in time and space, and so shadowy, that a question might be raised whether the whole affair had been anything more than the thoughts of a speculative man." His mood "robbed the actual world of its solidity," though Coverdale, a "devoted epicure" of his own emotions, can for a time enjoy his uncertainty (*BR*, 146). As he sits in the hotel thinking about Zenobia, Priscilla, and Hollingsworth, at times he blames himself for cold-hearted curiosity about them and at times he blames himself for not showing enough concern. Reconsidering those vacillating self-judgments, Coverdale now believes, "If I erred at all . . . it was through too much sympathy, rather than too little" (*BR*, 154). The one certainty is his uncertainty. He endures the penalty Dugald Stewart had described: sympathy nourished by imagination usually terminates merely in imagination.

His confusion increases when he calls on Zenobia in Boston. She is so ornately dressed and receives him so coldly that he wonders if she is now displaying her true self or whether "that were the truer one in which she had presented herself at Blithedale." When he says, "It appears all like a dream that we were ever there together," she rebukes his "poor and meagre nature, that is capable of but one set of forms, and must convert all the past into a dream, merely because the present happens to be unlike it" (*BR*, 165). She does not realize that Coverdale is equally uncertain about the present.

He continues to be baffled by the interconnected relationships of Zenobia, Priscilla, and Hollingsworth. Soon after he first met them, they became "the indices of a problem which it was my business to solve," and "the vortex of my meditations around which they revolved, and whitherward they too continually tended" (*BR*, 69–70). He tries to escape their "spheres" by leaving Blithedale, but they continue to dominate his waking thoughts. "These three had absorbed my life into themselves,"

170

he complains; he has lost his separate identity. Although he avoids discussing them with Boston acquaintances, he cannot put them out of his mind. "They dwelt in a profounder region. The more I consider myself, as I then was, the more do I recognize how deeply my connection with those three had affected all my being" (BR, 194–95). His inner drama has become his encompassing reality, enacted by figures beyond his comprehension.

They not only dominate his reveries but encroach upon his dreams. At three key points in the narrative, Coverdale tells of his mystifying but portentous nightmares. The first occurs on the night he arrives at Blithedale, the second on the night he tries to evade the problems of Blithedale by returning to Boston, and the third on the night he rejoins the Blithedale community. The first occurs when he is isolated by illness and the novelty of Blithedale, the second after he has deliberately pried into his friends' private lives, and the third when he realizes in horror that he would welcome disaster. All three dreams conform to Hawthorne's understanding that the dreaming mind produces apparently eccentric images dominated by a leading idea.

Coverdale cannot recall the first dream clearly, only its "confused sense"; yet he is certain it prophesied correctly. On his first feverish night, "I was in that vilest of states when a fixed idea remains in the mind, like the nail in Sisera's brain, while innumerable other ideas go and come, and flutter to-and-fro, combining constant transition with intolerable sameness. Had I made a record of that night's half-waking dreams, it is my belief that it would have anticipated several of the chief incidents of this narrative, including a dim shadow of its catastrophe" (BR, 38).

The second and longest dream—the only one described in detail—explicitly concerns his three friends, Zenobia, Priscilla, and Hollingsworth. An active image of obsessive pain replaces the static image of Sisera's nail: "Dreams had tormented me,

171

throughout the night. The train of thoughts which, for months past, had worn a track through my mind, and to escape which was one of my chief objects in leaving Blithedale, kept treading remorselessly to-and-fro, in their old footsteps, while slumber left me impotent to regulate them. It was not till I had quitted my three friends that they first began to encroach upon my dreams." He then describes his nightmare: "Hollingsworth and Zenobia, standing on either side of my bed, had bent across it to exchange a kiss of passion. Priscilla, beholding this—for she seemed to be peeping in at the chamber-window—had melted gradually away, and left only the sadness of her expression in my heart. There it still lingered, after I awoke; one of those un-reasonable sadnesses that you know not how to deal with, be-cause it involves nothing for common-sense to clutch" (BR, 153). Coverdale protects himself from the dream's troubling truths by claiming it defies common sense, but clearly it re-works a scene he had witnessed: Zenobia had pressed Hollings-worth's head to her bosom while Priscilla sadly observed them. The dream exaggerates Zenobia's gesture into a passionate kiss excluding both Coverdale on his bed and Priscilla at the win-dow. Further, it engages his earlier fantasies about Zenobia's sensuality and Priscilla's unsubstantiality. It comments on his friends' problems, and on his own ineffectual detachment. It also affirms what he never consciously understands: his sense that both he and Priscilla are outsiders to passion.

Before he tells of the dream he had on the night of his re-turn to Blithedale, Coverdale finds himself living in a day-dream in three different ways. First he describes the cheerful autumnal sights that met his eye on his return walk to Blithe-dale, the colored toadstools "mysterious growths" like "the emotions in my breast," while Hollingsworth, Zenobia, and Priscilla "glided mistily before me, as I walked" (BR, 205). Perceptions, emotions, memories, and fantasies are all over-laid. Coverdale brings back with him the confusions that had impelled him to leave. Feeling haunted by vagaries "of the

172

spectral throng, so apt to steal out of an unquiet heart," he wonders if Blithedale "had been nothing but dream-work and enchantment"; then he wonders whether his ominous "shifting fantasies" offer true portents of evil (*BR*, 206–207).

His anxiety is not dispelled even after he glimpses the Blithedale farm, surely "something real," then climbs once more into his hermitage; it increases after he encounters the strangely costumed individuals who had once been his companions. Undetected, he observes the group of masqueraders, "strange figures beneath the overshadowing branches; they appeared, and vanished, and came again, confusedly, with the streaks of sunlight glimmering down upon them" (*BR*, 209). They appear as unsteady as dream apparitions. Coverdale now finds himself, like Robin in "My Kinsman" and like Goodman Brown, the observer of a scene that seems to be a "dream-work and enchantment." Watching the incongruous figures dance to "Satanic music" in "a kind of entanglement that went nigh to turn one's brain," he betrays his presence by a laugh. He runs, but they pursue him, like spectral emanations of his own mind: "The whole fantastic rabble forthwith streamed off in pursuit of me, so that I was like a mad poet hunted by chimaeras" (*BR*, 210–11).

The scene reworks a notebook description of a costume party at Brook Farm that Hawthorne had observed as "a mere spectator," one that left him with a "fantastic impression" of the intermixture "of wild and fabulous characters with real and homely ones" (*AN*, 202). The *Blithedale* passage goes far beyond this impression. The masquers have two separate kinds of identity: they are real people in fabulous costume, yet they are creatures of Coverdale's haunted mind. He had hoped the familiar sights of Blithedale and its inhabitants would validate their reality and his own; but his pursuit by "chimaeras" only intensifies his uncertainty.

At the same time, the fantastic pursuit sustains the theater imagery which, like dream imagery, generates our sense of

173

Coverdale's separation from life. From the beginning, Coverdale describes people, events, dreams, and daydreams as if they belonged to a play he was watching. He likens his own role to "the chorus in a classic play" whose stage manager is Destiny. As choral observer, he can applaud, judge, and try to understand "the whole morality of the performance" (BR, 97), without participating in the real action or in its sequel in the "private theatre" of his mind. He had recognized Hollingsworth's selfishness and Westervelt's diabolism, but he never interrupted their plots. As his friends' lives intertwined, so did his fantasies about them; they occupied his "mental stage, as actors in a drama," while he sadly watched the performance, trying to "fathom the meaning and the moral," awaiting the catastrophe to end the action and release him from his choral role (BR, 156–57). His pursuit by the masquers does not end his role as anxious observer; it merely adds to his distress.

Then, in a "fitful mood" after he escapes, Coverdale "becomes quite lost in reverie." Stumbling over a pile of decaying firewood in the autumnal landscape, "I imagined the long-dead woodman, and his long-dead wife and children, coming out of their chill graves, and essaying to make a fire with this heap of mossy fuel!" (BR, 211–12). Like the woodman, and like the benighted wanderers he imagined at the beginning of the novel, Coverdale feels a need for heat and light that cannot be gratified. Only one of his fantasies in the novel indicates he was even capable of such gratification: on Sunday afternoons at Eliot's Pulpit with his three friends "(with my eyes of sense half shut, and those of the imagination widely opened,) I used to see the holy Apostle of the Indians, with the sunlight flickering down upon him through the leaves, and glorifying his figure as with the half-perceptible glow of a transfiguration" (BR, 119). Most of his fantasies are wistfully melancholy; and his reverie of the long-dead woodman's family presents a last spectral vision of human relationships he cannot share.

Immediately after, he is called to witness Zenobia's bitter

parting from Hollingsworth and Priscilla at Eliot's Pulpit. Again a spectator, Coverdale is more aware of anguish than ever before: he is in the middle of the action, not aloof in his hermitage or hidden by trees. The passionate scene is so disturbing that when he goes to sleep, a nightmare startles him awake. This third and final dream provides a prelude to the catastrophe he feared, desired, and did nothing to avert. He says, "I must have fallen asleep, and had a dream, all the circumstances of which utterly vanished at the moment when they converged to some tragical catastrophe, and thus grew too powerful for the thin sphere of slumber that enveloped them" (BR, 228). Sleep, as Hawthorne noted in "The Birth-mark," "cannot confine her spectres within the dim region of her sway" when the mind is apprehensive; and Coverdale wakens "in a tremble." By waking he protects himself from knowledge of the catastrophe in the dream, yet he retains enough foreboding to begin the search for Zenobia. The nightmare anticipates her suicide and Coverdale's discovery of it. Like his two other dreams, it tells truths his waking mind repressed even as it reveals Coverdale's horrified fascination with (and absorption by) other people's lives.

The dreamlike inconclusiveness of the entire romance can be attributed to the character of Coverdale. He says in his final chapter of "Confession" that he is dim and colorless, incapable of earnest belief or action. He has not been an active participant in the novel's chief incidents but a troubled observer, not a lover but a wistful observer of love, not a tragic figure but a choral voice. Zenobia sees him in Boston merely as a young man looking through a window. From the start, he was afraid to get "mixed up" in Blithedale, and his final retribution is inviolate detachment even from his own deepest self. His dreams propound mysteries he never fully understands, experiences he cannot even recall. But in the end he is no longer a self-protective bachelor puzzling over the Veiled Lady's message: as a self-critical narrator, Coverdale knows more about his own limits than he did in the spring of Blithedale's beginning. He still cannot fully understand the passions that joined and separated his friends; he still feels the same sorrow and helpless exclusion from experience that dominate his dreams and reveries. Not even the heat of the Blithedale summer could warm his heart, and so his mind cannot reach profound understanding. Coverdale had said, "By long brooding over our recollections, we subtilize them into something akin to imaginary stuff, and hardly capable of being distinguished from it" (BR, 104–105). *The Blithedale Romance* is the result of such brooding: fact and fantasy remain inextricably mixed in Coverdale's subtilized recollection.

Hawthorne's characteristic double attitude toward dreams is evident throughout *The Blithedale Romance*. By describing life at Blithedale as a daydream, he simultaneously praised and condemned it; and he is equally ambivalent about Coverdale's fantasies, reveries, and dreams. They offer truths not apparent to ordinary consciousness, but they withhold him from involvement in experience, and from the fullest development of his sensibilities. Through the "atmosphere of strange enchantment" that pervades the romance, Hawthorne suggests that dreams speak true, but cannot adequately substitute for real life. He had said so before, but not with such ironic understanding.

4. Apparitions from the Underground: The Marble Faun

In Italy, Hawthorne found the "Faery Land" with "an atmosphere of strange enchantment" that he had said "the American romancer needs" (BR, 2), a place rich in tradition. Everywhere in Italy, layers of time interpenetrated: the past visibly continued into the present through institutions, customs, legends, buildings, and works of art. But because Hawthorne found himself perplexed and finally overwhelmed in his efforts to assimilate his experience of the "various Italian objects, antique, pictorial, and statuesque" which "fill the mind" in Italy, the novel he based on that experience is to some

176

extent as shapeless and mystifying as a dream. "Side by side with the massiveness of the Roman Past, all matters, that we handle or dream of, now-a-days, look evanescent and visionary alike," he says; and he suggests that the novel's major characters were themselves "conscious of this dreamy character of the present" (*MF*, 3, 6–7). As Miriam, Hilda, Donatello, and Kenyon wander by torchlight through the Catacomb of St. Calixtus, they share "a sort of dream, in which reminiscences of church-aisles and grimy cellars—and chiefly the latter—seemed to be broken into fragments and hopelessly intermingled" (*MF*, 24). As through the catacomb, so through the novel the four wander in a sort of dream, where fragments of memory and perception intermingle, and spectral forms emerge from the darkness.

Hawthorne calls all of Italy and particularly the city of Rome "dreamlike"; he fancifully explains that the hills around Rome "being dreamed about so much . . . have taken the aërial tints which belong only to a dream" (*MF*, 101). More specifically, he develops localities as analogues for the dreaming mind. The novel's major events occur in three kinds of dream places: the underground, equivalent to the dark reaches of the unconscious, containing fears that all men share; residences high above-ground, equivalent to the private consciousness; and ground-level places of shared experience where private fantasies can interpenetrate with perceptions as in a daydream.

The dark and labyrinthine Catacomb of St. Calixtus, with its "intricate passages," deep recesses, and shallow burial niches, is the most richly suggestive equivalent for the dark corridors of the mind, like a Jungian figure for the collective unconscious. It must be reached by deliberate descent from the rationality of the daylight world, and it is too vast to be fully explored. Like the forest of "Young Goodman Brown," the dark streets of "My Kinsman, Major Molineux," or the Valley of the Shadow in "The Celestial Rail-road," it is a place of mystery and gloom where the wanderer is also a potential victim. In this ancient burial place beneath the "blessed daylight," Miriam is briefly separated from her friends; then she reappears accompanied by a wild-visaged figure—the "Spectre of the Catacomb," the chapter calls him. Proceeding through tortuous and cavernous passages, Miriam has involuntarily encountered an ominous figure from her past, the one she had most wanted to avoid; and he will henceforth shadow her (*MF*, 24–31).

The chapter in which this oppressive spectre is murdered, called, "On the Edge of a Precipice," begins at a legendary precipice and ends at a real one, both symbolic equivalents for the deepest reaches of human consciousness. As the four main characters stand with friends at the Forum, Kenyon tells the ancient legend of the chasm that suddenly opened there, to be closed only at the sacrifice of Rome's greatest treasure. He urges, "Imagine the great, dusky gap, impenetrably deep, and with half-shaped monsters and hideous faces looming upward out of it, to the vast affright of the good citizens who peeped over the brim!" Miriam immediately treats the chasm as a metaphor: " 'I fancy,' remarked Miriam, 'that every person takes a peep into it in moments of gloom and despondency; that is to say in his moments of deepest insight.' " The innocent Hilda protests that she "never peeped into it"; but Miriam warns her, "it will open for you. . . . The chasm was merely one of the orifices of that pit of blackness that lies beneath us, everywhere. The firmest substance of human happiness is but a thin crust spread over it, with just reality enough to bear up the illusive stage-scenery amid which we tread" (*MF*, 161–62).

Later in the chapter, they stand at the Tarpeian Rock at midnight, thinking of the traitors who had been flung to their death from that spot. One of their friends says it is time to leave: "We are literally dreaming on the edge of a precipice" (*MF*, 169). But Miriam remains behind with Donatello, and

Hilda, unnoticed, returns to join them. At this point, the Spectre appears and the "pit of blackness" opens for them all: Donatello pushes Miriam's tormenter from the edge of the Tarpeian Rock, Miriam stands beside him, and Hilda is a shocked witness. It is Donatello's first look into the dark chasm of consciousness and Hilda's first "peep"; and from this point on, all three are tormented by what they have seen. Beneath the "crust" of human happiness lies monstrous guilt, the sight Miriam had encountered long before.

By contrast with these commonly experienced underground localities, the places where Miriam and Hilda live and work and the ancestral tower where Donatello does penitence are coextensive with the particular consciousness of each one. The claustral chamber within each edifice defines its resident, each space delimited yet permitting egress to the outer world. Miriam's studio, like the haunted chamber of Hawthorne's love letters and his early tales, is equivalent to the troubled mind of a single sensitive individual. It is a shadowy place where strange and lovely fantasies appear, "one of those delightful spots that hardly seem to belong to the actual world, but rather to be the outward type of a poet's haunted imagination, where there are glimpses, sketches, and half-developed hints of beings and objects, grander and more beautiful than we can anywhere find in reality"; but the "delightful" spot also harbors Miriam's fears and sad memories. In this place of dreams, her art gives shape to dreams. Like the earlier artist-dreamers of Hawthorne's fiction, she is victimized by her own fantasies. Her portfolio of "domestic and common scenes" contains idealized images of the "life that belongs to woman," yet the lonely figure of Miriam herself always hovers in the background. Her drawings of vengeful women are more terrifying; "ugly phantoms that stole out of my mind," she calls them, "not things that I created, but things that haunt me." Among the haunting images is the face of the "Spectre of the Catacombs." The work of art most fully described is the one

179

most appropriate to the studio of consciousness: Miriam's self-portrait, conveying "some of the intimate results of her heart-knowledge." But everything there, even the dummy who serves as a model, is appropriate to Miriam's imagination: it is "now a heroine of romance, and now a rustic maid," like the artist herself. Her studio is on one of the highest floors of a building which is itself an analogue for Miriam, a large palace suffering from ruin and neglect (*MF*, 37–50).

Hilda's studio is at the top of a tower adjacent to a church, equivalent to her aspiring and virginal consciousness. A staircase leads higher up to a Virgin's shrine whose lamp she tends, and from her window she can feed the doves. Hilda has only "the doves and the angels" for neighbors, as Miriam comments after climbing to her room high above the "vanities and passions" of the street (*MF*, 53). The only object that we now see in Hilda's "turret home" is her copy of Guido's "Beatrice Cenci," a haunting portrait she achieved by letting the original "sink" into her heart. At this point Hilda is virtually devoid of personality; she could not, like Miriam, paint a self-portrait. Later, after she has witnessed Donatello's crime, Hilda looks at herself in a mirror which also reflects the "Beatrice." For a moment, Beatrice's expression of sorrowful "grief or guilt" seems "depicted in her own face"; and the composite image of mirror and portrait suggests that in Hilda's white consciousness, some awareness of dark mysteries is emerging (*MF*, 204–205). Later, after her strange disappearance, when Kenyon enters her "cool, airy, and secluded bower" and sees her white bed "enclosed within snowy curtains, like a tent . . . enough of Hilda's gentle dreams were lingering there to make him happy for a single instant" (*MF*, 404–405). By the end of the story we know that Hilda will leave her narrow curtained bed and become Kenyon's bride, but only after an interlude of imprisonment deep in the Convent of the Sacré Coeur. The convent's name suggests she learned secrets of the heart she had not learned as attendant of the Virgin's shrine.

Donatello's tower at his family's ancestral estate of Monte Beni resembles Hilda's only in that both are equivalents of the accessible consciousness. As he describes it to Kenyon, the old tower is appropriate to his time of soul-making: "it has a weary staircase and dismal chambers, and it is very lonesome at the summit!" At the first floor is a forlorn prisoner's cell with a few iron-grated openings and a single old stool, supposedly haunted by a holy monk who was once confined there. The "topmost chamber" is Donatello's bedroom which is also his oratory, filled with religious emblems of mortality and penitence—a skull, a crucifix, and religious pictures. Owls inhabit the chamber below it, and the battlements are above. Kenyon makes the implicit metaphor explicit: "With its difficult steps, and the dark prison-cells you speak of, your tower resembles the spiritual experience of many a sinful soul, which, nevertheless, may struggle upward into the pure air and light of Heaven, at last" (MF, 253–55). Donatello's tower does not lift him above the corruption and stench of the city, as Hilda's tower does; rather, it keeps him from the beautiful countryside. It is wholly a place of penitence, oriented inward and downward, though it may eventually lead upward. Donatello tells Kenyon he is thinking of entering a monk's cell; but we learn in the end that he is in prison, a more limited and punitive place of confinement than the tower afforded. Yet we recall that the monk's cell and the prison are in fact combined in Donatello's tower, close to the battlements open to "the pure air and light of Heaven"; possibly, as Kenyon had suggested, Donatello may eventually emerge from his prison of remorse.

As a third variant of place as an analogue for consciousness, two out-of-doors settings, one near the beginning and one near the end of the novel, develop Hawthorne's favorite metaphor of life as a dream. In both the scene of Donatello's brief frolic with Miriam in the Borghese Gardens and the longer scene of the Roman Carnival, strangely costumed figures join in a dance of life, joy and sorrow intermingling. Both the garden and the Roman streets are delimited yet horizontally extensive; unlike the labyrinthine underground of the catacombs, these are places of daydream, neutral territories where perceptions and fantasies can intermingle.

The Borghese Gardens where Miriam and Donatello enjoy their "sylvan dance" is a "lovely, dreamlike" spot; yet it is haunted by "dreamlike melancholy"—literally, the threat of malaria (*MF*, 73). To the sound of joyous music, Miriam and Donatello begin their wild dance. They are soon joined by costumed people of all ages and nationalities, all dancing as if "gone mad with jollity" (*MF*, 87). The scene recalls the riotous dances in "The Maypole of Merry Mount" and *The Blithedale Romance*, both soon terminated. Hawthorne extends his analogue by comparing the "wild ring of mirth" in the garden to carvings on a sarcophagus, figures of "merry-makers" interrupted by scenes of "doom and sorrow," an emblem of mortality (*MF*, 88).

While "Donatello's dance" is at its wildest, with Miriam the nymph to his faun, the satyr-like figure of her persecutor confronts her and she stops dancing. Their brief time of gaiety must end, she tells Donatello; she will "vanish from you quietly, among the shadows of these trees." The music stops, the dancers cease, and the "motley throng of rioters was dissolved as suddenly as it had been drawn together. In Miriam's remembrance, the scene had a character of fantasy" (*MF*, 89–90). Like all Hawthorne's burdened dreamers, she cannot prevent the intrusion of sorrow into her brief fantasy of shared mirth.

The longer and more complex Carnival scene is even more explicitly dreamlike. The Corso in Carnival, "peopled with hundreds of fantastic shapes," is like the parade at the climax

of "My Kinsman, Major Molineux" and the *Blithedale* masquerade, a dreamlike scene observed by a perplexed character who is uncertain if he is awake or asleep. The scene is a
trope for the dance of life, more so than the dance in the
Borghese Gardens: the street is "thronged with festal figures,
in such fantastic variety that it had taken centuries to contrive
them," a "mad, merry stream of human life" (*MF*, 439). Kenyon watches the "motley masquers" of the human comedy,
while he worries about Hilda's absence: "So remote from the
scene were his sympathies, that it affected him like a thin
dream, through the dim, extravagant material of which he
could discern more substantial objects, while too much under
its controul to start forth broad awake" (*MF*, 442).

This dreamlike experience becomes increasingly disturbing. To the accompaniment of martial music that "almost grew
to discord," as during the procession in "My Kinsman," a
parade of civic authorities appears, "illusive shadows, every
one" (*MF*, 443); then, while Kenyon stands watching "with his
dreamy eyes," Miriam and Donatello suddenly pass before
him, hand in hand, in costume and mask. He attempts to pursue them, but fails: "the crowd and confusion" are too great.
He is now enmeshed in his own nightmare. As an "anxious
and unquiet spectator," he becomes a target for practical
jokes, mocked like Coverdale by fantastic figures who seem
the emanations of his own inner torment. Absurd "apparitions" pelt him, then a gigantic "revengeful damsel" shoots
him with lime dust, perhaps Kenyon's symbolic punishment
for not giving Miriam or Hilda the sympathy they required.
Finally, a series of clowns, harlequins, and monstrous apparitions surround him, at once mocking and threatening: "The
affair was so like a feverish dream, that Kenyon resigned himself to let it take its course." The apparitions eventually vanish "as dreams and spectres do," and he is free to resume
his quest for Hilda. At this point he again encounters Miriam
and Donatello "straying through the grotesque and animated

scene," and Miriam gives enigmatic answers to his questions about Hilda before she and Donatello disappear. Kenyon passes his hand over his eyes and looks around, bewildered; the encounter "had made the scene even more dream-like than before" (MF, 444–48).

For all its irresolutions, perplexities, and foreboding, this scene reaches a happy ending. Kenyon is pelted by two last missiles, first a cauliflower, then "a single rosebud" thrown from a balcony, which "smote gently on his lips, and fell into his hand," as Hilda, the girl who threw it, is about to do. The cauliflower suggests Kenyon's summons by mundane reality, and the rosebud his opportunity for love. Ironically, the scene of joy is also a scene of gloom; the moment of Donatello's arrest is the moment Hilda is released from confinement. Kenyon beholds her on the balcony: "That soft, mirthful smile caused her to melt, as it were, into the wild frolic of the Carnival, and become not so strange and alien to the scene, as her unexpected apparition must otherwise have made her" (MF, 451). Then we briefly view the "chaos of mad jollity" through Hilda's eyes as, like a confused dreamer, she seeks "some object by which she might assure herself that the whole spectacle was not an illusion" (MF, 453). The "object" she finds is Kenyon. He relieves her confusion, and she does the same for him. In her presence, "his own secret sorrow and the obtrusive uproar of the Carnival alike died away from his perception" (MF, 454): his perplexing dream is dispelled.

Not only in the Carnival but throughout the novel, dreams define the way characters respond to experiences and the way they appear to others. Miriam, Donatello, and the Model all appear to be as strange and ambiguous as dream phantoms that go through metamorphoses yet remain recognizable; and even the more straightforward characters of Hilda and Kenyon are developed through their metaphorical involvement in dreams.

Miriam is initially described as "sprite-like" and "surrounded with misty substance" (*MF*, 23), but we soon come to know her as a haunted and enigmatic individual whose effect is most vividly suggested by her self-portrait: "She seemed to get into your consciousness and memory, and could never afterwards be shut out, but haunted your dreams, for pleasure or for pain; holding your inner realm as a conquered territory, though without deigning to make herself at home there" (*MF*, 47–48). She is at once haunted and haunting; her dreamlike effect results from her strong physical presence. As she furtively follows Kenyon and Donatello on their journey to Perugia, her presence "was like a dream that had strayed out of their slumber and was haunting them in the daytime, when its shadowy substance could have neither destiny nor outline. . . . After sunset, it grew a little more distinct" (*MF*, 299). Kenyon, who longs for Hilda, is aware of a kneeling woman; Donatello, too self-absorbed to see her, assumes the woman is a penitent like himself. They are both right; but each receives Miriam as his own distinctive dream.

Miriam's role as a haunted dreamer becomes explicit from the moment the Spectre who becomes her Model appears, though her "thralldom" is never fully explained. The combined metaphor of dungeon and dream expresses her feeling of victimization: "Is the dark dream, in which I walk, of such solid, stony substance, that there can be no escape out of its dungeon? Be it so!" she concludes; but nonetheless she will venture to share Donatello's joy. Like Clifford on his short train ride, she feels exhilarated, and through the prison metaphor Hawthorne accounts for this: melancholy people experience wild joy when "escaping from the dark region in which it is their custom to keep themselves imprisoned" (*MF*, 82–83). When Kenyon catches sight of her after the Model has ended her joyous interlude, the prison metaphor conveys his intuitive understanding of her predicament: "She has been in some sad dream or other, poor thing!" Kenyon tells Hilda, "and even now, she is imprisoned there in a kind of

cage, the iron bars of which are made of her own thoughts"
(*MF*, 112). A more complex image of Miriam as helpless
dreamer soon follows. She longs for Hilda's sympathy and Kenyon's advice; but "it was to little purpose that she approached
the edge of the voiceless gulf between herself and them.
Standing on the utmost verge of that dark chasm, she might
stretch out her hand and never clasp a hand of theirs; she
might strive to call out—'Help, friends, help!'—but, as with
dreamers when they shout, her voice would perish inaudibly
in the remoteness that seemed such a little way." In this "shivering solitude," her friends "turn to cold, chilly shapes of mist"
(*MF*, 113). She is alone in her life of nightmare, and escape is
impossible.

Her sense of impotence is most evident during the novel's
catastrophic event, Donatello's murder of the Model, described as a dream and remembered by Miriam as a dream:
"Miriam seemed dreamily to remember falling on her knees;
but, in her whole recollection of that wild moment, she beheld herself as in a dim show, and could not well distinguish
what was done and suffered; no, not even whether she were
really an actor and sufferer in the scene" (*MF*, 171). She
remembers the scene as a confusing nightmare. In a sense,
she remained innocent of the crime that Donatello and later
Hilda say her eyes invited. As in a dream, her will was suspended, and she was a confused and terrified observer of a
"dim show." Her curious paralysis and momentary amnesia
suggest that the murder was intolerable to her consciousness,
like the most horrifying moments of nightmare that we cannot
recall after waking. She never does completely recall what
was done and suffered, although she later accepts Hilda's and
Donatello's interpretations of her role. Yet since Donatello
has enacted her fantasies of vengeance, she is no longer completely isolated, and the obsessions that had emerged in her
art are now exorcised. From this point until the Carnival near

the end of the novel, her consciousness is dominated by Donatello's anguish and his rejection of her love.

To Donatello, the crime also seems to be a nightmare. He and Miriam both deliberately look at the dead Model to make sure the crime had actually occurred, "so like a dream was the whole thing" (*MF*, 174).[5] Later, in an inversion of Adam's argument to Eve, Miriam urges Donatello to think of his role in the crime as "but an ugly dream. For, in dreams, the conscience sleeps, and we often stain ourselves with guilt of which we should be incapable in our waking moments. The deed you seemed to do, last night, was no more than such a dream." Trying to ease his burden of guilt, she argues that the Model's face that continues to haunt him is an unreal dream vision "for you beheld it with dreaming eyes" (*MF*, 199–200). Although her argument establishes her tender sympathy for Donatello and her beliefs about gradations of moral responsibility, it is invalid. She says Donatello's crime was "but an ugly dream," but the ugly dream is real.

From this point on, real dreams torment Donatello. His suffering is a measure of his moral awakening, of his *Transformation*, which was the English title of *The Marble Faun*. He tells Kenyon about his recurring dream, the only actual dream in the novel, a recreation of the Model's death as a terrified observer might recall it. In the nightmare, a man falls shrieking from a precipice after "looking you in the face." He does not die in mid-air, as Kenyon suggests would happen in such a fall, but suffers horribly from "bruised flesh and broken bones! . . . I would fain fling myself down, for the very dread of it, that I might endure it once for all, and dream of it no more!" Startled by Donatello's passionate outburst, Kenyon warns that such a "vivid dream" could be dangerous: it might lead Donatello to the battlements "and act it-

5. Leonard Doane in "Alice Doane's Appeal" has a similar reaction to the corpse of the man he had murdered: he felt as if he were struggling in a dream.

self out as a reality!" Donatello himself recognizes the dream as an impetus to suicide in his qualified reply: "Whatever the dream may be, I am too genuine a coward to act out my own death in it" (*MF*, 261). His ordeal by nightmare continues the past crime into the present and threatens his future.

He is continually haunted by the dead figure of the Model whether he is awake or asleep. Looking at a shifting cloud, he says, "If I watch it a little longer, it will take the figure of a monk reclining, with his cowl about his head and drawn partly over his face, and—Well! Did I not tell you so?" He sees the Model as he had appeared laid out for burial. Kenyon, thinking of Hilda, sees a different "reclining figure" that "moves my heart by something indefinable that it suggests." Donatello next sees Miriam's face in the clouds, and Kenyon says, "No; not Miriam's" (*MF*, 265–66). Each projects onto the clouds what occupies his consciousness.

As the novel nears its close, Donatello's changes of garb and behavior make him seem increasingly like a metamorphosing dream figure. As he appears before Kenyon on the streets of Rome, wearing the white robe and mask of a religious penitent, the sculptor sadly recognizes "the glad Faun of his imagination and memory, now transformed into a gloomy penitent," like a sinister omen he could not interpret (*MF*, 393–94). In Donatello's later meetings with Kenyon on the Roman campagna and at the Carnival, he is clothed as a Roman peasant; but for the Carnival his face is "covered with an impenetrable black mask," and in that garb he submits himself to arrest for the crime that continues to obsess him.

For each of his transformations, Miriam undergoes a parallel change. In the Borghese Gardens, she had been nymph to his faun; when he is the death-haunted penitent of Monte Beni, she appeared "very pale, and dressed in deep mourning," her strength and warmth reduced to weakness and the chill of despondency (*MF*, 279). Then, right after Kenyon sees Donatello garbed as a Catholic penitent, he sees Miriam in a splendid coach, richly dressed, wearing a gem that "glimmered with a clear, red lustre," apparently "an emanation of herself" (MF, 396); while Donatello behaves like a subject of the Church, she plays her unexplained role as a mysteriously privileged subject of the State. When Donatello dresses as a peasant, she joins him as a contadina; and at the Carnival, her face is covered by the same kind of impenetrable mask he then wears. Her last appearance before Kenyon and Hilda, when Donatello is in prison, is again as his counterpart, "a female penitent," her face hidden "behind a veil or mask, which formed part of the garb" (MF, 459). Both are self-confined, whether by masks, veils, or prison; yet because their grief is shared, they are not wholly alone, as Miriam was at the beginning and Donatello was during his retreat at Monte Beni.

Even more wholly conceived as a figure of dreams is the spectral figure who had followed Miriam out of the catacombs. He always appears suddenly, as if by magic, or in a dream. When the four main characters emerge from the Capitoline Gallery near the novel's beginning, they are surprised to see his "dark, bushy-bearded, wild" figure, "partly concealed by one of the pillars of the portico" (MF, 19). We then learn they had encountered him before in the Catacomb of St. Calixtus, "a figure standing just on the doubtful limit of obscurity," clad in animal hides like a satyr, perhaps the spectre of the legendary "Man-Demon" who has haunted the catacombs for centuries (MF, 29–33). Hawthorne never explains what put Miriam in his "thrall"; but whether he is garbed as a satyr, model, or monk, he is the fullest development of the demon Hawthorne had introduced in "The Haunted Mind." He appears before Miriam at the Coliseum, that ancient site of violence, garbed as a pilgrim; then later that night he emerges before Miriam and Donatello at that "ominous precipice," the Tarpeian Rock, where Donatello hurls him to his death. When they visit the Capuchin church the

189

next day, they see his body in monk's robes. "It resembled one of those unaccountable changes and interminglings of identity, which so often occur among the personages of a dream." His face horrifies Miriam and Donatello: "It had a purplish hue upon it, unlike the paleness of an ordinary corpse. . . . The eyelids were but partially drawn down, and showed the eyeballs beneath; as if the deceased friar were stealing a glimpse at the bystanders. . . . The shaggy eyebrows gave sternness to the look." It is "the same visage that had glared upon their naked souls, the past midnight, as Donatello flung him over the precipice" (*MF*, 187–89), the same visage that has emerged in Miriam's sketches and that will henceforth torment Donatello's dreams.

The Model's demoniac identity is suggested not only by the myth of the man-demon, but by the resemblance to a figure in a time-honored work of art. One day Hilda notices among old drawings a sketch she is convinced Guido made for his painting of "The Archangel Michael Subduing the Demon," though the demon of the sketch "is entirely unlike the Demon of the finished picture." Kenyon agrees that the sketch portrays "a more energetic Demon," and one whose face he has seen before. Now Donatello articulates what all three have thought: "It is Miriam's Model." Whether the same demon had plagued Guido two hundred years before, or whether Guido had invented the face as "the utmost of sin and misery," the Model is identified with Guido's demon, the enduring earthly embodiment of evil (*MF*, 139–40). Looking at Guido's finished painting, Miriam passionately insists that victory against the demon is never a sure thing. If she tried to paint her version of "man's struggle against sin," she says, "I am sadly afraid the victory would fall on the wrong side" (*MF*, 184). Immediately thereafter, they all see the dead monk and recognize him as the Model. Hawthorne suggests that temporal death cannot put an end to this demon of many forms; across the centuries, he continues to haunt those who do battle with him. His is the sneering visage within the haunted mind, a face Hawthorne had depicted from the time of his early sketches.

If he is the apparition of evil, Hilda is the apparition of innocence. She is capable only of pure and gentle dreams, Kenyon thinks on his visit to her white bedchamber. Yet after witnessing murder, her lonely secret torments her; it puts her in "a chill dungeon, which kept her in its gray twilight and fed her with its unwholesome air, fit only for a criminal to breathe and pine in! She could not escape from it. In the effort to do so, straying farther into the intricate passages of our nature, she stumbled, ever and again, over this deadly idea of mortal guilt" (*MF*, 329–30). Even art galleries, which used to delight her, now seem "drearier than the whitewashed walls of a prison corridor" (*MF*, 341). By confessing her secret in St. Peter's she can emerge from her "chill dungeon"; but she cannot forget it exists nor accommodate the "deadly idea of mortal guilt." Kenyon's hypothesis that guilt and virtue may coexist shocks her: "She grew very sad; for a reference to this one dismal topic had set, as it were, a prison-door ajar, and allowed a throng of torturing recollections to escape from their dungeons into the pure air and white radiance of her soul" (*MF*, 385). Later, she performs a task for Miriam at the gloomy palace of the Cencis that leads to her mysterious imprisonment, and she emerges no longer a simple white-garbed girl. She is now clad in a domino and looks "bewildered"; but she no longer seems "strange and alien" in the complex scene of the human comedy she can now enter.

Kenyon, an intuitive artist-observer, is most aware of the separate and changing dreamlike characteristics of his friends; but we rarely enter his private imagination except to encounter his love for Hilda, "which it was his habit to confine in one of the heart's inner chambers" (*MF*, 263). Compared to the other characters, he is consistent and self-controlled.

Never is he in strange costume, never does he figure in people's dreams; yet he wanders through the long carnival scene as a bewildered dreamer.

Two symbolic objects near the end of the novel, both apparitions from underground, are conflations of Hawthorne's statements about the underlying truths in the dream of life. The first is the broken and earth-stained statue of Venus that Donatello and Miriam discovered while wandering on the campagna in their brief interlude of shared love. It lay underground, in the place of burial and decay, to be unearthed and recognized by individuals who must separately define its meaning. Donatello and Miriam, lovers about to part, know the value of this Venus, but Kenyon's worry about Hilda keeps him from wholehearted appreciation of it.

The second summary image is Miriam's bridal gift to Hilda, the bracelet of "seven Etruscan gems, dug out of seven sepulchres," its sad mystery intruding into a time of happiness. Like the Venus, the marriage gift comes from underground, the place of burial; and it offers a promise of survival through love. Together, the statue and the bracelet bring into the foreground of the narrative the earlier metaphor of the sarcophagus carvings: "You might take it for a marriage-pageant; but, after a while, if you look attentively at these merrymakers, following them from end to end of the marble coffin, you doubt whether their gay movement is leading them to a happy close" (*MF*, 88). Through its image of mortality, the sarcophagus is reminiscent of the tombstone over the graves of Hester and Dimmesdale at the end of *The Scarlet Letter*, its sombre "device . . . relieved only by one ever-glowing point of light" (*SL*, 264), and it recalls the torchlit Catacomb of St. Calixtus, a place of gloom, guilt, and death. Yet unlike the sarcophagus and the catacomb, both the broken Venus and the bracelet assert that a grave may be a place of treasure; and the images are sustained and reinforced by the image of

Italy itself, whose civilizations lie one on top of the other, going back and down to ancient Rome and the Etruscans.

All these images implicitly offer the same injunctions consistent with all Hawthorne's insights into the mind's response to its own dreams and daydreams: we should assimilate the past without being imprisoned by it, and we should live not only in our upper layers of consciousness, but descend to ground level and below. Such descent can be frightening and dangerous, Hawthorne asserts through the novel's burying grounds and dungeons, literal and metaphorical places of confinement. Miriam, looking at Hilda's copy of the "Beatrice Cenci," thinks of the girl "that slept in the dungeon" before going to her death (*MF*, 65); and as Kenyon walks through Rome in fear that Hilda has vanished "in some dark pitfall," he thinks of "the unsuspected dungeons" buried from sight beneath the Roman streets, used by ruffians "for murder, and worse crime" (*MF*, 412–13). Yet it is dangerous not to know that such dungeons and pitfalls exist. The novel warns that men must not ignore what lies below the surface of consciousness, whether guilt or love. Apparitions from the underground of an individual consciousness or a civilization may be figures of terror and torment; but they may be valuable treasures.

Hawthorne had welcomed Italy as "a poetic or fairy precinct, where actualities would not be so terribly insisted upon" as in America; but in writing *The Marble Faun*, he found himself limited rather than liberated by his material. Italy, like many of its paintings, proved too much for his imagination to assimilate. For example, he could praise a painting of "The Three Fates" as "a great symbol, proceeding out of a great mind," but complained, "If it means one thing, it seems to mean a thousand, and, often, opposite things"; and he was "perplexed and troubled" because he could never understand the "secret of grief or guilt" in the portrait of

Beatrice Cenci (x, 332, 505).[6] In consequence, some of the novel's symbolic objects and even plot lines can be perplexing. As Lathrop recognized, Italy remained "a sort of dream" for Hawthorne, haunting but incomprehensible. In fact, the Italian places and objects that served him best as symbols are variants of images associated with dreams in his earlier fiction— lonely chambers, dark labyrinths, mysterious portraits.

As Hawthorne was about to leave Italy, he said, "No place ever took so strong a hold of my being as Rome, nor ever seemed so close to me and so strangely familiar"; but he wished he would never see the city or any of its "objects" again (X, 506). The place had absorbed him more than he had absorbed it. At the beginning of *The Marble Faun*, Hawthorne referred to his novel as one of the "matters" that we "dream of" that seem "evanescent and visionary" by contrast with the Roman past. This explains some of its defects, yet also accounts for its haunting power.

5. *The Key to the Coffin: The Unfinished Romances*

In his introduction to "The Dolliver Romance" the manuscript Hawthorne was working on when he died, George Parsons Lathrop attributed his father-in-law's strange torpor during his last years to declining health, family illness, distress at the Civil War, and financial anxiety (XI, 9). Recent scholars have conjectured that Hawthorne was struggling during his last years with an old Oedipal problem and consequently with emergent "patricidal and incestuous thoughts."[7] But there is

6. The "Three Fates" is now attributed to Francesco Salviati. See Filippo Rossi, *The Uffizi and the Pitti* (London: Thames and Hudson, 1966), 286.
7. Crews, *Sins of the Fathers*, 251. Waggoner, *Hawthorne*, 233, also accepts the Oedipal hypothesis, and both are in accord with the psychoanalytically based theories of John H. Lamont in "Hawthorne's Unfinished Works," *Harvard Medical Alumni Bulletin*, XXXVI (1962), 13–20. Edward H. Davidson, in *Hawthorne's Last Phase* (New Haven: Yale University Press, 1949), 150–52, attributes Hawthorne's problems to poor health, too much writing, temperamental disjunction from the contemporary scene, loss of interest in moral problems, and inability "to fuse image and moral in a symbol." Christoph K. Lohmann, in "The Agony of the English

another explanation for the problems of the four unfinished romances.

Hawthorne was always diffident about his ability to create; even when he wrote "The Custom-House" at the height of his literary powers, he feared he had already lost what little ability he once had. But a note of anguish is added in letters he wrote to old friends during his last years. He told his friend and publisher James T. Fields of his reluctance even to begin writing "The Dolliver Romance." "I linger at the threshold," he wrote, "and have a perception of very disagreeable phantasms to be encountered, if I enter."[8] Lingering at the threshold of writing, he was also at the threshold of death. If he could not discover the meaning of the "disagreeable phantasms" he invoked or invented in the unfinished romances, if perhaps they had no meaning, the implications were barely tolerable. It might be pointless to search for meaning in dreams and impossible to fix such meaning in fiction, perhaps even to find it in life. In "The Custom-House," Hawthorne said he feared torpor of imagination; but now he confronted a worse fear.

A passage in "Septimius Felton," the long manuscript Hawthorne began writing in 1861, offers a model for his difficulties. At one point of the narrative, set at the time of the American Revolution, Septimius is trying to read a manuscript given to him by a young British soldier he had killed. After a restless night, he wakens and returns to the manuscript, "poring into its night, into its old, blurred, forgotten dream; and, indeed, he had been dreaming about it, and was fully possessed with the idea that, in his dream, he had taken up this inscrutable document, and read it off as glibly as he would a page of a modern sermon" (ELM, 52). The manuscript is like a dream of night

Romance," *Nathaniel Hawthorne Journal 1972* (Washington D.C.: NCR/Microcard, 1973), 219–29, argues that Hawthorne had trouble writing about an American claimant to an English estate because he was in conflict about the attractions of England as contrasted with those of America.

8. Hawthorne to James T. Fields, October 18, 1863, in *ELM*, 574.

with an inscrutable message for Septimius, and it enters his dream. It may be important, but it remains inaccessible to his waking consciousness.

The other unfinished romances similarly contain inscrutable messages that their author could not interpret. Symbols and transformations characteristic of dreams recur without the necessary leading idea to unify them. The symbols are essentially Gothic: a locked coffin filled with golden curls, a bloody footprint, a huge spider, an elixir of life, a poisonous flower growing on a grave, a bloody corpse. Hawthorne had made good use of such symbols in his earlier fiction: both a poisonous flower and a powerful elixir are central to "Rappaccini's Daughter," for example. But in his last years, he could no longer assimilate or "lubricate" them. They remained dream symbols that were portentous yet finally incomprehensible.

Repeatedly in the unfinished romances, the central character is uncertain whether he is dreaming or awake; at such times, nothing seems worth striving for. The heart of all mystery may be a void. As his career neared its end, Hawthorne was at the point Melville had reached over a decade before when he voiced the dread possibility that the meaning of Moby Dick's whiteness might be the absence of meaning, and the more horrifying thought that descent into man's consciousness might reveal an emptiness at the center. In his last fictions Hawthorne approaches the dark declaration of *Pierre* that man's best efforts may prove futile, and that human existence may be meaningless.

In the romance he began composing soon after his return to Concord (heavily edited by Julian and published in 1882 as *Dr. Grimshawe's Secret*), Hawthorne concentrates on the consciousness of an individual struggling to understand his present predicament and its implications for his past and his future. The search takes place in the chamber of his mind and in its external equivalent, a darkened chamber. Hawthorne's notes to himself mock his own irresolution; yet despite the narrative's abortiveness, its passages of daydreaming remain challenging and problematic. Such passages dominate the two overlapping but incomplete drafts of the romance. They define the central character, Ned Etherege, first as a child and then as a young man. The reader participates in his thoughts, memories, and fantasies, and sometimes in his quest for understanding. But his central problem is an extreme form of one that troubled his author: when Ned's perceptions and fantasies are indistinguishable, he fears they may have reflexive validity only within his own mind.

The story centers on an American orphan whose guardian encourages him to believe he is the heir of a noble English family. When Ned grows up and visits England, the scenery seems so familiar he feels he is dreaming. Twice he is nearly killed, once by being assaulted and once by poison. Each time he regains consciousness in a strangely familiar room whose other occupant also seems strangely familiar. Repeatedly through the novel the imaginary blends with the real and Ned's childhood fantasies intermingle with the experiences of England.

Hawthorne condones Ned's early predilection to daydreams as a prerogative of childhood that in his case has a special warrant. The lonely orphan spent his "dreamy childhood" living "with wild and beautiful visions, made out of his ignorance of what he was, which had given him all the kingdom of possibilities to choose his origin out of," and "he felt that, with all its shadowy gloom, there was a certain richness that made it better, probably, than the other boys' lives" (*ACM*, 119). Hawthorne's second draft expands on the richness of Ned's visions. He is subject to "vague reverie," but his friend Elsie sympathizes with "these unuttered thoughts or reveries," these "waking dreams" (*ACM*, 354). Together, the two make up "little dreams and romances, which all imaginative children are continually mixing up with their lives, making the common-place day of grown people a rich, misty, gleaming sort of fairy-land to themselves" (*ACM*, 367).

Both children are fascinated by Dr. Grimshawe's stories about an English mansion where a prisoner lies confined in a secret chamber; it seems so real that they plan to free the prisoner when they grow up, even though the chamber "assumed such a weird, spectral aspect to their imaginations, that they never wished to hear of it again." Like all Hawthorne's dreamers, the children are distressed by dark illusive mysteries. Nonetheless, "they lived a good deal of the time in a half waking dream, partly conscious of the fantastic nature of their ideas, yet with these ideas almost as real to them as the facts of the natural world, which are at first transparent and unsubstantial to children" (*ACM*, 364–67).

Such dreaming has its dangers. Ned spends more of his "real life" in the visionary English mansion than in his real house, leading "far too much an inward life for healthfulness, at his age." But he is fortunate to have Elsie "to keep life real, and substantial" while "he led her hand in hand through the same dream-scenery amid which he strayed himself." And as his scraps of poetry suggest, he has "the rudiments of a poetic and singular mind," capable of "taking outward things into itself, and imbuing them with its own essence, until, after they had lain there awhile, they assumed a relation both to truth and to himself, and became mediums to affect other minds with the magnetism of his own (*ACM*, 425–26). Here the young boy seems to be an alter ego of his author.

When Ned appears as a grown man on his first visit to England, he suddenly reenters the world of his childhood daydreams. Hawthorne condones this reversion, insisting that the visit is a well-earned vacation from a busy life devoted to public service. "The American is of course a lawyer," Hawthorne noted in a preliminary study; he is a man of practical affairs, a politician (*ACM*, 475). Yet this lawyer walks in the English countryside "through a kind of dream," as he perceives what "his dreaming childhood dreamt of" (*ACM*, 445, 257). Appropriately, he shows no real surprise when he encounters his friend Elsie for the first time since childhood, though he tells her of his peculiar sense of estrangement: "I seem to be in a land of enchantment, where I can get hold of nothing that lends me a firm support. There is no medium in my life between the most vulgar realities, and the most vaporous fiction, too thin to breathe" (*ACM*, 260).

From the start, Ned is confused by his sense that England is his childhood dreamland come true; but this is only the beginning of his disorientation. Later, he feels enmeshed in a dream that somehow gives access to long-forgotten experiences of childhood. He has been mysteriously assaulted and then slowly recovers in an almshouse chamber where he feels caught up in some "quaint dream of antiquity." In a note to himself Hawthorne says, "Throw into the first description of the chamber and the old man all possible dreamlike characteristics." He instructs himself at this point in both drafts to put Ned "in a feverish dream, that shall mix itself with the scene"; and he says, "We shall attach our story to the consciousness of this person, and endeavor to be present with his struggling recollections" as he tries to make sense of his "dreamlike perceptions." In the first draft, his struggle is troubled but not tormented. The curious chamber seems part of a "waking dream" somehow connected to his childhood. "What a strange, vivid dream!" he murmurs, annoyed at his state of mind and even angry at himself for it. But after he recalls that he had lived in such an almshouse in infancy, he resigns himself to the intermingling of memories and dreamlike perceptions. "Ah; I am still in my dream," he muses, "I will sleep a little more, and awaken, I hope, to a reality" (*ACM*, 131–37).

As a convalescent, Ned abandons himself to "meditations and reveries to which, in the abeyance of his active powers, he had latterly become addicted" (*ACM*, 142). He allows his "primal imaginative vein . . . to dream over the possibilities of his birth," and again Hawthorne condones this self-indulgence. "He felt an inclination to follow out this dream, and let it sport

199

with him, and by-and-by to awake to realities, refreshed by a season of unreality. At a firmer and stronger period of life, though Etherege might have indulged his imagination with these dreams, yet he would not have let them interfere with his course of action; but having come hither in utter weariness of active life, it seemed just the thing for him to do—just the fool's Paradise for him to be in" (*ACM*, 165–66). It might be argued that in writing the romance, Hawthorne was indulging himself, apologetically, for the same reason.

In the second draft, Ned's recovery of consciousness is more distressing. As he lies in the almshouse room, uncertain if he is awake or in a dream, he fancies himself "years back in life, thousands of miles away, in a gloomy cobwebbed room," perhaps with Dr. Grimshawe; but when he opens his eyes to see the apparition more clearly he "ceased to see it at all" (*ACM*, 447). Instead, what he sees in the declining daylight is a real chamber that seems part of his dream; the dreamlike reality is as distressing as the realistic dream. Extrication from one layer leaves him entangled in another.

He is further entangled when trying to make sense of the old man who enters the room and "seemed to enter into his dream, or delirium, whichever it might be"; and he concludes, "Yes; this must still be a dream, which, under the unknown laws which govern such psychical states, had brought out thus vividly figures, devices, words, forgotten since his boyish days." But despite his attempts to comprehend his dream state rationally, Ned feels frightened. "Though of an imaginative tendency, the stranger was nevertheless strongly tenacious of the actual, and had a natural horror at the idea of being seriously at odds, in beliefs, perceptions, conclusions, with the real world about him; so that a tremor ran through him, as if he saw the substance of the world shimmering before his eyes like a mere vaporous consistency" (*ACM*, 450). His mood of dreamy uncertainty threatens all certain knowledge about the concrete universe. It is no wonder that he trembles.

Nevertheless, as in the first draft, Ned yields to his mind's "strange illusiveness," willing to defer "solving the riddle in which he found himself involved."

In his present weakness . . . it was delightful to let all go; to relinquish all control, and let himself drift vaguely into whatever region of improbabilities there exists around the dull commonplace of life. . . . He, meanwhile, would willingly accept the idea, that some spell had transported him out of an epoch, in which he had led a brief trouble, of battle, mental strife, success, failure, all equally feverish and unsatisfactory, into some past century, where the business was to rest; to drag on dreamy days, looking at things through half-shut eyes; into a limbo where things were put away; shows of what had once been, now somehow parted, and still maintaining a sort of half-existence, a serious mockery; a state likely enough to exist just a little apart from the actual world, if we only know how to find our way into it. (*ACM*, 452–53)

Instead of the fool's paradise of the first draft, a condition of imaginative irresponsibility, Hawthorne offers the idea of a somnolent limbo, a serious mockery of life, a state we might well wish to enter.[9]

The passage continues with an even more unusual image for what the mind apprehends in dreams, corresponding to nothing else found in the novel: "Scenes and events that have once stained themselves, in deep colours, on the curtain that Time hangs around us, to shut us in from eternity, cannot be

9. The idea that through a "spell" Ned was involuntarily cast into a limbo is almost identical to the complaint to Longfellow in Hawthorne's 1837 letter. In "Septimius Felton" and the revision the Centenary edition entitled "Septimius Norton," a different kind of metaphorical limbo is given an even lower value. By his fanatical pursuit of the elixir, Septimius "had strayed into a region long abandoned to superstition, and where the shadows of forgotten dreams go, when men are done with them; where past worships are; where Great Pan went when he died to the outer world; a Limbo into which living men sometimes stray, when they think themselves sensiblest and wisest, and whence they do not often find their way back into the real world. Visions of wealth, visions of fame, visions of philanthropy; all visions find room here, and glide about without jostling" (*ELM*, 100; *cf.* 353). Hawthorne implicitly contradicts his praise of such visions in "The Hall of Fantasy" and *The Blithedale Romance*; he now suggests it is neither sensible nor wise to stray among "the shadows of forgotten dreams."

quite effaced by the succeeding phantasmagoria, and sometimes, by a palimpsest, show more strongly than they" (*ACM*, 453).

Memory closes in around the dreamer. Here Hawthorne not only implicitly adopts Upham's notion of the dreaming imagination as merely a receptive power, neither cognitive nor creative, but limits it even further. His earlier veils and masks have turned now into a curtain of time; the mind, as in senility, confronts merely events long past. Hawthorne's tone is one of tranquil acceptance. He has paid a high price to keep his demons of guilt and shame concealed. For a time, Ned yields like Coverdale after his illness to "slumbrous luxury," the "dream in the midst of which he lay, while its magic boundaries involved him, and kept far the contact of actual life," and he even delights in his ability to "let one spontaneous and half-definite thought loiter after another" (*ACM*, 457–58). But unlike Coverdale, he reaches no new insights.

A brief episode in the second draft indicates how seductive such a passive and irresponsible state of mind might seem to Hawthorne as he struggled with the composition of his romance. During Ned's childhood, a gentle schoolmaster is hit on the head while trying to deflect an attack on Dr. Grimshawe, and he describes his state of mind during his convalescence: "The grossness, the roughness, the too great angularity of the actual is removed from me. It is a state that I like much." The teacher even suggests, "It may be, this is the way that the dead feel, when they awake in another state of being, with a dim pleasure, after passing through the brief darkness of death." For this sensitive individual as for Poe's heroes, dreaminess is a superior alternative to the "angularity of the actual" (*ACM*, 387). The passage does not probe the mind's dark mysteries, yet the schoolmaster presents a hypothesis that Hawthorne must have found attractive: an eternal state of languor would forfeit the prospect of heaven but avoid the prospect of hell.

Hawthorne identifies this schoolmaster with the kindly pensioner who nurses Ned in his convalescence, a man who seems at first a figure in Ned's dreams and who calls himself a dreamer. In the first draft Hawthorne wrote a long note to himself about making this character "some strange sort of dreamer," though he never resolved what strange sort. Through him, Hawthorne approves dreams yet denies them significance. The pensioner attributes his dreaminess simply to his age, and earlier, Ned had observed other old men at the almshouse indulging in a "quiet dreaminess about things past" (*ACM*, 166). Such dreaming is not a mode of self-knowledge or even a curative convalescent state, but merely a reduced mode of existence. "'An old man,' said the pensioner, quietly, 'grows dreamy as he waxes away; and I, too, am sometimes at a loss to know whether I am living in the past or the present, or whereabouts in time I am—or whether there is any time at all.'" This last resonant phrase echoes and extends Ned's doubts about his own location in space and time when he daydreams. Yet the pensioner ends in wistful self-denigration: "But I should think it hardly worth while to call up one of my shifting dreams more than another" (*ACM*, 217). He concludes that his dreams are merely the backward-looking indulgences of old age, and Hawthorne does not hedge that conclusion.

Yet there is a more complicated yet strangely irresolute series of interconnected daydreaming episodes near the end of the first draft that seem closer to the haunting daydreams of Hawthorne's earlier fiction—episodes that again require entry into Ned's mind on the threshold of consciousness. The occasion is Ned's visit to Brathwaite Hall, the English mansion that had dominated his childhood dreams. From the moment he approaches it, he feels the same sense of unreality as when he had first walked in the English countryside; again his perceptions seem indistinguishable from his fantasies. On a front stair he perceives a rusty stain, the legendary "Bloody Footstep" that had haunted his childhood dreams and affected his waking imagination. His obsession with the footstep Hawthorne explains as one of those "bugbears and private terrors which grow up with people, and make the dreams and nightmares of childhood, and the fever-images of mature years, till they haunt the deliriums of the dying-bed, and after that, possibly, are either realized or known no more" (*ACM*, 283). The word "possibly" suggests that such bugbears may survive a dreamer's death. An even stranger kind of transcendence is suggested once Ned enters the labyrinthine house and has "thoughts, or dreams" of self-dissolution, fancying that "his every part and peculiarity had once fitted into its nooks, and corners, and crannies" (*ACM*, 285). His very identity seems coeval with this manor house, in part because of Dr. Grimshawe's stories that shaped his childhood fantasies, but also for another reason.

As with the image of the curtain of Time, Hawthorne is concerned with more than private consciousness. Brathwaite Hall is his most elaborate analogue for all men's inner consciousness, with its bloodstained threshold, its dark old rooms, its labyrinthine passages, and its concealed stairway leading to a windowless chamber. It is an ancient place of guilt and suffering. Places are identified with some aspect of the inner self throughout the romance. Dr. Grimshawe's cobweb-filled study is said to resemble "the inner chambers of his brain" (*ACM*, 94); and he says of his prepared guest room, "In most hearts, there is an empty chamber, waiting for a guest" (*ACM*, 115). The small dark-paneled almshouse chamber where Ned first convalesces is a more extensive analogue, representing Ned's inner consciousness as he daydreams of his childhood and infancy. But the mansion is a far more extensive symbol, a heuristic riddle of life: it is "like dark-colored experience, the reality; the point of view where things were seen in their true lights; the true world, all outside of which was delusion, had here— dreamlike as it sometimes seemed—the absolute truth" (*ACM*, 299). Reality, by definition, sometimes seems dreamlike. Brathwaite Hall is equivalent to Ned's mind, but apart from it.

Once inside its walls, he behaves like an impotent dreamer,

living in a spell or a "darkened dream," passively waiting "for whatever should come to pass." The state is partly pleasant and partly painful, as if he were irresponsibly adrift in his lonely childhood dream world; this state pervades page after page of the draft. Dr. Grimshawe himself "seemed to pass continually" through Ned's nighttime dreams, uttering some incomprehensible command; even when he wakes up, Ned feels he is still dreaming. This time his passivity does not lead to pleasant languor but to nightmare anxiety; Ned fears his host intends him harm, a fear that is wholly justified. Feeling helplessly "under a spell," Ned can do "nothing but dream troubled dreams" (*ACM*, 297).

There is a final stage for these troubled dreams. The secret chamber of the mansion is the place the whole romance has been leading to from the moment we heard how it tormented Dr. Grimshawe and disturbed young Ned and Elsie. Once Ned entered Brathwaite Hall, "It seemed as if, underneath this manor-house, were the entrance to the cave of Trophonious; one visit to which made a man sad forever after" (*ACM*, 299).[10] The dark chamber that in fact is concealed beneath the "dark-colored" mansion is Hawthorne's consummate version of the dungeon in the depths of the haunted mind. Here Ned lies imprisoned for a time, here the true heir of Brathwaite had been imprisoned for most of his life, and here rests the supposedly treasure-filled coffin that Ned has long sought. Within this dark chamber, as in the almshouse room, Haw-

10. Trophonious was an ancient Greek architect who, with his brother Agamedes, designed a king's treasury impervious to all thieves but the architects themselves. They robbed the king, Agamedes was caught, and Trophonious killed his brother to protect himself. Later Trophonious became a famous oracle whose reputation for truth was second only to the oracle at Delphi. In the cave of Trophonious, Pausanias reported, "some learn the truth by sight, others by hearing. In the process, it seems, the petitioners were literally paralyzed with fright, though they later recovered." See Edward Tripp, *Crowell's Handbook of Classical Mythology* (New York: Thomas Y. Crowell, 1970), 588. The components of the legend—the treasury with its secret entry, robbery, fratricide, the cave with its oracle, and even the petitioners' response to their experience in the cave—seem so similar to Hawthorne's that one can only wonder why he made no use of it.

thorne follows Ned's recovery of consciousness, fascinated by the process itself. But something more seems at stake. After his host poisons him, Ned feels on the brink of some marvelous revelation: there seems to be "an opening of doors, a drawing away of veils, a lifting of heavy, magnificent curtains, whose dark folds hung before a spectacle of awe;—it was like the verge of the grave." He feels "as if he were passing through the gates of eternity" (*ACM*, 307). Perhaps he may be about to discover what lies beyond the curtain of Time.

In fact he discovers nothing of the sort. What he enters is simply another state of uncertainty about whether he is in a dark room with someone beside him, or "whether he dreamed it." Amid his "mixed and jumbled" fantasies, he can retrieve "pre-Adamite" childhood fantasies that were ordinarily inaccessible; like Hester on the scaffold, he can escape present distress by paying attention to his inner pageant, "willing to look at the scenes that were unrolling for his amusement, as it seemed; and willing, too, to keep it uncertain whether he were not back in America, and in his boyhood, and all other subsequent impressions a dream or a prophetic vision." This "dim, twilight place . . . of half awakeness" is "so like his own half-awake state that he lay in it a longer time, not incited to finish his awaking, but in a languor, not disagreeable, yet hanging heavily." But this neutral territory is not a place of imagination or understanding; it is merely a place of memory and suspended consciousness. Ned is like a character in one of Poe's colloquies who wakens after death: "It was, in fact, as if he had been asleep for years, or centuries, or till the last day was dawning" (*ACM*, 308–309). But he reaches no new knowledge. As soon as he begins to distinguish reality from "delusive shows that bewildered him," he tries to dispel his dream state completely: he stamps on the floor and reaches out to touch the hand of his companion in the dark chamber, proving to himself that the room and its two occupants are real. That is all he finally does ascertain.

Hawthorne described the chamber from a different point of view near the end of the first draft, as if he himself were trying to recapture and comprehend a place that seemed "dim, dim as a melancholy mood": "There is—or there was, now many years ago, and a few years also, it was still extant—a chamber, which when I think of, it seems to me like entering a deep recess of my own consciousness, a deep cave of my nature; so much have I thought of it and its inmate, through a considerable period of my life. After I had seen it long in fancy, then I saw it in reality, with my waking eyes; and questioned with myself whether I was really awake" (ACM, 335–36). At this point, Hawthorne and Ned seem virtually identical. The chamber is a cave of despair where a wasted old man has lived a nightmare life, tormenting himself for an unspecified crime, and where a younger man tries to understand the old man's predicament while attempting to make sense of his own.

The romance's interconnected themes—entry into the self, encounter with secret guilt, search for an ancestral heritage, and search for concealed treasure—are objectified in this place. It is a consummate place of dreams, thickly carpeted, hung with tapestry, illumined with a faint light "that makes noon-day look like evening twilight" and "a coal fire, a dim smouldering fire" (ACM, 338–39). When Ned enters this room, however, he encounters not his own repressed fears and desires, but those Dr. Grimshawe had imprinted years before. Even his encounter with the prisoner of the secret chamber does not seem particularly important except as a strange fulfillment of a childhood fantasy. Hawthorne never made up his mind about Ned's or Dr. Grimshawe's relation to the prisoner, nor even why he was imprisoned; the old man is merely a pathetic victim. Through him, Hawthorne has nothing new to say about human guilt.

Ned's search for his patrimony is equally inconclusive. Hawthorne never decided who Ned's father was, or even whether Ned is the rightful heir of the English estate. Yet the search makes some sense: it validates Ned's childhood dreams, and it demonstrates a democrat's desire for the patterned life of an aristocrat. It also suggests an older theme, that an ancestral heritage carries with it the stain of guilt.

The search for hidden treasure is crucial to the Grimshawe manuscripts and also to "The Ancestral Footstep" and "Septimius Felton." In each of these romances, the hero possesses a silver key to an unknown treasure that is in some sense a gift from the dead. This is literally true in "Septimius Felton" where Septimius obtains his key from the young British soldier he killed; in the Grimshawe narrative, Ned finds the key in a grave; and in "The Ancestral Footstep," an embryonic version of Grimshawe, the hero inherits it. But Hawthorne could not decide on the significance of the key, or how it connects the past to the present. In each romance the silver key opens different kinds of treasure chests, each with different contents.

The fewer than ninety pages of "The Ancestral Footstep"— written in 1858 before Hawthorne turned to *The Marble Faun* —contain several separate versions of unlocking the treasure chest. In the first, a girl leads the hero to the miniature palace that had figured in his dreams, for whose secret chamber he has the key. He "dreamily" inserts the key in the lock that has not been turned for three hundred years; but ironically, all that remains within is a pinch of dust, evidence of the vanity of human wishes (*ACM*, 28–29). The variant near the end of the manuscript is more indeterminate, although the hero is more active in it. He is alone in the bedroom containing the "mimic" palace, and after he falls asleep and dreams about it, some "association" leads him to press a square of pavement which parts to reveal a keyhole. His antique key fits it, and he opens a secret compartment where he finds sealed documents. He immediately closes the compartment, planning to examine the documents in the presence of a witness, but we learn no more about them (*ACM*, 77–79). As Hawthorne worked with the idea of a secret compartment, he could not decide whether it should contain something valuable or valueless, significant or meaningless, or whether it should be empty. A "dreamy" curiosity is never gratified.

In "Septimius Felton," the silver key Septimius had inherited from the dying British soldier opens an iron-bound box the soldier had inherited from his part-Indian aunt, curiously symbolizing his double heritage of European society and American wilderness. The rugged box, lined with delicately carved ivory, contains old genealogical papers and the missing clue to the recipe for an elixir of life that the soldier had also given to Septimius. But the girl who drinks the elixir immediately dies. And although Hawthorne suggests that Septimius eventually claimed an estate in England, it is never established that the box's contents enriched his life in any significant way.

What the silver key opens in the Grimshawe manuscripts is a coffin filled with golden curls. Hawthorne had heard of such a coffin while in England, and it obsessed his imagination as he tried to write this romance. Still, he could not settle how the dead young woman had been connected to the guilt-stained family who might be Ned's ancestors. That coffin is in a sense contained in another, the mansion's secret chamber, reached by pressing a secret place in the floor and then descending a winding stair. Here an aged prisoner has for decades endured a living death, and rescuers enter only after the old man is dead. Not until then does Ned unlock the coffin, discovering the golden hair that has no value except to stimulate tender sensibilities. It seems almost the residuum of Hawthorne's talent as a writer. Hawthorne could never decide what dreadful secret was to be concealed in the mysterious chamber or in the locked compartment of all the Ancestral Claimant manuscripts. All the coffin contains is evidence of mortality and mutability.

The central character of every one of the unfinished romances sometimes worries that he may be lost in a dream and that he may never be certain whether he has emerged. His plight is an unrelieved version of Oberon's. Hawthorne acknowledges that dreams can be pleasant compensations for the deprivations of childhood, illness, or old age, and that all men are subject to nightmares in which they are "startled at their own wickedness" (*ACM*, 403); but what most torments each hero is not recognized wickedness, but fear that he might be immersed in experience whose significance he can never determine. "The Dolliver Romance" and "Septimius Felton" pursue the possibility of earthly immortality, and at one point Hawthorne speaks of our sense of an "undying principle" within us which promises "spiritual immortality" (*ACM*, 13); but the main focus in all the last romances is on mortality, mutability, and epistemological uncertainty. Thus, Septimius daydreams as he tries to concoct his elixir and then realizes "he had been in a dream, superinduced by too much watching, too intent thought; so, that living among so many dreams, he was almost afraid that he should find himself waking out of yet another, and discover that the vase itself, and the liquid it contained, were also dream-stuff" (*ELM*, 168). Earlier, he felt his companions and his surroundings were all unreal: "It was a moment, such as I suppose all men feel (at least, I can answer for one) when the real scene and picture of life swims, jars, shakes, seems about to be broken up and dispersed, like the picture in a smooth pond, when we disturb its smooth mirror by throwing in a stone; and though the scene soon settles itself, and looks as real as before, a haunting doubt keeps close at hand, as long as we live, asking—'Is it stable? Am I sure of It? Am I certainly not dreaming? See; it trembles again, ready to dissolve'" (*ELM*, 101; *cf*. 354). Dr. Dolliver's uncertainty is simply attributed to old age: he is unsure whether "his senile predicament was but a dream of the past night." When he walks on the streets, he has "that nightmare feeling which we sometimes have in dreams, when we seem to find ourselves wandering through a crowded avenue, with the noonday-sun upon us, in some wild extravagance of dress or nudity" (*ELM*, 464). Messages from the past are unclear; perceptions cannot be trusted; and memory contains an indeterminate admixture of fantasy. Hawthorne was approaching Prospero's conclusion that we are such stuff as dreams are made on.

In one of his studies for the Septimius story, Hawthorne said he intended the reader "to see how all that is highest and holiest in this life depend on death and the expectation of it" (*ELM*, 511)—a conviction expressed at least as early as "The Lily's Quest." But nagging questions persisted as he wrote. In the first manuscript, the face of the dead English soldier has an expression of "great joy and surprise," an intimation of "God's Providence" (*ELM*, 32–33). In the revised manuscript, however, Septimius cynically wonders whether such an expression might simply be the result of Nature's "contemptuous kindness" as she provides "a thrill of the very highest rapture" as the culmination of earthly experience (*ELM*, 246). Undoubtedly Hawthorne empathized with the patriarch who tells Septimius about the debilities of old age but cannot be sure what will follow. Although he hopes for an interval of sleep preceding an afterlife, he says, "My faith is good but my sight is dim" (*ELM*, 298). Hawthorne might have said the same.

He did sometimes suggest in the last romances that the afterlife might merely be an extended but unintelligible form of dreaming. Davidson's edition of *Dr. Grimshawe's Secret* and the Centenary edition of *The American Claimant Manuscripts* enable readers to share Hawthorne's anxieties as he tried to find a way to connect Ned's past to his present and a way to connect centuries of a family's experience both in England and America. Yet the legendary bloody footprint exists only as a rust-colored stain; the silver key unlocks only a coffin, containing nothing of any use. The novel is filled with ominous but empty symbols. What the Grimshawe manuscripts ultimately suggest is that as Hawthorne neared death, he seriously considered the possibility that the afterlife might be a kind of limbo, a state like the languorous dreaminess both Ned and the schoolmaster experience during convalescence, a state free of guilt, anxiety, and the "angularity of the actual." In the *French and Italian Notebooks*, Hawthorne had interpreted Judgment Day as "all future days, when we see ourselves as we are," a time when punishment for sins "will be the perception of them" (X, 205); but in the Grimshawe narratives and the other unfinished manuscripts, no one reaches such perception. By making dreaming a condition of self-evasion, Hawthorne might have been trying to accommodate his own fears of annihilation.

Writing of the unfinished romances, Davidson says, "Sometimes Hawthorne tried to cast experience in the form of a dream, as though the hazy intangibility of dream would mediate between the disparate claims of life." Indeed, in all his fragmentary romances, Hawthorne was trying to make dreams perform such tasks of mediation; but it is primarily because those dreams do not take the hero into his own deepest abysses that the mediation does not succeed. The dreams are usually generalized conflations of a personal past, a bewildering family past, and a bewildering present. Davidson suggests that Hawthorne thought possibly "the very mystery of dream would solve the difficulties which a hero, bent on destroying the fixed ethical system, imposed on the narrative." But through his dreams as through his waking actions, the hero is trying to comprehend his own life, not to destroy an ethical system. If his dreams do not make a great deal of sense, it is because his creator could not determine their leading idea. Eventually, Davidson says, Hawthorne "abandoned his theory of romance and tried to write a moral fable for his own time." Hawthorne never did abandon the theory: in the end, he simply could not make it work.[11]

In the preface to *Our Old Home*, written in July, 1863, while he was laboring on "The Dolliver Romance," Hawthorne acknowledged that he could no longer transform notebook sketches into fiction that "would convey more of various modes

11. Edward H. Davidson, "The Unfinished Romances," in Roy Harvey Pearce (ed.), *Hawthorne Centenary Essays* (Columbus: Ohio State University Press, 1964), 154–56.

of truth than I could have grasped by a direct effort." He could not enter his own familiar dream world: "The Present, the Immediate, the Actual, has proved too potent for me. It takes away not only my scanty faculty, but even my desire for imaginative composition, and leaves me sadly content to scatter a thousand peaceful fantasies upon the hurricane [of the Civil War] that is sweeping us all along with it, possibly, into a Limbo where our nation and its polity may be as literally the fragments of a shattered dream as my unwritten Romance" (*OOH*, 4). Hawthorne's concern with the mind relaxed in dreams and daydreams continued to generate most of the power in these last romances, but the metaphor of the shattered dream implicitly explains their radical incompleteness.

V
Disagreeable Phantasms

Hawthorne always regarded dreaming as crucial to the individual moral life, because the dreamer penetrates beyond life's surfaces to explore his private interior world, encountering whatever "disagreeable phantasms" might there await him. Dreams are not readily decoded messages from supernatural powers, calculated simply to inform or to deceive; rather, they are emanations from the mind of the dreamer that he can neither control nor wholly understand—though he may sometimes glimpse, or think he glimpses, regions of the ideal or the infernal. But Hawthorne's imperative to the dreamer, whether himself or a character in his fiction, was always an equivocal warning: he should reflect upon his inner experience, yet not too intently or persistently. Thus, he warned that "it is dangerous to look too minutely" at the images drifting across the "inward sky"; he asked Sophia to interpret a troublesome dream but not to educe any "sombre omens"; and he deplored his fictional dream-obsessed writer as a man unfit for ordinary life even though his "glance comprehends the crowd, and penetrates the breast of the solitary man."

Hawthorne's profound ambivalence necessarily entered into his fictional exhibitions of the images of dreams, the process of dreaming, and the character of the dreamer. A character may regard the images of his dream as bizarre and incoherent admixtures of fantasy, memory, and sense perception; yet Hawthorne always suggests that there is some "leading idea" behind them. That idea may, however, be difficult or even impossible to determine, or too horrifying for the dreamer to admit to waking consciousness.

Thus Hawthorne represents the act of dreaming as an escape that is also an encounter—an escape from the problems of waking life only to encounter them again at a deeper level. At the same time, dreaming is a radical form of isolation yet a mode of aggregation and conservation. The dreamer is separated from society and alone in his interior world, yet his dreams establish his communal identity as they incorporate imaginary and real figures from his past and his present life. Whenever Hawthorne rendered dreaming as an autonomous act, he insisted that it enables man to live through the whole range of his faculties and to respect both his own complexity and his interdependence with other men. Dreaming is a curious act of self-completion: old men of childhood, young men of the future, guilty men of their hidden deeds and desires. Dreaming warns men of their limitations, yet it helps them determine their options of belief and action. Thus if dreaming is an act of evasion, it is also an act of synthesis and self-assessment.

Hawthorne judged the dreamer according to the use he makes of his dreams. A dreamer is deplored as a pathetic creature, a trapped and wasted man, to the extent that, like Clifford, he remains confined within his dream world. He is condemned as self-deceived if, like Giovanni or Goodman Brown, he gives absolute credence to a single strand of truth within a complicated dream. Or he may be praised if, like Robin or Hester, he makes tentative efforts to understand his dreams and to modify his behavior according to that understanding.

Such understanding Hawthorne sought for himself and urged through his fiction. The characters we are most moved to praise are those who accept their own admixtures of sin and sorrow and their own areas of mystery. The kind of dignified self-comprehension that leads to this limited self-transcendence is attainable only through the imagination, whether for the character of a story, its writer, or its readers.

Whether he pursued the drift of daydream or the confrontations of nightmare, what most engaged Hawthorne's attention was the mind's movements from outer to inner reality and within its own interior world. Always the process was more important to him than the event, the dreamer's responses more significant than what he envisioned. Nonetheless, Hawthorne worried about the importance and authenticity of such visions. His judgments of dreaming always exhibited painful irresolutions, though his particular judgments depended on whether he was treating the dream as an idle fantasy, a form of thought, or a mode of self-exploration.

Especially during his bachelor days, Hawthorne worried that dreams might be merely idle fantasies, and he often voiced his society's casual conviction that dreams are transitory and insubstantial, and the dreamer an indolent individual. Dreaming might be condoned for the very young or the very old, or as a brief escape from a dull or painful waking existence, but the judgment that a dream is "only a dream" suggests that it is insignificant and unimportant. Hawthorne pushed this judgment a step further to suggest that dreaming could be dangerous, a cause and expression of psychic debilitation, as when he complained to Longfellow that he was an enchanted dreamer unable to extricate himself from his dream world. Whenever Hawthorne wrote of "vagrant fantasies" or "wild vagaries," he worried as the Scotch philosophers did that dreaming might become an end in itself, a form of self-indulgence and self-depletion. The dream world would then be no more than a limbo, a cold world of shadows. In the early tales, the habitual dreamer might be marked for an early death; in the last romances Hawthorne more pessimistically suggested a worse penalty—a long life. These assumptions about the mere dream and the mere dreamer lie behind Hawthorne's recurrent self-deprecation as a writer. To the extent that his fictions simply embodied dreams, they could be dismissed as insignificant and unimportant. The implicit imperative is that the dreaming imagination must be validated against the waking world and merged into it. This Hawthorne attempted in his life and in his fiction.

More often than he conceived of dreams as idle fantasies, Hawthorne treated them as a form of thought that is not only normal but necessary, a way of going beyond perplexing sense impressions to deeper understanding of the world we inhabit —in short, as a mode of problem-solving. Set loose by sleep or glimmering light, the mind can move through the dream or daydream to make juxtapositions and identifications not bounded by ordinary logic or the limitations of time or space. Thus Giovanni's dream equates Beatrice and the curious purple flower; Robin's imagination superimposes his country home on the moonlit city street; and Coverdale, both in his sleeping and waking dreams, tries to figure out the knotted relationships of his three friends. But even while Hawthorne valued such dreaming, he warned of its limits. Not only might the dreamer, like Coverdale, remain perplexed by his dream-thought, but worse, he might like Giovanni mistake partial insight for absolute truth.

The third kind of dreaming is at once most characteristic of Hawthorne and his fiction yet most enigmatic: the dream as a mode of self-exploration, a means of entry into the self that may lead to painful self-confrontation. Throughout his fiction, Hawthorne explored the inner life through the metaphor of a cave or chamber in whose dark recesses men may encounter monsters of guilt and shame, though sometimes buried treasure. Exploring the cave is analogous to entering a dream. A dreamer may be terrified or occasionally delighted by particular discoveries, or by illusive hints of what lies beyond the enclosure; but what he apprehends of his own interior life usually evades full understanding. What is concealed within Aylmer's nightmare of excising his wife's birthmark, for example, is too painful, even too dangerous, to acknowledge even to himself.

The unfinished romances continue these patterns with some important changes. Hawthorne was moving toward solipsism in his last years. Neither as he prepared to write his fiction nor within the fiction could he successfully effect the merger of the actual and the imaginary: both seemed equally blurred to begin with. Consequently, the last protagonists do not experience the pains of hell in dreams or daydreams. Their "disagreeable phantasms" are like the messages in "Bartleby the Scrivener" that end up in a dead letter office. Each protagonist suffers, though rarely is he responsible for it. There is no private hell in these romances, and little hope of heaven. The dreamer cannot penetrate beyond the confusions of mortal existence.

From Hawthorne's early fiction to his last romances, treasure chests and coffins are symbolically interchangeable. Chillingworth searched into Dimmesdale's soul "like a treasure-seeker in a dark cavern" or "like a miner searching for gold; or, rather, like a sexton delving into a grave, possibly in quest of a jewel that had been buried on the dead man's bosom, but likely to find nothing save mortality and corruption"; and Hilda's bracelet of gems comes from Etruscan sepulchres. These metaphors offer complex moral judgments—that man is mortal and guilt-stained, yet may possess some redeeming spiritual treasure. But often in Hawthorne's last years, such judgments must have seemed overly simple. When a seeker finds a long-sought treasure in the unfinished romances, it is usually valueless; and it may even prove poisonous, like the splendid flower growing from the grave in "Septimius Felton." The hair filling the coffin in the Grimshawe manuscripts and the pinch of dust in the secret compartment of "The Ancestral Footstep" convey the same message: there is no gold, no jewel; there is only evidence of mortality uncovered by a confused and lonely individual. This is far more disturbing than the image of treasure turned to dross in the early tales. Yet these abortive fictions never move to final despair. In his early tales and letters, Hawthorne had described himself as a solitary and dream-haunted man who could be wakened by love, and who then became free— or relatively free—to reenter his dream world. That freedom he exercised and wrote about even when he was distraught by the phantasms of his own dreams. But the last romances show that at the end of his life, Hawthorne was agonized by the insoluble secrets of mortality—questions about what lies beyond the curtain of Time, even about the importance of life itself. After their last meeting in 1856, Hawthorne had said of Melville that he can "neither believe, nor be comfortable in his unbelief" (*EN*, 433). The reverse seems true of Hawthorne in his last years: he could neither disbelieve, nor be comfortable in his belief.

No longer sustained by faith in an ideal realism, Hawthorne could no longer assimilate experience within a controlling imaginative framework. In England, he had been disturbed by the grandeur of Lichfield Cathedral because he knew he could never "melt it into one idea, and comprehend it that way"; in Italy he had felt distressed by a great painting like "The Three Fates," because "if it means one thing, it seems to mean a thousand, and, often, opposite things." In the unfinished romances, he was unable to melt perceptions or legends into single ideas, so he could not comprehend them or fit them in his narrative; repeatedly when a symbol seems to mean one thing, it also seems to mean opposite things. What had earlier been difficult was now virtually impossible. He kept trying to "dream strange things," but he could rarely "make them look like truth."

From his earliest years as a writer to his last, Hawthorne described his tentative ventures into his consciousness with a mixture of self-respect and self-mockery, confidence and fear. He limited these inner ventures, fearing his own darkest secrets; and he carefully limited what to tell his readers. Throughout his career, his narratives display his irresolution about the ultimate importance of his inner drama and his tensions about how much of it to display. Yet paradoxically, by displaying the dreaming minds of fictional characters, he was at once escaping and confronting his deepest problems, sometimes even dominating them. He could be simultaneously impersonal and personal as he articulated the mysteries that tormented and fed his imagination.

Hawthorne fulfilled the ambition he had expressed near the beginning of his career: "To write a dream, which shall resemble the real course of a dream, with all its inconsistency, its strange transformations, which are all taken as a matter of course, its eccentricities and aimlessness—with nevertheless a leading idea running through the whole." He had added, "Up to this old age of the world, no such thing ever has been written"; but repeatedly and cumulatively he did what he set out to do. With what can be called a pragmatic pluralism, he drew on any literary conventions, psychological terminology, or philosophical tenets that seemed useful to him, extrapolating what he believed, suspected, hoped, and feared, guided by his insights into his own dreaming mind.

Hawthorne entered a dreaming mind not as an occasion for thrilling adventure in the Gothic manner, nor to express Romantic wonder. He did not seek the bizarre but the ordinary. His point was that the ordinary is always extraordinarily mysterious, that intertwined with common experience are truths too terrible to utter and uncertainties too terrible to bear. The dream is a way of rendering such mysteries as it offers the dreamer self-knowledge and simultaneously suggests the limits of that knowledge, including the limits that, in the interests of self-preservation, he imposes on himself.

What Melville applauded and today's critics value is Hawthorne's refusal to accept the benign sentimental values and opinions that crowd the surface of life. He pushed past masks and even past the skull beneath the skin to the strange subterranean world within man's mind. His fiction is never more complex than in its pursuit of those dark truths men conceal even from themselves.

Our view of Hawthorne has been impoverished by our inadequate attention to the way the problems central to his vision of himself are central to his fiction. He agonized about how he could come to comprehend himself, assimilating his own perceptions, locating his own creative powers, and coming to wisdom about the dark concerns of the isolated individual and of men's shared existence. Dreams were central to his processes of self-exploration, of self-definition, even of self-evasion. As a romancer, Hawthorne was also a philosopher and psychologist, trying to understand the mind on the borders of consciousness, as it mediates between the real world and truths of the imagination. For him, composing fiction was a form of dreaming, and his stories and romances should be read as the literature of dreaming. Repeatedly, they are about the mind's uncertain struggles toward self-understanding; and their course is "the real course of a dream."

Selected Bibliography

WRITINGS OF NATHANIEL HAWTHORNE

Centenary Edition of the Works of Nathaniel Hawthorne. Edited by William A. Charvat *et al.* 18 vols. projected. Columbus: Ohio State University Press, 1962—.

The Complete Works of Nathaniel Hawthorne. Edited by George P. Lathrop. 12 vols. Boston: Houghton Mifflin, 1887–88.

Dr. Grimshawe's Secret. Edited by Edward H. Davidson. Cambridge: Harvard University Press, 1954.

English Notebooks. Edited by Randall Stewart. New York: Modern Language Association of America, 1941.

Letters of Hawthorne to William D. Ticknor, 1851–1864. 2 vols. Newark, N.J.: Carteret Book Club, 1910. Reprint (2 vols. in 1). Washington, D.C.: NCR/Microcard, 1972.

Love Letters of Nathaniel Hawthorne. 2 vols. Chicago: Society of Dofobs, 1907. Reprint (2 vols. in 1). Washington, D.C.: NCR/Microcard, 1972.

BOOKS AND PARTS OF BOOKS

Aaron, Daniel. *The Unwritten War: American Writers and the Civil War.* New York: Knopf, 1973.

Abrams, Meyer H. *The Mirror and the Lamp.* New York: Oxford University Press, 1953.

Bachelard, Gaston. *The Poetics of Space.* Translated by Maria Jolas. Boston: Beacon Press, 1969.

Baym, Nina. *The Shape of Hawthorne's Career*. Ithaca: Cornell University Press, 1976.

Bell, Millicent. *Hawthorne's View of the Artist*. Albany: State University of New York Press, 1962.

Borges, Jorge Luis. "Nathaniel Hawthorne." In *Other Inquisitions, 1937–1952*. Translated by Ruth L. C. Simms. Austin: University of Texas Press, 1964.

Bridge, Horatio. *Personal Recollections of Nathaniel Hawthorne*. New York: Harper, 1893.

Brown, Charles Brockden. *Edgar Huntly*. Philadelphia: McKay, 1887.

Brown, Herbert Ross. *The Sentimental Novel in America*. Durham: Duke University Press, 1940.

Brown, Thomas. *Lectures on the Philosophy of the Human Mind*. Edinburgh: William Tait, 1833.

Brownell, W. C. "Hawthorne." In *American Prose Masters*. New York: Scribner, 1909.

Chandler, Elizabeth L. *A Study of the Sources of the Tales and Romances Written by Nathaniel Hawthorne Before 1853*. Smith College Studies in Modern Languages (Northampton, Mass.: Smith College, 1926).

Charvat, William. *The Origins of American Critical Thought, 1810–1835*. Philadelphia: University of Pennsylvania Press, 1936.

Cleaveland, Nehemiah. *History of Bowdoin College*. New York: Putnam, 1908.

Crews, Frederick C. *The Sins of the Fathers: Hawthorne's Psychological Themes*. New York: Oxford University Press, 1966.

Davidson, Edward H. *Hawthorne's Last Phase*. New Haven: Yale University Press, 1949.

Doubleday, Neal Frank. *Hawthorne's Early Tales, A Critical Study*. Durham: Duke University Press, 1972.

Elder, Marjorie. *Nathaniel Hawthorne: Transcendental Symbolist*. Athens: Ohio University Press, 1969.

Emerson, Ralph Waldo. *The Complete Works of Ralph Waldo Emerson*. Edited by Edward Waldo Emerson. 12 vols. Boston: Houghton Mifflin, 1903–1904.

Feidelson, Charles, Jr. *Symbolism and American Literature*. Chicago: University of Chicago Press, 1953.

Fogle, Richard Harter. *Hawthorne's Fiction: The Light and the Dark.* Norman: University of Oklahoma Press, 1952.

Freud, Sigmund. *The Interpretation of Dreams.* Vols. IV and V of *The Complete Psychological Works of Sigmund Freud.* Translated by James Strachey. 23 vols. London: Hogarth Press, 1962.

Frothingham, O. B. *Transcendentalism in New England.* New York: Putnam, 1886.

Frye, Prosser. "Hawthorne's Supernaturalism." In *Literary Reviews and Criticisms.* New York: Putnam, 1908.

Garber, Marjorie B. *Dream in Shakespeare.* New Haven: Yale University Press, 1974.

Grave, S. A. *The Scottish Philosophy of Common Sense.* Oxford: Clarendon Press, 1960.

Halliburton, David. *Edgar Allan Poe: A Phenomenological View.* Princeton: Princeton University Press, 1973.

Hart, James D. *The Popular Book.* Berkeley: University of California Press, 1961.

Hatch, Louis. *The History of Bowdoin College.* Portland: Loring, Short, and Harmon, 1927.

Hawthorne Centenary Essays. Edited by Roy Harvey Pearce. Columbus: Ohio State University Press, 1964.

Hawthorne, Julian. *Nathaniel Hawthorne and His Wife.* 2 vols. Boston: Houghton Mifflin, 1884.

———. *Hawthorne Reading.* 1902. Reprint. Folcroft, Pa.: Folcroft Press, 1969.

Jacobson, Richard J. *Hawthorne's Conception of the Creative Process.* Cambridge: Harvard University Press, 1965.

Lathrop, Rose Hawthorne. *Memories of Hawthorne.* Boston: Houghton Mifflin, 1897.

Lesser, Simon O. *Fiction and the Unconscious.* Boston: Beacon Press, 1957.

Lundblad, Jane. *Nathaniel Hawthorne and the European Literary Tradition.* Cambridge: Harvard University Press, 1947.

Male, Roy R. *Hawthorne's Tragic Vision.* Austin: University of Texas Press, 1957.

Martin, Terence. *The Instructed Vision.* Bloomington: Indiana University Press, 1961.

Matthiessen, F. O. *American Renaissance.* New York: Oxford University Press, 1941.

Messer, W. S. *The Dream in Homer and Greek Tragedy.* New York: Columbia University Press, 1918.

Riley, I. Woodbridge. *American Philosophy: The Early Schools.* New York: Dodd, Mead, 1907.

————. *American Thought from Puritanism to Pragmatism and Beyond.* New York: Holt, 1915.

Roback A. A. *History of American Psychology.* New York: Library Publishers, 1952.

Robinson, Daniel Sommer, ed. *The Story of Scottish Philosophy.* New York: Exposition Press, 1961.

Schneider, Herbert W. *A History of American Philosophy.* New York: Columbia University Press, 1946.

Singer, Jerome L. *Daydreaming.* New York: Random House, 1966.

Slotkin, Richard. *Regeneration Through Violence.* Middletown: Wesleyan University Press, 1973.

Smith, David E. *John Bunyan in America.* Bloomington: Indiana University Press, 1968.

Stewart, Dugald. *Elements of the Philosophy of the Human Mind, I.* Vol. II of *The Collected Works of Dugald Stewart.* Edited by William H. Hamilton. 11 vols. Edinburgh: Thomas Constable, 1854.

Stewart, Randall, ed. *The American Notebooks.* New Haven: Yale University Press, 1932.

————. *Nathaniel Hawthorne.* New Haven: Yale University Press, 1948.

Upham, Thomas C. *Elements of Mental Philosophy.* New York: Harper, 1841.

Waggoner, Hyatt. *Hawthorne: A Critical Study.* Cambridge: Harvard University Press, 1963.

Winters, Yvor. *Maule's Curse.* New Haven: Yale University Press, 1938.

ARTICLES

Benson, Eugene. "Poe and Hawthorne." *Galaxy*, VI (1868), 742–48.

Blow, Suzanne. "Pre-Raphaelite Allegory in *The Marble Faun.*" *American Literature*, XLIV (1972), 122–27.

Coad, Oral S. "The Gothic Element in American Literature Before 1835." *Journal of English and Germanic Philology*, XXIV (1925), 72–93.

Colacurcio, Michael J. "Visible Sanctity and Specter Evidence: The Moral World of Hawthorne's 'Young Goodman Brown.' " *Essex Institute Historical Collections,* CX (1974), 259–99.

Cook, Reginald. "The Forest of Goodman Brown's Night: A Reading of Hawthorne's 'Young Goodman Brown.' " *New England Quarterly,* XLIII (1970), 473–81.

Cowley, Malcolm. "Hawthorne in the Looking-Glass." *Sewanee Review,* LVI (1948), 545–63.

Davidson, Frank. "Toward a Re-evaluation of *The Blithedale Romance.*" *New England Quarterly,* XXV (1952), 374–83.

Davis, Merrill R. "Emerson's 'Reason' and the Scotch Philosophers." *New England Quarterly,* XVII (1944), 209–28.

Dryden, Edgar R. "Hawthorne's Castle in the Air: Form and Theme in *The House of the Seven Gables.*" *ELH,* XXXVIII (1971), 294–317.

Kesselring, Marion. "Hawthorne's Reading, 1828–1850." *Bulletin of the New York Public Library,* LIII (1949), 55–71, 121–38, 173–94.

Kimbrough, Robert. " 'The Actual and the Imaginary': Hawthorne's Concept of Art in Theory and Practice." *Transactions of the Wisconsin Academy of Sciences, Arts, and Letters,* L (1961), 277–93.

Lamont, John H. "Hawthorne's Unfinished Works." *Harvard Medical Alumni Bulletin,* XXXVI (1962), 13–20.

Laser, Marvin. " 'Head, 'Heart,' and 'Will' in Hawthorne's Psychology." *Nineteenth Century Fiction,* X (1955), 130–40.

Levin, David. "Shadows of Doubt: Specter Evidence in Hawthorne's 'Young Goodman Brown'." *American Literature,* XXXIV (1962), 344–52.

Liebman, Sheldon W. "The Origins of Emerson's Early Poetics: His Reading in the Common Sense Critics." *American Literature,* XLV (1973), 23–33.

Lohmann, Christoph K. "The Agony of the English Romance." *Nathaniel Hawthorne Journal 1972.* Washington, D.C.: NCR/Microcard, 1973, pp. 219–29.

Pancost, David. "Hawthorne's Epistemology and Ontology." *ESQ,* XIX (1973), 8–13.

Pattison, Joseph C. " 'The Celestial Railroad' as Dream-Tale." *American Quarterly,* XX (1968), 224–36.

227

————. "Point of View in Hawthorne." *PMLA*, LXXXII (1967), 363–69.

Ringe, Donald. "Hawthorne's Night Journeys." *American Transcendental Quarterly*, X (1977), 27–32.

————. "Hawthorne's Psychology of the Head and Heart." *PMLA*, LXV (1950), 120–32.

Ross, Donald. "Dreams and Sexual Repression in *The Blithedale Romance*." *PMLA*, LXXXVI (1971), 1014–17.

St. Armand, Barton Levi. "Hawthorne's 'Haunted Mind': A Subterranean Drama of the Self." *Criticism*, XIII (1971), 1–25.

Schorer, C. E. "Hawthorne and Hypnosis." *Nathaniel Hawthorne Journal 1972*. Washington, D.C.: NCR/Microcard, 1973, pp. 239–44.

Schroeder, John. "Alice Doane's Story: An Essay on Hawthorne and Spenser." *Nathaniel Hawthorne Journal 1974*. Washington, D.C.: NCR/Microcard, 1975, pp. 129–34.

Schroeder, John W. " 'That Inward Sphere': Notes on Hawthorne's Heart Imagery." *PMLA*, LXV (1950), 106–19.

Shulman, Robert. "Hawthorne's Quiet Conflict." *Philological Quarterly*, XLVII (1968), 216–36.

Sprague, Claire. "Dream and Disguise in *The Blithedale Romance*." *PMLA*, LXXXIV (1969), 596–97.

Stewart, Randall, ed. "Recollections of Hawthorne by His Sister Elizabeth." *American Literature*, XVI (1945), 316–31.

Stoehr, Taylor. "Hawthorne and Mesmerism." *Huntington Library Quarterly*, XXXIII (1969), 333–60.

————. " 'Young Goodman Brown' and Hawthorne's Theory of Mimesis." *Nineteenth Century Fiction*, XXIII (1969), 393–412.

Trollope, Anthony. "The Genius of Hawthorne." *North American Review*, CXXIX (1879), 203–22.

Turner, Arlin. "Hawthorne's Literary Borrowings," *PMLA*, LI (1936), 543–62.

Waggoner, Hyatt. "A Hawthorne Discovery: The Lost Notebook, 1835–1841." *New England Quarterly*, XLIX (1976), 618–26.

Warren, Austin. "Hawthorne's Reading." *New England Quarterly*, VIII (1935), 480–97.

UNPUBLISHED MATERIALS

Hawthorne, Nathaniel. Correspondence. Henry W. and Albert A. Berg Collection and Duyckinck Collection of the New York Public Library; the Houghton Library, Harvard University; and the Huntington Library.

——. "The French and Italian Notebooks." Edited by Norman Holmes Pearson. Ph.D. dissertation, Yale University, 1941.

Hawthorne, Sophia. Correspondence and holograph manuscript. Henry W. and Albert A. Berg Collection, New York Public Library.

Pearson, Norman Holmes. 'The College Years of Nathaniel Hawthorne." M.A. thesis, Yale University, 1932.

Index

231

Nathaniel Hawthorne
and the Truth of Dreams